COMMODITY MARKETS AND THE GLOBAL ECONOMY

In an era defined by financial upheaval, few parts of the economy have witnessed the kind of volatility seen in commodities markets. In this book, Blake C. Clayton, a Wall Street analyst and Adjunct Fellow at the Council on Foreign Relations, draws on the latest thinking from academia and the private sector to deliver a clear-eyed analysis of pressing questions at the intersection of commodity markets, natural resource economics, and public policy. The result is a work that challenges the conventional wisdom about how these markets function and provides a fresh perspective on what public policy can do to improve them.

Blake C. Clayton is an equity analyst at Citigroup in New York, where he covers oil and gas companies and master limited partnerships. Prior to joining Citigroup, Dr. Clayton was a Fellow at the Council on Foreign Relations, where he currently serves as Adjunct Fellow on Energy. He holds a doctorate from Oxford University.

Commodity Markets and the Global Economy

BLAKE C. CLAYTON

Citigroup and Council on Foreign Relations

CAMBRIDGE
UNIVERSITY PRESS

CAMBRIDGE
UNIVERSITY PRESS

32 Avenue of the Americas, New York, NY 10013-2473, USA

Cambridge University Press is part of the University of Cambridge.

It furthers the University's mission by disseminating knowledge in the pursuit of education, learning, and research at the highest international levels of excellence.

www.cambridge.org
Information on this title: www.cambridge.org/9781107616929

© Blake C. Clayton 2016

First published 2016

Printed in the United Kingdom by Clays, St Ives plc

A catalog record for this publication is available from the British Library.

Library of Congress Cataloging in Publication Data
Clayton, Blake C. (Blake Carman), 1982–
Commodity markets and the global economy / Blake C. Clayton.
pages cm
978-1-107-61692-9 (paperback : alk. paper)
Includes bibliographical references and index.
ISBN 978-1-107-04251-3 (hardback : alk. paper)
1. Commodity exchanges. 2. International economic relations. 3. Geopolitics. I. Title.
HG6046.C5737 2015
332.64′4–dc23 2015012676

ISBN 978-1-107-04251-3 Hardback
ISBN 978-1-107-61692-9 Paperback

Contents

v

Foreword

Commodity markets have been the source of extraordinary global disruptive change since the start of this century. They have also suffered the consequences of the very changes they triggered. In this sense what has occurred within the commodities sector stands alongside the growth of global terrorism, the increased failure of nation-states, the challenge to the sanctity of national borders, and the rise to prominence of China, India, and other emerging market countries and the relative decline of power and influence of the United States, Europe, and Japan as key features of the geo-economic and political landscape over the past decade and a half.

In many ways commodity markets have been at the core of global politics and economics since the start of the twenty-first century and were certainly a main feature of the last decade, the so-called "Commodity Super Cycle Era," when prices of food, fuel, industrial metals, bulks, and gold reached ever increasing record levels at least in nominal terms until these commodity prices themselves were significantly important in driving the world economy into recession in 2008. Partly this has been a function of the growing dominance of emerging markets in the world economy and the concentration of new commodity demand, itself associated with rapid if not frenetic fixed asset investment and strong industrial production in the non-OECD world. Partly too it has been a function of the collapse of the Soviet Union and the end of bipolarity with its focus on nuclear weapons and arms control. Increasingly international politics are being played out through persistent but lower levels of conflict that have affected commodity flows and also through financial instruments – including commodity instruments – that provide "safer" ways to promote national (and often group level) objectives.

The first decade of this century was dominated by the so-called commodity supercycle, a period of time when virtually all commodities witnessed extraordinary increases in prices accompanied by equally extraordinary increases in capital investment in search of new sources of production of everything from food staples to fuel requirements to sustain growth. Simultaneously the seemingly exponential spurt in commodities prices was accompanied by, and to some degree itself driven by, an explosion of investor flows designed to tap into the expected returns from commodities.

The second decade of the century has been more nuanced: global growth has been challenged, especially in emerging markets and especially in China, leading to substantially lower growth paths for commodity demand. Commodities themselves have experienced more diversified performance, as investments in new supplies of oil, natural gas, iron ore, coal, food staples, and most base metals have created more abundance, particularly given the disappointing level of economic growth that has taken hold around the world.

Common to both decades so far has been both the growing prominence of financial flows in commodity price determination, with managed money capable of exacerbating fundamentals by going long or short on specific commodities, and what we might understand as the "volatility of volatility," sustaining both periods of high and of low realized volatility, with abrupt and unexpected changes from the one to the other.

This book by Blake Clayton is unified by its focus on what is new and what is persistent about commodities in the global economy and what has brought them to the fore of public debates both national and global over the past fifteen years. It is a brave and distinguished effort to enhance our understanding of the geo-economics of commodities. Underlying the world of commodities and what distinguishes that world from so many other parts of the international economy has been the dramatic lack of consensus both within and across countries about how much of commodities sector should be treated as private interest versus public good, how much should be left to markets to find appropriate adjustments, and how much should be in the hands of the state. If anything, this unresolved and perennial debate about commodities has become a central part of public debate over the past decade and a half, witnessed by the dramatic re-concentration of commodity enterprises under the state in Russia and debates in all advanced economies about the appropriate relationship between government, the banking system, and commodities.

This should not be surprising. Commodities constitute the largest part of physically traded goods internationally, whether in terms of volume or value; and within commodities the two largest commodity sectors broadly encompass food and fuel. With prices for these two basic elements of consumption – particularly across emerging markets – having experienced a dramatic roller-coaster ride during this century, there is no puzzle as to why the regulation of these two particular sectors has become the center of domestic and global debates. A five- to tenfold increase in underlying prices, which is what occurred across commodities in the short span of 2003–2008, was bound to raise questions about the proper role of government and the proper way to organize the commodity chains when governments themselves have so much as stake.

Nor has the debate over private versus public coincided cleanly as between advanced economies and emerging markets. Volatility in global food markets, the subject of Chapter 3, has become one of the central themes of the G-20, the quintessential twenty-first-century organization, itself founded in 1999 to bring together nineteen countries plus the European Union to meet on global issues that could no longer be "managed" by the seven largest advanced economies meeting without the participation of finance ministers, central banks, and heads of state from the major emerging economies of the world. Within the G-20 European countries, including especially Germany, many have been convinced that agricultural commodities should not succumb unduly to the influence of finance flows, and therefore should be off limits to investments by public and private pension funds. Even in a period of substantially lower prices for food staples and meat, the debate still rages in parts of Europe.

Two age-old issues in the politics surrounding commodities highlighted by Clayton under the evolving conditions of this century revolve around diverging and often asymmetric relations between importers and exporters of raw materials and around sovereigns working to stem the influence of the private sector in particular, or markets in general, as they try to foster and preserve comparative advantage. Much of this book is infused by these two tensions as they have played out in recent years, including the time since the book manuscript was completed. Indeed, the intellectual construct of these chapters in looking at these two traditional issues in their new context helps us in understanding the dramatic events that have played out in the oil market in late 2014 and through 2015.

When it comes to international petroleum, for example, the inherent conflict of interests between exporters and importers has been dramatically impacted by the growth of three forms of unconventional oil and natural gas during the twenty-first century – whether coming from deep water, oil sands, or shale oil and gas. Perhaps the most disruptive of the consequences of these new sources of supply has been their role in depriving what has been regarded as the world's most successful cartel, the Organization of

Petroleum Exporting Countries (OPEC), of its ability to successfully target prices well above production costs in order to maximize their revenue.

Two critical factors made for OPEC's success: its control of relatively lower-cost supply and the asymmetry of consequences of higher prices as between oil-producing countries and oil importers or consumers. By late 2014 it became clear to OPEC's largest producer, Saudi Arabia, that if it used its traditional means of cutting supply to balance markets in oversupply, it would not only not reduce the abundance of light, sweet crude in the world (what comes from the shale revolution), but it would, in fact, continue to subsidize new unconventional oil. Because of the robustness of new unconventional oil and its technological improvements driving down underlying costs, the conclusion for the Kingdom of Saudi Arabia and therefore for OPEC has been to stop being a swing producer and placing the burden of adjustment on new sources of supply – a process that appears to have increased long-term price volatility.

The other factor was the asymmetry of the impact of price increases. For oil-producing countries a price increase has a strong impact on their revenue given the role of oil and gas production in their economies (often well above 50% of GDP), but it has only a marginal impact on advanced economies, where energy costs tend to be under 10% of GDP. As a result, the oil-producing countries historically could succeed in efforts to keep a wedge, if not a growing one, between production costs and market prices. But now, with unconventional oil becoming increasingly available at lower prices, the original asymmetry is turned on its ahead, particularly as all three sources of unconventional hydrocarbons are abundant outside of OPEC. So unconventional output makes it asymmetrically more difficult for OPEC countries to achieve and sustain higher prices.

Clayton's examines in depth the 2011 release of strategic stocks by the international energy agency and the debates around that release as perhaps the quintessential issue raised by the disruptive changes abounding around commodities in this century. When should strategic stocks be released? Which countries need to get involved, including oil producers that could have a negative impact by withdrawing oil from the market? The new order questions not only when these strategic assets should be released but also what level of stocks might be desirable, and logistically how has the infrastructure of such stocks, especially in the United States, need to be revamped, perhaps moving them to other parts of the country. This is an issue that is likely to grow in importance as Saudi Arabia ends its role as a swing producer and also reduces its spare production capacity. The SPR issues embody the four major themes of Clayton's essays: the tensions and inherent conflict of visions between commodity-importing and -exporting countries; markets and sovereigns vying for comparative advantage; the tensions in an inter-dependent global economy between national and international solutions; and the frequent difficulties in reconciling opposing forces of physical and financial markets.

Perhaps the biggest of the issues confronting commodity markets and the global economy relate to financial flows. The debates over the consequences of speculation in commodities markets, the core of Chapter 4, have subsided significantly in the aftermath of the Commodity Super Cycle, but they have not gone away. If anything, the low-interest-rate environment in this era of quantitative easing globally has increased the size and volatility of financial flows into and out of commodities. Over the twelve months before the publication of this book, there were two periods when total net length of managed money in oil reached peaks not dreamed of even in 2008. In the spring of 2014, as ISIS took over larger segments of the Sunni Triangle area of Iraq and as tensions in Europe grew over Russia's re-annexation of Crimea, net length of investors in financial oil reached their then record length and pushed "deferred" oil – contracts for settlement in 2017 and 2018 – to well over $100 a barrel from the previous high of $90. And then, through the summer and into September, that record net length turned into a net short position for Brent oil trading for the first time in history. As the Bank for International Settlements (BIS) noted (BIS Quarterly Review, March 2015), the decline in prices that occurred in the second half of 2014 cannot be explained by market fundamentals; rather, "the steepness of the price decline and very large day-to-day price changes are reminiscent of a financial asset." The BIS also noted that the size of indebtedness in the oil sector also played a role.

The rise in oil prices in 2015 has a similar relationship to financial flows, which by May 2015 reached another level of net length, this time concentrated in the prompt contracts of trading in the oil market. It is unclear how this record length will be played out as this book reaches the public. But one thing is clear – the world is only beginning to understand the volatility and finicky-ness of financial flows into commodities. If anything, conditions are becoming significantly less transparent and "controllable" than they were thought to be in 2008 when regulators in OECD countries started to reign in financial flows. Now, with a significant amount of metals inventories moving into warehouses that are not monitored by major exchanges like the London Metals Exchange (LME), and with many of these used to buttress securitized financing, it seems clear that volatility will not diminish any time soon, even if a world of relatively "cheap money" changes as central banks move away from quantitative easing. This is the sort of puzzle that confronts commodity markets as the century proceeds. Clayton's book goes a long way in establishing a framework for understanding the issues that are now front and center in commodity markets.

Edward L. Morse
Managing Director, Global Head of Commodity Research at Citigroup

Acknowledgments

The majority of this book was written while I was a Fellow at the Council on Foreign Relations (CFR) in New York, where I spent two years following stints at Oxford and Louis Capital Markets. CFR was an ideal environment for researching, writing, and rewriting the manuscript, providing me with the time, freedom, and intellectual resources I needed to explore the broad range of topics touching finance, economics, and public policy discussed in this book. I am particularly grateful to Richard N. Haass and James M. Lindsay for their generous guidance regarding and support for my work while at CFR. I would also like to thank Michael Levi, whose critical insights and editorial judgment improved my work.

Following CFR, I joined Citigroup in the summer of 2013 as a securities analyst covering oil and gas companies and energy master limited partnerships. Once again, at Citi, I have had the privilege and good fortune to work among supportive colleagues whose expertise and research acumen sharpened my arguments and improved my earlier drafts. I am grateful to Jonathan Rosenzweig, Jon Rogers, and Michael Artura for their support for the book. I am also indebted to Faisel Khan, whose support and expertise with regard to the energy industry and commodity markets has been invaluable. I also owe thanks to Edward Morse, global head of commodity research at Citi, for his support and remarkable knowledge of the asset class. Thanks also go to Vikram Bagri, Mohit Bhardwaj, Aakash Doshi, Eric Genco, Trieu Huynhtan, Sophie Karp, Eric Lee, Ryan Levine, Richard Morse, Nick Raza, Tony Yuen, and Mirek Zak for their insights.

I am grateful to the other scholars and experts whose critiques and feedback have shaped and honed my arguments in this book, including Trevor Houser, Lou Lazzara, Bob McNally, Mark Skousen, Benn Steil, and John Tysseland. Sabina Frizell, Kate Gavino, Alexandra Mahler-Haug, and Cole Wheeler provided excellent research and editorial assistance. This book would not have been possible without the vision and support of my editor, Karen Maloney, and the talented team at Cambridge University Press. I owe a special thanks to my wife, Amy, for her patience and encouragement throughout the time-consuming book-writing process.

This book was made possible by the generous support of the Alfred P. Sloan Foundation as part of the Council on Foreign Relations' Project on Energy and National Security. I alone am responsible for the book's contents.

The Revenge of the Old Economy

In an era defined by financial upheaval, few other markets have undergone as profound a transformation over the past decade as commodity markets. Part of the change, certainly, has been in price levels: Both futures prices and volatility levels have spiked to levels not seen since the 1970s, only for volatility to dip to the placid levels more typical of the mid-1990s, as of the time this book was written. For resource producers, whether nations or companies, such generally heady price environments have marked an era of almost unprecedented bounty, while their consumer counterparts have often languished as the cost of basic materials, including essentials like food and fuel, have soared. But prices are as much symptom as cause. Behind the price swings has been a range of factors spanning trends in economic development (an increasingly wealthy Asian consumer base), demographics (a restless rising generation in the Middle East), economics (declining real interest rates across the West), geology (massive disagreement over the hydrocarbon reserve base, coupled with technological advances that have challenged the Malthusian paradigm), and politics (an OPEC at turns emboldened and in disarray). Beyond these trends, the structure, players, and pricing dynamics that make up the landscape of modern commodity markets have also undergone a sea change, with vast new sources of liquidity and rapid securitization changing the way many of the world's oldest goods change hands.

Perhaps the most remarkable aspect of the mostly erstwhile commodities boom was the unexpectedness, at least for mainstream experts, of its arrival. This was a case of boom not merely following bust, but actually being borne – suddenly – of it. In the latter half of the 1990s, the market for hard assets was as soft as nearly any time in the hundred years prior. The relative geoeconomic stability that defined the second Clinton administration, coupled with its strong dollar policies, had depressed commodity prices in dollar-denominated terms. When the Asian financial crisis bit into economic growth in the emerging world in 1998, oil prices and commodity complex more broadly tanked. At $1.24, a gallon of retail gasoline in the United States was cheaper in real terms than it had been at any time since the Arab embargo of 1973.[1] Many experts saw cheap oil as the new normal – a long-term status quo that was almost certain to persist over the next several decades, a stable feature of the Great Moderation underpinned by technological improvements along resource supply chains.

Two pieces of popular commentary from 1998 capture the ultra-bearishness prevalent at the time – which for energy consuming countries, like the United States, was wonderfully good news. "In the old days the question was low or high prices, and everything rode on those numbers," wrote one commentator. "Now the question is low or very low prices."[2] A futuristic array of new information technologies, the growing role of natural gas in the energy mix, and the diverse sources of oil around the world meant that the "[oil] industry has changed fundamentally since previous shocks that seemed to portend ever higher prices." There was no need to fear an energy crisis redux. "If you are having haunting visions of long lines and $2.50-per-gal. gasoline, relax."[3] As late as seven years later, market prognosticators were hard-pressed to see how oil prices could rise any higher than $35 per barrel or so in the decade ahead.[4] Yet only three years later, it would be closer to $135 per barrel – not $35 – and analysts would have to come to grips with the risk of a superheated crude market, or Oil.com, as Edward Morse dubbed it.[5] And yet such sharp reversals, difficult to discern ex ante, would come again with the global financial crisis that struck in 2007 and the strong rebound across most of the complex less than half a decade later, which was underpinned by the prevailing dovish rate environment.

The commodity cycle of the past two decades – still underway and hardly uniform in its dynamics across the diverse goods that make up the commodity complex – has proceeded in five stages, broadly speaking. The first

---

[1] U.S. Energy Information Administration, "Table 5.24 Retail Motor Gasoline and On-Highway Diesel Fuel Prices, 1949–2011 (Dollars per Gallon)," *Annual Energy Review*, September 27, 2012.

[2] David E. Sanger, "Singing the Cartel Blues," *New York Times*, March 29, 1998.

[3] Daniel Yergin and Joseph Stanislaw, "How OPEC Lost Control of Oil," *Time* 151 no. 13 (April 6, 1998), 58.

[4] Doug Leggate et al., "2005 Oil Sector Outlook," Citigroup Equity Research: Oil Companies – Majors, February 18, 2005.

[5] Edward Morse and Michael Waldron, "Oil Dot-com," Lehman Brothers Energy Special Report, May 29, 2008.

phase was stage setting: the lull of the late 1990s, marked by a dearth of capital investment in producing assets and infrastructure as supply-side productivity soared. The value of the dollar-denominated capital stock of oil, coal, iron ore, aluminum, and copper across several major national suppliers (the United States, China, Australia, and Brazil, among others) stagnated between 1990 and 2000. Productivity in base metals production in key producers rose over the course of the decade, rising as high as 10% per year in China and Chile on average. In the U.S. oil and gas patch, the average age of the capital stock rose from roughly six years in 1990 to ten years by the turn of the century, as relatively poor cash returns led to a pullback in upstream capital expenditure. Sector-wide cost and commodity price deflation, coupled with confidence-inspiring productivity increases, made for a market environment in which the prospect of declines in inventories that might have been unsettling in an earlier era were greeted with relative calm, as the pace of investment into productive assets like oil rigs and storage facilities were pressured by low profit margins.[6]

But chronically low rates of investment would bite back. This second phase, the revenge of the so-called Old Economy – those industrial sectors that had been on life support near the end of the twentieth century, left for dead by investors who favored the tech-driven New Economy – stretched from 2001 to 2008. Surging demand challenged the outer limits of productive capacity across most resources, egged on by a collection of macroeconomic and political trends that caused the complex to reignite. The proximate cause of the boom was an industrializing Asia – mainly China – whose capital- and heavy-industry intensive growth phase was compounded by an urbanizing, nascent middle class there and in other major developing economies, who were taking to roadways, buying durable goods, and consuming high-caloric diets in record numbers. A surge in biofuel demand in the European Union and the United States, driven by aggressive government mandates seeking to supplement transportation fuels with biofuel, mainly ethanol, rededicated what was once food-producing farmland to fuel production and exerted upward pressure on the prices of substitutes, like edible oils, to disastrous effect on the affordability of basic foodstuffs among the world's poor, who suffered rampant price inflation. Expansions in production capacity – structurally slow when it comes to supplying natural resources, particularly in the extractive industries – were painfully delayed. This was part economics – the outgrowth of a decade and a half of

---

[6] Christian Lelong et al., "Investor Returns Will Survive the Productivity Comeback," Goldman Sachs Commodities Research, April 24, 2014.

underinvestment – and part politics, as Riyadh and other sovereign producers reaped a windfall from a tightening market. Supply shortfalls were amplified by geopolitical uncertainties, particularly in oil, across a war-ridden and post-Saddam Iraq, a tumultuous Nigeria, and a Chavista Venezuela, with terrorist violence wreaking havoc in Saudi Arabia and North Africa. Rising oil prices spilled over into the markets for food and minerals, the production of which relies heavily on oil, as the cost of crude saw electricity generators turn to gas, coal, and uranium. All told, food and agricultural product prices reversed their downward trend of the prior two decades, whereas energy and metals prices spiked to levels rarely seen in the preceding century.[7]

The third phase of the cycle was one of collapse – the epic meltdown of 2008 and 2009. In the financial sector, the domino effects of an economic recession in the United States, which precipitated the collapse of the domestic housing sector and metastasized, via derivative linkages, to the financial sector, iterated back into the real economy worldwide. Among hard assets, metals were the bellwether of the downturn, plummeting in the spring of 2008. The S&P GSCI Metals index, which gauges the returns of futures contracts in the sector, fell nearly 60% between March and December 2008, with major industrial metals – such as copper and lead – logging worse performance in the last four months of the year than occurred during the worst years of the Great Depression between 1929 and 1933.[8] Agricultural and energy prices withstood well into the summer, with Brent crude's stunning race to $143 per barrel cresting in July 2008 – in the midst of a U.S. recession, no less, and on the cusp of a global one – on North Sea supply woes and a healthy dose of market exuberance. From July 2008 to their nadir in February 2009, the International Monetary Fund (IMF) Energy Index lost more than two-thirds of its value. As is typical of major sell-offs, the routing was both fundamental – the freezing up of bids on supply chain capacity, the laying up of productive assets, the contango-inducing rush of goods into storage, the drying up of lines of credit on which traders depend – and forward-looking, driven by fear of a second Great Depression in the West and concomitant severe pullback in developing Asian growth. This was boom and bust on a scale that would have been hard to imagine even two years earlier, despite the sector's reputation for jarring whiplash.

---

[7] Thomas Helbling, Valerie Mercer-Blackman, and Kevin Cheng, "Riding a Wave," *Finance and Development* 45 no. 1 (March 2008): 10–15.

[8] Ambrose Evans-Pritchard, "Metal Prices Fall Further than During Great Depression," *Telegraph*, December 2, 2008.

If the third phase of the cycle was the collapse associated with the Great Recession, the fourth phase, could be termed the Great Divergence. It did not take long after the crash for most commodities' futures prices to snap back to form, though not quite to the exalted levels of 2008. Brent crude priced in U.S. dollars reentered triple digit territory in the early days of 2011; copper had surpassed its boomtime highs, breaching $4 per ton in New York in December 2010. The resurgence had several drivers: the bottoming out of effective interest rates in G10 economies, effectuated by central banks as a means of mitigating deflationary risks and encouraging borrowing rates; an emerging Asia in China, India, and Indonesia that had muscled through the downturn relatively unscathed; and a newly bullish crude market, in which Saudi mentions of a $75 "fair" price of oil, robust non-OECD demand, and still-tepid non-OPEC supply growth led traders to foresee fundamentals improving rapidly.[9] Oil was not the only beneficiary. Many commodities rebounded strongly from 2009 to 2011, buoyed by similarly favorable macroeconomic tailwinds and a developing-market-centric growth paradigm that, while diminished, was far from defeated.

But across the commodity complex, including within families of related goods (i.e., energy, agriculturals, etc.), a great parting of ways was beginning to play out, in a trend that would only amplify over the next half decade. Forecasts of a return to the perfect storm of the 2000s, though superficially compelling, were shallow. In reality, the mobilization of capital and supply responses was having enormously various effects among commodities in price responses and time horizons. Nowhere was this contrast more vivid than in the markets for North American natural gas versus Brent crude oil. The former, thanks to a sustained shale-driven climb in production and a lack of viable export routes, collapsed Henry Hub prices, not to mention regional basis differentials, forcing Henry Hub spot prices below $5 per MMBtu almost without a pause from 2009 onward. The North Sea crude marker, in contrast, has turned structurally short: declining regional production, down from a peak of 8.6 mb/d in 2004 to 2.4 mb/d, has forced European refiners to pull barrels from elsewhere and kept the curve in chronic backwardation.[10] Meanwhile, industrial metals and non-food agricultural goods prices broadly have grinded lower since their 2011 highs in

[9] Bassam Fattouh and Christopher Allsopp, "The Price Band and Oil Price Dynamics," *Oxford Energy Comment,* Oxford Institute for Energy Studies (July 2009); Jeff D. Colgan, "The Emperor Has No Clothes: The Limits of OPEC in the Global Market," *International Organization* 68 no. 3 (2014): 599–632.

[10] Seth M. Kleinman et al., "Energy Weekly: Brent is also a Broken Benchmark," Citi Commodities Research, February 17, 2014.

U.S. dollar terms. Metals market conditions eased thanks to a step change downward in Chinese growth rates and supply-efficiency increases after a decade-long surge in capital expenditure from less than $5 billion in 2000 to roughly $140 billion in 2012. Grains and soft commodities flat price returns, for their part, turned negative on surplus output, acreage growth, and rising inventories. Yet across industrial and precious metals, as elsewhere, the specific dynamics guiding, for example, copper, where returns on capital expenditure surged between 2008 and 2012, symptomatic of a cyclical supply response, have differed greatly from those of gold, which stayed aloft until 2013, supported by concerns over inflation from massive expansion of central bank balance sheets. With the evaporation of those fears and declining European sovereign tail risks, investors abandoned the yellow metal amid the rising opportunity cost of holding gold at a time of soaring equity prices in the United States. The exceptionally synchronized movements of commodities prices in a single direction, typically upward, that had prevailed from 2003 to 2009, gave way to more fragmented trajectories.[11]

The fifth epoch of the cycle – a sudden and severe crash in crude oil prices – played out as this book was going to press. Seaborne crude benchmarks, resistant to the glut that had defined the U.S. natural gas market the half decade prior, succumbed to incessant waves of new, largely North American supply, in the autumn of 2014. Defying the skeptics, the continual surge in the productivity of shale wells combined with a rebound in Libyan production and Saudi production in excess of 9 million barrels per day that refused to taper in the face of an oversupplied market, at the risk of losing market share. Chinese demand growth, the catalyst of the bull market of the preceding decade, had softened, while consumption in the developed world appeared to be in secular decline. A strengthening U.S. dollar, benefitting from an expectation of higher real U.S. interest rates in response to a domestic economy with visible signs of momentum (5% GDP growth in the third quarter of 2014), also weighed on the oil complex. As of the time this book was written, Riyadh has dropped all pretense of maintaining crude prices in or near triple digit territory, intent instead on preserving market share by ferreting out unmitigated North American supply growth and calling on their OPEC brethren, as well as Moscow, to shoulder the load.

Over the course of these five chapters of market history, the changes to commodity markets ran deeper than the ebb and flow of supply, demand,

---

[11] Edward L. Morse, "Commodities Inflection Point: 2014 Annual Market Outlook," Citi Commodities Research, November 18, 2013.

and price. At least two aspects of these markets underwent structural changes whose effects will likely outlast the current price cycle. The first of these changes is regulatory. The Dodd-Frank Wall Street Reform and Consumer Protection Act (or simply "Dodd-Frank Act"), enacted in July 2010, greatly expanded the power of the Commodity Futures Trading Commission, or CFTC, to conceive and implement rules designed to promote financial stability. In the ensuing years, the CFTC has issued provisions governing which parties can participate in these markets as well as the reporting and position limits to which they must adhere, seeking to mitigate the systemic risks associated with market participants that are too big to fail, whose investments pose a threat to the stability of the broader marketplace, or where ordinary consumers and producers are left at a disadvantage. Although the effects of the Dodd-Frank Act in commodities markets are still taking shape, with new rules being codified every few months since September 2010, certain consequences of the law have already hit, including the retreat of most major Wall Street banks from physical commodity trading and the gradual flow of trading from over-the-counter to exchange-cleared transactions.[12] Critics of the rules argue that, by reducing liquidity in commodity derivative markets and potentially leading to cash-flow risk for physical producers and consumers who have to abide by the stricter collateral requirements on exchanges, the law could backfire, increasing price volatility and counterparty risk.[13]

The second structural change to commodity markets to occur over the past decade has been their so-called financialization, or the increasing popularity of these goods as an investment vehicle in derivatives markets, which has altered both the amount of money flowing into and out of commodity-linked securities, as well as the types of market participants who hold these securities. The magnitude of growth in interest in these markets by institutional investors is astounding, jumping from $15 billion in 2003 to more than $200 billion in 2008.[14] U.S.-listed exchange traded funds (ETFs) and passive index assets under management stood at roughly $275 million as of

---

[12] An online list of the CFTC's Final Rules, Guidance, Exemptive Orders, and other actions stemming from Dodd Frank is available at http://www.cftc.gov/LawRegulation/DoddFrankAct/Dodd-FrankFinalRules/index.htm.

[13] For a brief overview of these arguments, see Andrew Peaple, "Commodities Firms Fear Dodd-Frank Effects," *Wall Street Journal*, March 12, 2011. For a more scholarly overview, see Craig Pirrong, "Clearing and Collateral Mandates: A New Liquidity Trap?," *Journal of Applied Corporate Finance* 24 no. 1 (Winter 2012): 67–73.

[14] Ing-Haw Cheng and Wei Xiong, "The Financialization of Commodity Markets," Working Paper for the Annual Review of Financial Economics, 1.

the end of 2013.[15] By way of background, a typical commodity index fund takes a long position in a near-term futures contract (or a linked swap), selling the security as the contract nears maturity and assuming a new long position in the next contract, creating an asset that seeks to capture positive spot price movements and the associated roll yield. Because the rising flow of funds into commodity-linked securities between 2003 and 2008 largely mirrored the rising prices of these goods, some analysts have argued that they were the causal force behind the bull market. Although there is little empirical evidence for this view, it remains a popular one among some commentators, making the topic of financialization a contentious one in the popular media and infusing what might otherwise be arcane debates over CFTC rule implementation with a rare degree of public concern, owing to worries over high gasoline prices in the United States and economic welfare in the developing world. A close reading of the evidence suggests that at least two aspects of the way commodity markets function do in fact appear to have changed over the past decade; however, the way in which information is disseminated within the market and the risk-sharing that occurs among producers, consumers, and intermediaries or investors has altered. These changes are discussed later in this chapter.

For many people in the developed world, tremors in commodity markets can seem arcane – gyrations in a market with little direct impact on them, beyond the occasional pain at the pump or a fluctuation in their savings account. In reality, however, these markets matter hugely to the course of world affairs and global markets in at least three ways. First, in terms of human welfare and economic development, these markets are among the most important in the world. Poor people spend a large majority of their income on food, and farmers, who represent a larger share of the population in poor countries than rich ones, depend on it for their livelihood. Whether in Ghana, Guatemala, or Vietnam, the lowest quintile of the population typically spends between 60% and 75% of their household budgets on food.[16] The price of wheat or soybeans – an abstraction for many people in New York or Paris – can tip the scales toward progress or poverty in less privileged parts of the world. Second, fluctuations in commodities prices, particularly oil, the 800-pound gorilla of the commodity complex

---

[15] Edward L. Morse, "Commodities Inflection Point: 2014 Annual Market Outlook," Citi Commodities Research, November 18, 2013, 7.

[16] "Recent Trends in World Food Commodity Prices: Costs of Benefits," in Food and Agriculture Organization, *The State of Food Insecurity in the World: How Does International Price Volatility Affect Domestic Economies and Food Security?* (Rome, Italy: Food and Agriculture Organization of the United Nations, 2011): 14.

in terms of physical volumes traded, inevitably reverberate throughout the broader economy in an outsized way. What happens in the oil market does not stay in the oil market. A lurch by gasoline and diesel prices in one direction or another, particularly in a moment of economic stress, as in 2007, can speed economic growth or cause it to grind to a halt. Some economists believe that the Great Recession was precipitated, through direct and indirect channels, by the historic spike in oil prices from 2005 onward, just as they feared the resurgence of oil prices in 2010 and 2011 could cause the world economy to contract once again.[17] Finally, the strategic importance of many commodities – whether rare earth elements, uranium, or oil – means these markets often set the stage on which the most vexing problems in international affairs play out. Indeed, some historians argue, not implausibly, that access to oil had a decisive effect on the outcome of the two world wars of the twentieth century, and that the security of the global oil trade has likewise played a leading role in Western strategy in the Middle East from the days of Roosevelt and Churchill in Arabia and Persia to Obama and Cameron in Libya.[18] More recently, natural gas trade linkages have formed the critical context in which Moscow and Ukraine have quarreled over the Crimea and, elsewhere in the world, the acquisition of oil wealth by the Islamic State of Iraq and Syria has catapulted it to prominence as a regional military force.

The epic bull market of the mid-2000s might be the stuff of history – but commodities are still king.

---

[17] See James D. Hamilton, "Oil and the Macroeconomy," Working Paper (August 24, 2005), Chapter prepared for Steven N. Durlauf and Lawrence E. Blume (eds.), *The New Palgrave Dictionary of Economics*, Second Edition (U.S. and UK: Palgrave Macmillan, 2008), http://dss.ucsd.edu/~jhamilto/JDH_palgrave_oil.pdf (Accessed September 16, 2014); Lutz Killian, "Not All Oil Price Shocks Are Alike: Disentangling Demand and Supply Shocks in the Crude Oil Market," *American Economic Review* 99 no. 3 (2009): 1053–1069; James D. Hamilton, "Historical Oil Shocks," NBER Working Paper 16790, National Bureau of Economic Research (February 2011); International Monetary Fund, World Economic Outlook: *Tensions from the Two-Speed Recovery: Unemployment, Commodities, and Capital Flows* (Washington, DC: International Monetary Fund, April 2011); and James D. Hamilton, "Nonlinearities And The Macroeconomic Effects Of Oil Prices," *Macroeconomic Dynamics* 15 no. S3 (November 2011): 364–378.

[18] Daniel Yergin, *The Prize: The Epic Quest for Oil, Money, and Power* (New York: Simon & Schuster, 1992); Daniel Yergin, *The Quest: Energy, Security, and the Remaking of the Modern World* (New York: Penguin Press, 2011); Amos N. Guiora, "Intervention in Libya, Yes; Intervention in Syria, No: Deciphering the Obama Administration," *Journal of International Law* 44, Case Western Reserve University School of Law (2011): 251–276; Sam Raphael and Doug Stokes, "Globalizing West African Oil: US 'Energy Security' and the Global Economy," *International Affairs* 87 no. 4 (July 2011): 903–921.

WHERE FROM HERE: FOUR FORCES SHAPING THE COMMODITY MARKET LANDSCAPE

Four pairs of opposing forces – four guiding tensions – will determine the landscape on which the major battles of commodities markets will be fought over the coming decade. This book, a collection of essays that are introduced later in this chapter, explores a set of public policy debates at the nexus of these four fault lines. They consist of the inherent tension between (1) net importing and net exporting countries in the search of economic gains; (2) sovereign states (and state-owned enterprises) and private-sector companies vying for competitive advantage; (3) international cooperation and nationalism as opposing means of addressing failures in resource markets; and (4) the physical and financial aspects of the modern commodity trade. Collectively, these tensions underlie a broad range of seemingly disparate debates in the resource sector, ranging from the debate over the causes of and appropriate means of mitigating harmful volatility in global food markets, the rise of Chinese national oil companies in oil production overseas, the legal clash over how to regulate speculation in commodity derivative markets, or the idiosyncratic campaign in the United States for a return to the gold standard.

The structurally opposing interests of net commodity importers and exporters, the first of the four guiding tensions in commodity markets, has economic origins but geopolitical manifestations. Countries that predominately export a good are generally motivated to keep its price high enough to maximize their short-term revenues yet low enough to keep demand for it intact over the long term. For net importers, on the other hand, natural resources, whether crude or processed, are materials whose economic value stems from the fact that they are used as inputs in another product's supply chain (iron ore into steel) or consumed as a means of growing the economy (diesel for cars and trucks). The economic antagonism between the two sets of countries is intrinsic: the price environment that is good for one is typically not preferred by the other. At stake, as trading partners seek to turn the market to their advantage, are the macroeconomic health of the home country (for instance, the impact of trade performance on the volatility of exchange rates, fund flows on interest rates, and exogenous price-level pressures on domestic inflation, for instance) as well as sector-specific economic outcomes (say, the health of an exporter's mining and minerals sectors or an importer's manufacturing and automotive industries). Yes, there is the potential for cooperation between importers and exporters – every seller needs a buyer, and vice versa, so interests overlap in fundamental ways – yet any analysis of the competitive dynamics that shape the commodity trade must begin at the fact that in a very real sense, the national interests of net buyers and sellers are often conflicting. A host of factors govern the intensity of that competition, from the degree to which the given commodity can be substituted for by the buyers to the extent to which the exporting country's fiscal pulse depends on its trade in that good.

In a market like energy, the most tectonic geoeconomic shifts often happen as a country transforms from net exporter to importer or vice versa, or as a country moves from a minor to major exporter or importer. Both of these two dynamics – a change in net export/import status and the rise of a major importer/exporter – have constituted arguably the two major storylines in the world oil and gas trade since the turn of the millennium. China's transition from a minor to a major net importer in oil and switch from a net exporter to importer of coal, with knock-on effects across global energy markets, is a perfect example. The country was a net oil exporter until the early 1990s; it is now the world's largest net importer of petroleum and other liquid fuels, not to mention the biggest energy consumer worldwide, a title it claimed in 2010. Coal in China had a similar storyline: historically a net exporter, the Middle Kingdom became a net importer in 2009 and is now both the world's largest producer and consumer. If a single explanation had to be given for the stunning surge in world oil prices over the past decade, the unprecedented pace of Chinese consumption growth during the 2000s and the flatlining of oil production outside of OPEC, would be a good candidate. The rapid shrinking of net oil imports into the United States, the world's largest oil consumer, has also redrawn the map of the global oil trade. A net importer of gasoline and diesel for the past half century, the United States became a net importer of petroleum producers in 2011. Although still a major net importer of crude oil, imports have fallen by one-third since 2008. Trade flows in oil between the United States and West Africa, once a major exporter to the U.S. Gulf Coast, have slowed to a trickle, while Middle Eastern exporters, who not long ago saw the United States as a reliably expanding market, have embraced a rising Asia. Meanwhile, in the natural gas market, the United States has seen net imports fall dramatically to roughly 100 Bcf per month and with Henry Hub prices well below European and Asian counterparts, will likely export 8 to 9 Bcf of liquefied natural gas daily by 2020. While tempting to overstate the geopolitical implications of these changes so far, were these trends to continue, they would put increasing downward pressure on prices, which could hurt the economics of current net exporters, as well as provide the Washington policymakers with greater freedom of action in their dealings with other energy exporters, in addition to stimulating economic growth at home.

But the clash of sovereign interests is only one facet of the evolving state of international competition in commodity markets. Another theme of the past decade, which promises to continue into the coming one, is the clash of sovereign states and state-owned enterprises with their pivate sector peers. This is not a new phenomenon. The East India Company, granted a monopoly on trade to the east of the Cape of Good Hope by Queen Elizabeth I in 1600, pioneered the state-backed enterprise centuries ago, even though, with a standing army that dwarfed those of most European states at the time, the firm was a far cry from the current commercial behemoths.[19] Aside from their shared status as at least partially government owned, state-owned enterprises differ widely, whether in terms of the degree to which they are privately owned, cater to the will of their state sponsor, or operate domestically or abroad. In China alone, nearly 80,000 such state businesses operate far from the international spotlight, in mundane corners of the economy like restaurant management and shopping mall operations – a world apart from a Saudi Aramco, producer of 3.4 billion barrels of oil in 2013, or China Mobile, with roughly $100 billion in revenues, in U.S. dollar terms.[20] Yet the ubiquity – and in many sectors, dominance – of state-owned companies on today's business landscape in sectors as diverse as telecommunications and oil and gas production gives lie to the notion that the International Monetary Fund-supported privatization movement of the past three decades has truly reoriented the commanding heights of the global economy, particularly in the energy and materials sectors. Such companies account for a massive amount of global stock market capitalization: 80% of China's, perhaps unsurprisingly, but also more than 60% of Russia's and 35% of Brazil's.[21] Ranked in terms of their reserve base, the thirteen largest energy companies in the world are state owned and operated, controlling three-quarters of the world's oil. Even the largest non-state oil company by market capitalization, ExxonMobil, is only the eighth largest by that metric, lagging behind names like National Iranian Oil Co., Petróleos de Venezuela, and Petronas.[22]

This public-private fault line, which runs down the middle of the oil industry, among other sectors, raises critical questions for businesses, investors, regulators, and policymakers alike, whether they sit in countries dominated or mostly devoid of state-run firms. For business executives,

---

[19] "The Company that ruled the waves," *The Economist*, December 17, 2011.
[20] "Fixing China Inc," *The Economist*, August 28, 2014; Saudi Aramco, *Energy is Opportunity: Annual Review 2013*; China Mobile Ltd. *Annual Report 2013*.
[21] "The Company that Ruled the Waves," *The Economist*, December 17, 2011.
[22] Ian Bremmer, "The Long Shadow of the Visible Hand," *Wall Street Journal*, May 22, 2010.

many of the questions are practical: Can they compete with businesses that enjoy significant government support, particularly given the propensity of countries that favor the state-capitalism model to do business with each other? How trustworthy are foreign joint-venture partners when it comes to sharing valuable intellectual property or sensitive confidential data, when their political equity holders could seek it for nationalistic purposes? Investors face similar dilemmas. Private shareholders in the publicly traded vehicles attached to some national oil companies, prizing risk-adjusted returns, must come to grips with the fact that these firms' mandates typically extend beyond financial considerations. Yet they must balance these concerns against the potential financial gains these companies stand to gain from state-support, whether via sweetened financing terms or diplomatic muscle to close deals over prime drilling acreage. For U.S. regulators, in the decade prior to the domestic shale boom, the most pressing question regarding state-owned enterprises was how to help American firms compete with them abroad. Since China National Offshore Oil Corporation's (CNOOC) failed 2005 bid for Unocal, and increasingly in the ensuing years as merger-and-acquisition activity in the U.S. oil patch has intensified, Washington has been forced to grapple with questions that are typically the province of OPEC and the exporting states: Should foreign firms of any flag, including potential adversaries, be allowed to buy U.S. energy infrastructure and reserves? Can the dangers of increased intellectual property theft and cyber-security breaches posed by foreign direct investment in a sector of prime importance to national security be mitigated? Do the benefits from that investment, particularly in a post-recessionary U.S. environment starved for jobs and shovel-ready jobs, outweigh the security risks, and indeed the broader trade-related economic dangers of the country signaling it is not open for foreign business? No matter one's vantage point, navigating an industry whose largest participants have conflicting and sometimes contradictory aims inevitably involves complex tradeoffs.

"In the geopolitics of energy," observes Citigroup's Edward Morse, "there are always winners and losers," a truth that applies not only to the companies but to countries, whose vital interests are intertwined with commodity revenues and the domestic price of these essential goods.[23] Because nations are loath to yield their sovereignty when vital questions of national interest are at stake, market failures in strategic sectors like energy and food production, whose aggregate economic pain could be lessened via international

---

[23] Edward L. Morse, "Welcome to the Revolution: Why Shale is the Next Shale," *Foreign Affairs* 93 no. 3 (May/June 2014): 3–7.

economic cooperation, are often left unsolved. This tension – between joint versus individual action by states to address dysfunctions in commodity markets – is the third of the four tensions this book discusses. It is particularly intense in markets like these in which the stakes are often zero sum. The urge for countries, particularly exporters, to adopt policies that harm importers is often particularly intense when markets are under stress, which can make matters worse, in an economically destructive feedback loop.

Nowhere is this dynamic more apparent than in global food markets. In 2010, as a severe drought in Russia wreaked havoc on crops and caused vicious wildfires to spread across the country, Moscow, trying to stem the pain, imposed a ban on grain exports, repeating a similar clampdown two years earlier. Taking traders and food producers by surprise, the move sent prices soaring to levels not seen since the 2007 and 2008 food crisis. U.S. wheat futures rose by 80% between June and August, and pushed up the price of other grains, including corn and barley, in the process. Russia, seeking to take care of its own, promised to award $1.2 billion in subsidies to its farmers and open its grain silos without action to regions in need. Moscow was on the giving end of the price spike, but consumers, particularly the poorest segment of the population in emerging market nations, were on the receiving end, with analysts worrying about the inflation effects on food prices in North Africa and the Middle East, where panic buying had ensued.[24] It was a classic case of a national action, in a moment of market stress, worsening the economic pain for everyone else. It should not be surprising that Moscow or any other nation would take a similar course, if it thought doing so would protect its own economic interests. Such thinking is the stuff of international relations and undergirds the complex calculus that informs national trade policies. The tension between national self-interest and the possibility of aggregate net gains from cooperative action among states is thus structural, an intrinsic part of the political landscape on which state-level economic policy is crafted, which can have major effects on how events unfold in global commodities markets.

Balancing these interests must be done in the context of a commodity market whose structure has changed deeply since the 1970s, in light of the so-called financialization process that has occurred over the past three decades. The dual nature of these markets as allocators of physical goods but also of investment capital, which sits in global financial capitals far from the oil well or grain silo, is the fourth dynamic tension in these markets whose

---

[24] Catherine Belton, Jack Farchy, and Javier Blas "Russia Grain Export Ban Sparks Price Fears," *Financial Times*, August 5, 2010.

evolution will chart the course of the sector over the coming decade. Public debate over the role of speculation in commodity markets is too often ahistorical, assuming that the surge of capital into commodity-linked financial securities over the past decade has given rise to a public-policy problem that is altogether new. It is not. In reality, public officials have fretted – and at times voiced outrage – over the perceived malign role of brokers and middlemen in the commodity trade, who grease the wheels at the market but draw criticism for the fact that they market their profit without the sweat of actually producing or consuming anything concrete, since at least the nineteenth century. Of such marketers, no less than Abraham Lincoln remarked that "for my part, I wish that every one of them [speculators] had his devilish head shot off." Vladimir Lenin, on the other side of the spectrum, felt the same. "As long as we fail to treat speculators the way they deserve – with a bullet in the head – we will not get anywhere at all."[25] The perennial fear among such critics is that profiteering by these middlemen cause prices to rise and fall beyond their fair value, harming producers' and consumers' ability to hedge their risk – the use for which forward grain markets were invented centuries ago – and hurting the businesses and consumers who would benefit from more stable, less unpredictable prices.

This debate remains one that can stir passions today, particularly when the prices of food and other essential goods are surging, as they were in 2008 and 2011, which was enough to bring a host of public officials to call for stricter policing of commodity derivative markets as a way of taming prices. The issue is more complicated to understand, let along regulate, than it was in Lincoln's time. A much broader array of commodities are traded on exchanges today than was the case even forty years ago – recall that crude oil contracts were not exchange-traded as recently as the 1970s oil crises (the longest-running oil futures contract was for heating oil, launched by the New York Mercantile Exchange in 1978). Electronic trading now dominates these markets, rather than the open-outcry method of price discovery that was the hallmark of these markets in places like Chicago and New York. The number and sophistication of the financial products tied to physical commodity benchmarks has also proliferated, as has the global breadth of commodity exchanges and the amount of money that pumps through them on a daily basis. The outcome of the debate over the helpfulness or harm caused by the presence of purely speculative traders to price formation is more than academic. Regulation of these exchanges and products has implications for

---

[25] Both quoted in David S. Jacks, "Populists Versus Theorists: Futures Markets and the Volatility of Prices," *Explorations in Economic History* 44 no. 2 (April 2007): 343–344.

everyday people, many of whom invest in these markets directly (sometimes unknowingly, via pension and 401(k) accounts).[26] Investments aside, price action at the NYMEX hits the pocketbooks of U.S. consumers directly via the gas station, the grocery aisle, and the jewelry store. For economies whose fate is closely tied to commodity export revenues, and for those consumers in the poorest parts of the world, ensuring that prices reflect what supply-and-demand fundamentals truly warrant is both a major fiscal and pocketbook issue.

This book is an exploration of scholarly debates that touch on at least one of these pivotal tensions: between producing and consuming nations, sovereign states and state-owned enterprises versus private-sector companies, international cooperation and economic nationalism, and the physical and financial layers of the modern global commodities market. Given the complexity of the markets involved and the range of interests at stake, none of these debates is easy to resolve. Many raise age-old questions about the optimal role of the state in the economy, the proper boundaries of the private sector and public life, and the trade-offs inherent in different monetary and trade regimes, not to mention market structures. No policy prescription can entirely eliminate these tensions. The aim of this book, instead, is to shed light on the conceptual issues that underpin the most pressing debates about commodities markets, drawing on some of the best-informed research from the academy, private sector, and think tanks, and to offer ideas about how public policy can improve outcomes for businesses and consumers alike.

---

[26] One popular exchange traded fund (ETF), the iPath Dow Jones-UBS Commodity Index Total Return ETF, is now among the top twenty most widely distributed in U.S. 401(k) retirement plans.

2

A Twenty-First Century Supercycle? Long-Term Trends in Metal and Energy Prices

In the eyes of some market analysts, the tripling of commodity prices between 2003 and 2006 was more than simply another bull market – it was the upswing of a so-called commodity supercycle, a protracted boom driven by roaring Chinese demand growth. For some skeptics, the supercycle concept was theoretically underdeveloped, more marketing than substance. It is true that proponents of the idea, operating outside the realm of university economics departments, left its theoretical dimensions underspecified. But a closer examination of long-term price data for commodities, and the economic concepts that underlie them, suggest that prolonged periods of rising and falling prices are intrinsic to these markets, both phases of the cycle sowing the seeds of the other. The duration and magnitude of the bull market that began shortly after the year 2000 are not uncharacteristic of other booms that have taken place over the past century. In terms of short-term horizons, supply and demand behavior for many commodities helps account for the relatively high volatility of these markets. Over very long periods of time, however, the inflation-adjusted prices of primary commodities show a stagnating or slightly declining trajectory.

THE ORIGINS OF THE COMMODITY SUPERCYCLE IDEA

Alan Heap, a commodity strategist at Citigroup, published what became the most widely cited articulation of the commodity supercycle thesis in a March 2005 note, *China: The Engine of a Commodities Super Cycle*.[1] Heap argued that a commodity supercycle was already underway. This boom was responsible for the postmillennial takeoff in natural resources. He defined

---

[1] Alan Heap, "China: The Engine of a Commodities Super Cycle," Citigroup Smith Barney, March 31, 2005.

a supercycle as a "prolonged (decade or more) trend in real commodity prices driven by urbanization and industrialization of a major economy." The upswing portions of these cycles last between ten and thirty-five years, Heap argued, making the timing of a full cycle last as many as seventy years. In his view, two supercycles had occurred in the prior 150 years. The first one stretched from the late 1800s through the early twentieth century, fueled by the materials-intensive economic expansion of the United States, while the second cycle ran from roughly 1945 through 1957 in tandem with the postwar reconstruction of Europe and Japan. The third such cycle was just taking off, in his view.

How did the current commodity supercycle come about? As Heap saw it, it was a purely a demand-side phenomenon, as were other supercycles. It came to pass owing to a sustained jump in commodity-intensive economic growth globally. Domestic demand for raw materials in China was the "engine" of the current supercycle, and the country's hunger for industrial metals was the best signal of the broader structural change unfolding in natural resource prices. The Middle Kingdom was straining global production capacity. The country's share of global industrial activity had doubled to 12% in just seven years. Its economic growth was incredibly natural resource-intensive, requiring three times as much commodity consumption per unit of output as the United States did. Although increased capital expenditure would ultimately help mitigate the amplitude of the price cycle, Heap argued, the response would be slow in coming, thus allowing the boom to extend over several decades. Increasing production costs had blunted the per-dollar ability of new capital expenditure to bring about production gains. Moreover, production lead times had lengthened because of environmental permitting and sustainability issues, leaving the supply side to play catch-up as demand soared. Although Heap used the example of the copper market to make his case, he argued that other commodities were in a similar pattern, implying that the supercycle dynamic would drive gains in primary resource prices.

The notion that recent years' gains in commodity prices were not merely cyclical gains, but rather an early manifestation of a decades-long bull run, found many proponents in the investment community. Indeed, the term "commodities supercycle" soon became commonplace in financial lexicon. The head of BlackRock's natural resources team, Graham Birch, described the current supercycle in 2007 as "one of only six in the last 250 years, similar to the surges in demand during the European Industrial Revolution and the opening up of the United States in the 1800s." But in contrast to Heap, BlackRock emphasized poor long-term supply growth as

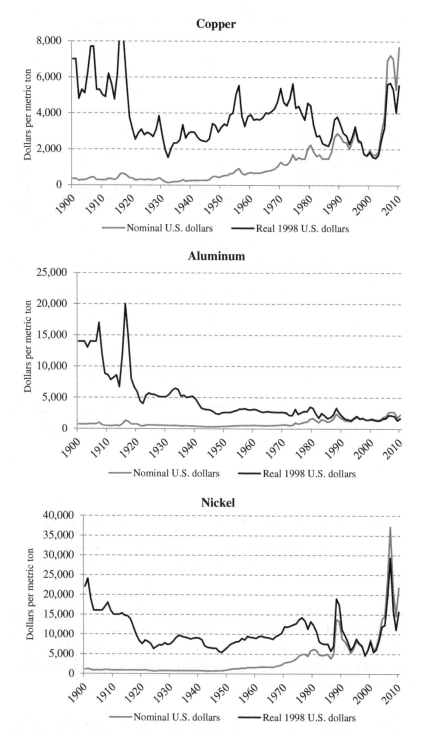

Figure 1. Real and Nominal Spot Metals Prices (1900–2010). *Source:* Thomas D. Kelly and Grecia R. Matos, "Historical Statistics for Mineral and Material Commodities in the United States," U.S. Geological Survey Data Series 140 (Online, 2013 Version).

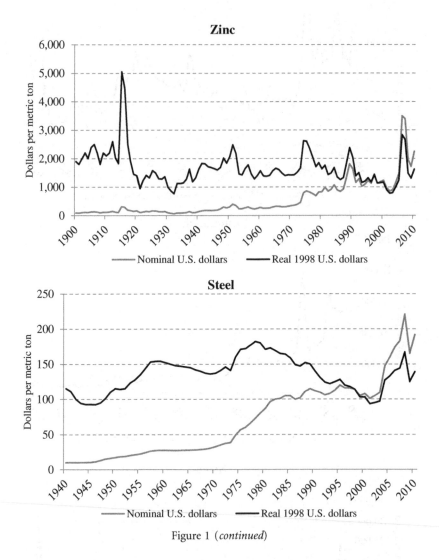

Figure 1 (*continued*)

being as responsible for the supercycle as demand was. Yet the investment manager shared the view that China was firmly at the center of the picture, as consumer spending in the Middle Kingdom and "other emerging markets in Asia and Latin America" was bringing about greater demand for resource-intensive consumer durables.[2]

---

[2] BlackRock, "Further Demand and Constrained Supply Underpin Commodities," November 23, 2007.

During the mid-2000s, booming commodity prices helped popularize the supercycle thesis. A World Bank index of commodity prices climbed 109% between early 2003 and 2008. That number never topped 60% in any boom in the twentieth century. From trough to peak, oil prices rose 1145% in nominal terms between December 1998 and July 2008. Noting that "booms and busts are relatively common occurrences in commodity markets," a 2009 World Bank report emphasized that the price spike of the previous five years was differed from its predecessors "in important ways."[3] According to a United Nations report, it was "among the most marked of the past century in its magnitude, duration, and the number of commodity groups whose prices have increased."[4] This boom was proving more resilient to production growth and had more than twice the effect on nominal commodity prices as measured by the World Bank index (up 131% in nominal terms from trough to peak). Moreover, it included not only those commodities with the highest trade-weighted value, such as oil, but also exotic raw materials, such as rhenium and cobalt.

But when commodity prices suffered an awesome collapse in the latter half of 2008, the chorus of voices on Wall Street trumpeting the investment virtues of the purported commodity supercycle fell silent. The S&P GSCI (formerly the Goldman Sachs Commodity Index), a world-production weighted index, collapsed from 890 points in July 2008 to just 306 points by February 2009. The stunning collapse in front-month oil prices, with Brent sinking from $146 per barrel in mid-2008 to $36 per barrel five months later, was a decline of historic proportions. To many, the price declines cast serious doubts on the legitimacy of the supercycle theory. As the December 2008 article "So Long, Super Cycle" in the *Financial Times* reported, "the severity of the crisis has surprised natural resources companies' executives, commodity traders and Wall Street bankers alike.... The sudden plunge poses a fundamental question: is this just a temporary blip within an upward trend, with prices likely to rebound in the medium term, or is it the conclusion of another commodities cycle of boom and bust, with a period of relatively stable prices coming ahead?" It continued by saying that a "growing minority" in the natural resources industry and among Wall

---

[3] John Baffes, Donald Mitchell, Elliot (Mick) Riordan, Shane Streifel, Hans Timmer, and William Shaw, *Global Economic Prospects: Commodities at the Crossroads 2009* (Washington, DC: The World Bank, 2008), 53.

[4] Christian Nellemann, Monika MacDevette, Ton Manders, Bas Eickhout, Birger Svihus, Anne Gerdien Prins, and Bjørn P. Kaltenborn (eds.), *The Environmental Food Crisis: The Environment's Role in Averting Future Food Crises.* A UNEP Rapid Response Assessment (United Nations Environment Programme, February 2009).

Street analysts now doubted the "rosy view" that the boom would continue, and that these same executives would admit as much – but only in private.[5]

Among the most skeptical analysts was Jeffrey Christian of CPM Group. In his judgment, commodity supercycles were nothing more than a Wall Street marketing ploy to accommodate a resurgence of investor interest in commodities. Speaking at World Bank Extractive Week in March 2009, Christian said:

Part of this marketing pitch was a great deal of talk about "Commodities Supercycles." There's not quantitative historical evidence of commodity supercycles, and when you hear terms like that, as with "The New Economic Paradigm" that supposedly justified the never-ending stock market boom that collapsed in 2000–2001, you must realize immediately that you are not listening to reasoned research, but rather to marketing hype. Terms like the Commodities Supercycle are used by brokers and others trying to sell investors products based not on research and analysis, but on hype.[6]

In alluding to "the new economic paradigm," Christian equated the idea of supercycles with the "new era economic thinking" rampant during the tech boom of the late 1990s. The theory was that a fundamental shift in the world economy, in that case supposedly brought on by the invention and popularization of the Internet, would lead asset prices on a long-term, even permanent, climb to new highs. As Robert Schiller shows in *Irrational Exuberance*, this sort of new era economic thinking has accompanied every major stock boom in the twentieth-century in the United States. But each time, the eventual collapse in equity prices puts an end to such talk, at least until the next boom.[7] For Christian, the commodity supercycle argument had no more merit than any of these theories, and the sensational price collapse of 2008 was proof.

The idea that the world was in the throes of a commodity lift-off was as hard to deny in 2005 as it was to defend in early 2009. At either moment, prices appeared to bear out one or the other conclusion, and in dramatic fashion. Some analysts, such as Francisco Blanch of Merrill Lynch, foresaw a resurgence in the secular price surge after prices hit rock bottom the year following the collapse of Lehman Brothers. "The commodity supercycle is not over, just resting," he told the *Economist* in May 2009.

[5] Javier Blas, "So Long, Super Cycle," *Financial Times*, December 10, 2008.
[6] Jeffrey M. Christian, "The Effects of the Financial Crisis on Metals Markets," Remarks at World Bank Extractive Industries Week, March 4, 2009 (accessed at worldbank.org in May 2015).
[7] Robert J. Shiller, *Irrational Exuberance*, 1st and 2nd eds. (Princeton, NJ: Princeton University Press, 2000, 2005).

The rapid price rebound from the lows of 2009 provided a new spark to the discussion. Indeed, the robustness of the recovery led some to wonder whether rumors of the death of the commodity supercycle were not exaggerated. Between December 2008 and June 2009, the price of Brent crude oil more than doubled, ultimately returning to $126 per barrel in April 2011, within spitting distance of its 2008 peak. That upward move in crude oil was propelled to some extent from the events of the Arab Spring in 2011, particularly the loss of Libya's 1.2 million barrels per day (mb/d) of Qaddafi-era crude exports. The recovery was not only in oil, however, so unrest in the Middle East and North Africa cannot be the whole explanation. The Rogers International Commodity Index total return product also doubled between February 2009 and April 2011. Even the S&P GSCI non-energy spot index – which excludes oil – jumped by 115% between its 2008 nadir and April 2011. That is not only a recent high, but perhaps most remarkably, it is actually 13% higher than its 2008 peak.

This resurgence challenged the view that commodities were dead in the water after the credit crisis. Prices were able to rebound in spite of subpar growth in many OECD countries. One observer at the *Financial Times* put the issue well in January 2011:

Clearly, at the top of the economic cycle, consumers will be so desperate to get their hands on raw materials that they will pay well over the cost of production. So the current surge in commodity prices, at a time of spare economic capacity in the rich world, suggests one of two things is going on. Either the needs of the developing world are causing demand growth to outstrip supply for an extended period, or new sources of supply can be found only at higher cost. Both explanations add weight to the idea of a "commodity supercycle", a long-term surge in prices that might last 15–20 years.[8]

Other voices agreed that high or rising commodity prices would not disappear anytime soon. Jim Rogers said in August 2011 that he saw the supercycle lasting another twenty to twenty-five years. For its part, the *Economist* argued that the forces that prompted the creation of the supercycle notion were still in force. "There are good reasons to suspect that prices will stay high for a while yet," it declared.[9]

And yet by 2013 it was becoming clear that the structural drivers of the broad commodity price increases of the past decade had begun to wane. The first, and perhaps most important factor, was a downshift in Chinese economic growth from its astronomical annual gains of roughly 10% on average

---

[8] "Buttonwood: Material Concerns," *The Economist*, January 13, 2011.
[9] "Commodities Markets: A Rocky Patch," *The Economist*, May 12, 2011.

between 2005 and 2011. But the composition of that growth has also been evolving, a trend they expected to continue. No longer would the Middle Kingdom's growth be as closely tied to raw materials-intensive manufacturing and investing. Instead, consumer spending and services would begin to make up a bigger share of the pie, reducing the commodity-intensiveness of future marginal output gains. Changes on the supply side of global commodity market fundamentals were also underway. "What first occurred in US natural gas – a marshaling of capital and a new supply surplus – is being replicated across most commodities, including critical industrial and bulk commodities, and in other longer-lead time products such as oil, even with risks to supply disruptions."[10] These developments would make for more idiosyncratic conditions across individual commodity markets, significantly reducing the likelihood of a repeat of the broad-based bull market of the prior decade.

THE ECONOMIC THEORY OF SHORT- AND LONG-RUN COMMODITY PRICE FORMATION

Understanding the economic theory behind how commodity prices behave can help make sense of the debate about where these vital markets are headed. It can also shed light on the likely implications of a sudden disruption in supplies or a gradual downshift in demand. The theory also illuminates certain oft-cited properties of commodity prices, such as their tendency to rise and fall suddenly and unpredictably, their boom-and-bust nature, and the counterintuitive downtrend in commodity prices over long periods of time.

The schematics in Figures 2 and 3 illustrate aspects of commodity price behavior over short and long time horizons.[11] As Figure 2 illustrates, the price at a given moment settles at P_1 where the supply and demand schedules meet at S and D_1. Over short periods of time, production capacity is set in stone, limiting how much supply can be created. Therefore, the supply schedule S, otherwise known as the supply curve, represents the variable costs of producing a given amount of the good in light of existing production

[10] Edward L. Morse, Heath R. Jansen, Daniel P. Ahn, Jon Bergtheil, Aakash Doshi, Viswanathrao Kintali, Seth Kleinman, Eric G. Lee, Ulhas Shenoy, Johann Steyn, David B. Wilson, and Anthony Yuen, "The New Abnormal: 2013 Commodities Outlook," Citi Commodities Strategy, November 19, 2012.

[11] This section on the basic elements of commodity price formation is based on the explication in Radetzki's 2008 textbook. See Marian Radetzki, *A Handbook of Primary Commodities in the Global Economy* (Cambridge and New York: Cambridge University Press, 2008).

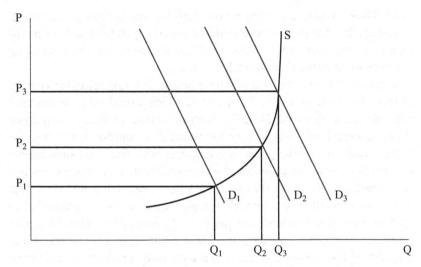

Figure 2. Short-Run Price Determination. *Source:* Marian Radetzki, *A Handbook of Primary Commodities in the Global Economy*, (Cambridge and New York: Cambridge University Press, 2008), 58.

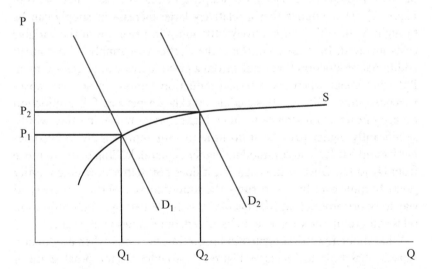

Figure 3. Long-Run Price Determination. *Source:* Marian Radetzki, *A Handbook of Primary Commodities in the Global Economy*, (Cambridge and New York: Cambridge University Press, 2008), 58.

units. These variable costs depend on many factors, including operational efficiency, differences in natural endowment (the quality of soil or ore, for example), and labor costs. Producers are incented to keep up output as long as prices are covering their variable costs.

Supply or demand may also shift temporarily, affecting prices for a period of time. Demand may rise, for instance, which would shift the demand schedule to the right from D_1 to D_2. Such an increase in demand may come about as a result of many factors: for example, an upturn in the business cycle, a rush to buy the good by consumers who fear a possible supply interruption, or a rise in prices of a commodity that consumers use as a close substitute. Whatever the cause, the jump in demand would mean that additional units of production, with higher variable costs, would need to be drawn on, which would raise prices to P_2. A sudden decline in supply could also bring about higher prices. As in Figure 2, that would mean that S would shift to the left. Problems that force some production capacity to shut down from one moment to the next – such as bad weather, a strike, or an accident – could cause this type of price increase.

The degree to which a shift in supply or demand affects prices is attributed in large measure to capacity utilization at the time. When there is plenty of excess production capacity, the supply schedule is close to flat (see S in Figure 2). That implies that a relatively large increase in supply can be brought forth with comparatively little jump in prices given the variable costs involved. In these conditions, the elasticity of supply – how much additional production that results from a given increase in prices – is high. But what about when short-term production bumps up against capacity constraints? The supply schedule quickly steepens as full production capacity nears. No matter how much higher prices move, in other words, significantly higher prices can do little to spur more supply. It becomes harder and harder to accommodate higher demand, leading prices to move from D_2 to D_3. Once at full capacity, it does not matter how much loftier prices become over the short run – the supply curve is vertical, there is no way to boost production when capacity is 100% tied up. High utilization rates will prompt new capacity to be added, but doing so takes time.

What about how prices form over longer time horizons, when production capacity has time to increase? Figures 3 provides a conceptual sense of how supply and demand schedules interact to form the price levels toward which market prices are moving over a longer window. The long-run supply schedule represents the average total cost of marginal production at different output levels, allowing for capacity to change over time. It is relatively costly to bring on the first supplies, given the limited nature of ultra-low-cost resources to exploit, whether farmland or minerals. But the supply curve becomes flatter at higher cost levels, which allow for a relatively large number of resources to be exploited economically.

The elasticity of both short- and long-run supply depends on the specific commodity in question. The steepness of a short-run increase in price depends on several factors, including the amount of the good in storage, the size of the demand shift, and the shape of the short-run supply curve. Likewise, the time it takes for a given commodity's price to fall, as well as the magnitude of the decline over the full adjustment period, will vary depending on the market context and particular attributes of the good in question. Generally speaking, extracted goods like oil and metals have higher long-term price elasticities of supply than do agricultural goods (i.e., relatively higher prices are needed to spur additional supplies of the former than the latter). It tends to be easier to boost farm output – for example, by bringing new land into production, switching crop plantings based on price signals, and investing in yield-enhancing technologies – than for those that are essentially mined, where investment cycles and project lead times can be long and often subject to delays.

Two competing forces play an important role in shaping prices over long periods of time, assuming constant demand growth. The first is improvements in technology. Thanks to technical innovation, mankind has continually found ways to produce natural resources more efficiently, putting downward pressure on the supply curve. But an opposing force, depletion, also matters. As demand grows, producers are forced to use ever-more marginal land or other inputs, which can cause average total marginal costs to rise. Generally speaking, over the very long run, technological progress has proven the victor, enabling production to grow without concurrent increases in real prices.

The traditional Hotelling model, on which much of the scholarship in the field of exhaustible resource economics is based, predicts ever-increasing long-run prices for finite geological resources such as hydrocarbons and metals.[12] The intuition behind Hotelling's theory is straightforward. Someone who owns a finite resource will want to sell it at a time that maximizes its aggregate worth. He or she will incorporate into any production decision the fact that if the good is sold today, the chance to sell it tomorrow disappears. Thus, the owner will calculate how much of the good to bring to market at any given time based on what the current marginal revenue net

---

[12] Harold Hotelling, "The Economics of Exhaustible Resources," *Journal of Political Economy* 39, no. 2 (1931), 137–75.

of extraction costs could yield as productive capital earning a market rate of interest. The implication of this rule is that market forces will attach a so-called scarcity rent to the price of an exhaustible resource. That scarcity rent should increase over time at the prevailing rate of interest.[13]

Yet, however compelling and artful Hotelling's theory, it is at odds with observed behavior of prices over the centuries. The prices of most commodities have been essentially stagnant or fallen in real terms over the centuries as a result. For some, especially those where politics come into play, such as crude oil, the long-term price path has not trended downward, but rather has been defined by epochs marked by distinct price behavior.[14] Currently, oil prices are quite high – a multiple of what they were over much of the twentieth century. But it is an exception, not the rule, among commodities. These empirical trends will be discussed in more depth later in the chapter.

There are generally two ways to reconcile the Hotelling rule's prediction of rising real exhaustible resource prices with their observed price trajectories. The first is that the market perceives the Earth's endowment of these vital resources as so vast, and their ultimate extinction so far in the future, that any actual scarcity rent the market attaches to them is a negligible component of their current price. While the scarcity rent may be growing at the rate Hotelling would predict, marginal extraction costs are the overwhelming price determinant in practice. Another way of reconciling the rule with empirical price patterns is that technological gains have lowered marginal extraction costs, and with them the real price of finite commodities, over long periods of time, eclipsing the net effect of any rising scarcity rent on market prices.[15] However, it would not be impossible for the Hotelling formulation to show greater empirical validity at some point in the future for a given commodity, should market perception shift or a binding, measurable geological reserve-size limit come into view.

Capacity expansion can help lower costs over time, allowing prices to fall to a theoretical long-run equilibrium level, but they also push short-term costs higher. The commodity boom of the past decade is an example of

---

[13] For a useful discussion of the Hotelling rule, see Tobias Kronenberg, "Should We Worry about the Failure of the Hotelling Rule?," Paper prepared for Monte Verità Conference on Sustainable Resource Use and Economic Dynamics, June 4–9, 2006, Ascona, Switzerland. Center of Economic Research at ETH Zurich.

[14] Eyal Dvir and Kenneth S. Rogoff, "Three Epochs of Oil," NBER Working Paper No.14927, National Bureau of Economic Research (April 2009).

[15] James D. Hamilton, "Oil Prices, Exhaustible Resources, and Economic Growth," in *Handbook Of Energy And Climate Change*, ed. Roger Fouquet (Edward Elgar Publishing, March 2013), 29–57.

this dynamic. A lack of spare production capacity across a wide variety of commodities in the early 2000s helped spark a fierce market rally. These higher prices stimulated investment in new capacity. Although this additional capacity is now beginning to help lower prices, it is part of the reason why prices have been so high during the boom years. Demand for scarce investment inputs all along the production supply chain has been intense, bidding up their prices. But this cost increase is temporary. Once the production bottlenecks are removed, whether for more roads or more drill bits, marginal costs decline, and the new production capacity (and typically higher inventories) helps cool off markets.

Other dynamics inevitably complicate the price formation process just described. Some commodities are produced jointly. Often pairs of polymetallic ores (copper and nickel, for example, or lead and zinc) and agricultural products (leather and beef) fit this description. As a result, high prices for the commodity that forms the more important part of the revenue stream can mean that its partner is produced beyond what its own economic merits would allow. Politics also frequently interferes with market function. Rarely if ever does a commodity market, in the real world, amount to a perfect monopoly, despite the casual usage of that term in the popular press. As Marian Radetzki observes, "what occurs is jointly implemented and crudely determined cuts in capacity utilization by the leading producers in markets where such action is believed to result in higher aggregate revenue and profits."[16]

Applying short-run supply and demand curves as a means of analyzing day-to-day market prices is not as easy as the smooth curves in these economic models suggest. In practice, prices tend to trade in "ill-defined and unstable broad bands."[17] The supply and demand schedules are typically too opaque and unsteady to make precisely pinpointing where prices should be trading based on them possible. Why is that so? One reason is that publicly available data regarding current supply and demand conditions in a given commodity market are almost without exception incomplete, infrequently issued, and often contradictory. This problem of transparency has only worsened as China and other countries that disclose less data than do the United States and other advanced Western economies have assumed a more prominent place in the market.

But the issue goes beyond data. Figure 4 depicts a short-run supply curve, composed of profit-maximizing firms. The horizontal axis shows aggregate

---

[16] Marian Radetzki, *A Handbook of Primary Commodities in the Global Economy* (Cambridge and New York: Cambridge University Press, 2008), 60.
[17] Ibid., 61.

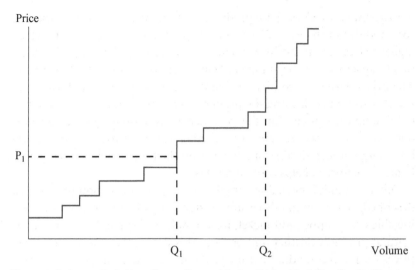

Figure 4. Industry Cash Cost Curve. *Source*: Marian Radetzki, *A Handbook of Primary Commodities in the Global Economy*, (Cambridge and New York: Cambridge University Press, 2008), 62.

production volume, with each step of the curve representing a given plant's limited production capacity. The vertical axis shows the price level, with each plant having a set average variable production cost (also known as cash cost). Economic theory would predict that when prices fall, quantities produced would also decline, as plants take production offline in response to prevailing market prices failing to compensate them for their out-of-pocket costs.

Yet, often producers do not behave as this simplified theory would predict in that they choose to keep producing. Why? To begin with, closing and reopening a plant, such as an oil refinery, can be costly. If the firm foresees the downturn in prices as temporary, it may decide it is more advantageous to stay in production than shut down. Those costs that are fixed (which the cash cost curve does not depict) versus variable for a given plant may also fluctuate over time and have an element of unpredictability. Labor, for example, is theoretically a variable cost. But in practice, there are frictions and limitations to hiring and firing workers over short time horizons. So too with other expenses, such as nonessential services. The larger the portion of a plant's expenses that ownership deems fixed, the lower the supply schedule becomes, leaving the plant to produce at levels that might not have been economical in other conditions. Moreover, some producers choose to hedge their output using derivatives markets. That offloading of risk allows them to continue covering their cash costs even if they confront market prices that would be too low to be economical had they not sold their output forward. Prevailing market prices typically play a role in determining commodity producers' costs. When high prices allow for exceptional profits, firms typically become more casual in maximizing operational efficiencies, and costs along the supply chain get bid up. But when prices fall and times are lean, cash costs often fall owing to lower input costs and market-driven pressure to increase efficiency. Finally, some producers, such as state-owned enterprises, may not be strictly profit maximizing, as the model assumes. Even those that are can still be subject to political pressure – to maintain output even when it does not make economic sense, for example – and changes in public policy, which can shift short-term supply and demand schedules from one day to the next.

LONG-TERM HISTORICAL COMMODITY PRICE FLUCTUATIONS

Several conclusions about long-term cycles in commodity markets emerge from an empirical analysis of these phenomena. First, the reality of prolonged commodity booms, as well as the timing of those cycles over the past 150 years, is broadly supported by the historical record. Heap's formulation of the mechanisms that underlie these protracted cycles, however, is imperfect, in that it does not recognize that such booms also have an essential supply-side component. Changes in the level of competition in a given market can have significant implications on the timing and duration of its long-term price cycles, as the history of the crude oil market demonstrates. When turning points do occur – their timing is notoriously difficult to predict – they tend to be sudden and deep; the result of both supply and demand inelasticities at work and the possibility of long-term overhangs in production capacity and inventories. The response of commodities as a class to the recent recession – a sharp crash quickly followed by a renewed upward surge only months later – illustrates another key feature of these booms: they are not immune from the vicissitudes of the business cycle, though they are marked by an unusual degree of resilience to cyclical downturns. Additionally, the timing and amplitude of commodity booms vary across individual commodities, though they display a significant amount of co-movement in related families of commodities and at times across the class more broadly. Lastly, the data show that despite these boom periods, real commodity prices tend to decline, not rise, over very long periods of time.

Commodity market booms can last well beyond the time frames associated with short-run economic fluctuations. Normal upswings and downswings in economic activity "happen at irregular intervals and last

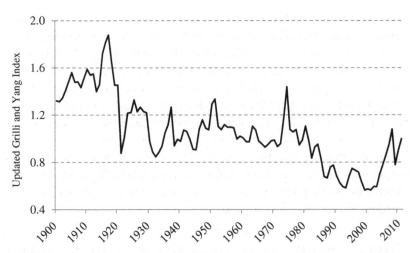

Figure 5. Real Non-Energy Commodity Prices (1900–2010). *Note:* The updated Grilli and Yang commodity price index is deflated using the manufacturing unit value index, a trade-weighted index of major developed country exports of manufactured commodities to developing countries. See Stephan Pfaffenzeller, Paul Newbold, and Anthony Rayner, "A Short Note on Updating the Grilli and Yang Commodity Price Index," *World Bank Economic Review* 21 no. 1 (2007), 151–63. *Sources:* Grilli and Yang (1988); World Bank; Pfaffenzeller et al. (2007).

for varying lengths of time," as Christina Romer points out. The very term "business cycle" can be misleading; after all, these oscillations can be highly asymmetric and defying easy timing, even over relatively brief spans of time. Some are long, such as the 1981 recession, which lasted sixteen months, whereas the one in 1980 held for only six months. And the three recessions that occurred between 1973 and 1982 contrast sharply with the eight booms years starting in 1982.[18]

But larger cycles of booms and busts have also transpired over the course of history, as the index reveals. The authors of the IMF study, Paul Cashin and John McDermitt, define a large boom as a period during which industrial commodity prices increase by at least 25%, while large slumps, by the same token, show declines of at least the same magnitude.[19] This approach filters out less significant directional price movements. By their criteria, seven large booms and slumps occurred between 1862 and 1999, based on an extension of the Grilli and Yang commodity price index.[20] The longest boom in the

---

[18] Christina D. Romer, "Business Cycles," Concise Encyclopedia of Economics (1993).

[19] Paul Cashin and C. John McDermott, "The Long-Run Behavior of Commodity Prices: Small Trends and Big Variability," IMF Staff Papers 49 no. 2 (2002).

[20] For the technical details of the Grilli and Yang commodity price index, as well as the commonly used extension of the data through 2003 by Pfaffenzeller et al., see Stephan

series lasted an extraordinary thirty-nine years, from 1868 to 1907. The second longest lasted a still impressive twenty years, beginning in 1931. Had the authors' data extended through 2011, they would have determined that the next longest boom would have happened from 2001 to 2008.

These long booms were followed by prolonged periods of stagnating or declining prices, resulting in bull-bear market cycles that when measured from trough to trough lasted several decades. After the large upcycle from 1868 to 1907, prices then slipped to a nadir in 1915. That complete cycle lasted a full forty-seven years. The next one, from 1915 to 1931 on a trough-to-trough basis, had a duration of sixteen years. Then the longest of all, with a boom from 1931 to 1951 followed by a slump from 1951 to 1971, had a complete cycle of forty years. Were commodities prices to continue rising over the next twenty to twenty-five years, as some financial analysts have argued they will, that would mean a boom lasting more than ten years less than the one that occurred between 1868 and 1907 and just a few years more than the one that occurred after the Great Depression and World War II.[21]

In the case of metals markets, for instance, the boom that began in 2003 has proven durable. Yes, metals prices were cut off at the knees in 2008, but it was only a matter of months before they were back in historically high territory. The S&P GSCI Industrial Metals Index, which had peaked at 536 points in May 2007, rose from the ashes of early 2009 to reach 498 points by April 2011 (see Figure 6). That rebound contrasts with the fact that the index almost never rose higher than 200 points between its beginnings in 1977 until the boom was well underway in 2004.

What mechanisms help explain these dramatic long-term price fluctuations? Making sense of them requires coming to grips with the underlying economic dynamics. The IMF's *World Economic Outlook* published in October 2008 provides a good if incomplete summary of the structural drivers of the commodity boom of the 2000s:[22]

In the current boom, the supply-side constraints were not the result of sharp, temporary supply reductions, but instead reflected protracted, inelastic supply responses

Pfaffenzeller, Paul Newbold, and Anthony Rayner, "A Short Note on Updating the Grilli and Yang Commodity Price Index," *World Bank Economic Review* 21, no. 1 (2007), 151–63.

[21] Jim Rogers, *Hot Commodities: How Anyone Can Invest Profitably in the World's Best Market* (New York: Random House, 2004).

[22] International Monetary Fund, *World Economic Outlook: Financial Stress, Downturns, and Recoveries* (Washington, DC: International Monetary Fund, October 2008): 86.

Marian Radetzki, Roderick G. Eggert, Gustavo Lagos, Marcos Lima, and John E. Tilton, "The Boom in Mineral Markets: How Long Might It Last?," *Resources Policy* 33, no. 3 (September 2008): 125.

Figure 6. S&P GSCI Industrial Metals Index (2000–2012). *Source:* Bloomberg, as of December 31, 2012

in the face of higher demand and rising prices. In the oil market and, to a lesser extent, in some metals markets, "time-to-build" lags appear to have increased during the current cycle.... In the face of rapidly growing demand, this slow capacity expansion has led to a perpetuation of low inventory and spare capacity levels, which have sustained the pressure on prices. This fear of the current boom has given rise to the notion of a "supercycle" in commodity prices – a period with secular trend increases in commodity prices because of the need for a substantial buildup in capacity.

What ought to be added to this delineation are the supply issues that bedeviled OPEC production in key exporters such as Iraq, Venezuela, and Nigeria, all of which saw politics interfere with dependable commercialization of their prodigious reserves. No single factor alone explains the dramatic rise in prices, as the IMF explains. Instead, when the right combination of supply and demand stimuli confronts the intrinsically inelastic nature of production and consumption of some goods, and where inventories and spare capacity are low, the result can be a fierce upward rise in prices. Broader macroeconomic forces, including a decline in the value of the U.S. dollar against other major currencies and falling interest rates, can amplify the boom. These macroeconomic factors are described in more detail in Chapter 3, which explores the so-called food crisis of the mid-2000s.

The global economic boom between 2003 and 2006 forms the structural backbone of the current boom. Real-world GDP grew by more than

4% each year from 2004 through 2007, which the IMF points out was the first time that level of growth on a global level had been achieved since the early 1970s. Still, despite this impressive economic expansion, the real question is why buoyant prices and industry profits for most of the eight years since 2003 have apparently not been sufficient to generate the capacity additions necessary to bring prices more closely in line with marginal production costs. It is difficult to generalize about the timeline required to bring greenfield capacity online given the numerous factors at play, from political conditions among both investing countries and host countries to the particulars of the mineral deposit being targeted to funding conditions in global markets.[23]

The upswing portion of a secular commodity cycle akin to the one currently underway cannot be chalked up purely to increases in global demand. The history of commodities markets shows conclusively that a jump in demand, even a large one, is not enough by itself to cause a decades-long increase in prices. A look at the aluminum market over the course of the twentieth century makes that clear. Global aluminum output rose fortyfold for a full three decade span, from 1939 to 1969, yet real prices trended downward over that time.[24] The example of crude oil is even more dramatic. Between the years 1965 and 1970, global oil consumption exploded from 30.8 million barrels per day to 45.4 million barrels per day, an astounding annualized growth rate of 10%. But real prices over those same five years hardly followed suit. Instead, they declined, according to the posted price for Arabian Light at Ras Tanura, Saudi Arabia.[25] Despite the outward shift in the demand curve, the supply response was sufficient in both of these cases to ensure that real prices did not rise on a sustained basis. These episodes were not historical anomalies. Climbing demand, even if structural in nature, is not sufficient to provoke a commodities supercycle.

Still, an enduring growth in demand for a particular commodity is a necessary condition for an upward supercycle, even if it is not sufficient without the right conditions on the supply side. Of the four global commodity price spikes since 1900 that the World Bank identifies, all but one of them was preceded by a more gradual upward trend in prices over the prior decades, spurred by rapid demand growth that took place in connection with

[23] Marian Radetzki, Roderick G. Eggert, Gustavo Lagos, Marcos Lima, and John E. Tilton, "The Boom in Mineral Markets: How Long Might It Last?," *Resources Policy* 33, no. 3 (September 2008): 125.

[24] Ibid.

[25] For consumption and price data, see *BP Statistical Review of World Energy 2011* (London: BP, June 2011).

economic expansion. The four notable spikes in real non-energy commodity prices it names took place in 1917, 1951, 1974, and 2008.[26]

Each of these four spikes occurred after at least a decade of major infrastructure investment and/or strong global growth. The first of them, which took place in the closing decades of the twentieth century and reached its zenith in 1917, was mainly the result of the economic coming of age of the United States, coupled with an industrial build up in Europe prior to World War I. The next sustained uptrend in prices occurred as the world moved out of the Great Depression into World War I and then into postwar rebuilding in Europe and Japan. The real economy grew at an average rate of 4.8% between 1950 and 1957. In the case of the 1974 oil crisis, global growth had been running at nearly 5% on average in the five years prior. The movement from 2003 to 2011 to a higher plane occurred within the context of industrialization in the so-called BRIC economies and with global growth running from 2003 to 2008 at an annual average 3.5% (post-2008 data is not shown in the graph).[27]

The fact that commodity prices often rise and fall together, broadly speaking, for prolonged periods squares with the notion that changes in global demand are partly responsible for secular commodity booms, although they alone are insufficient.[28] These fluctuations in consumption, linked to natural resource-intensive phases of economic development, play a role in driving cycles, as the industrialization and urbanization processes through which development often takes shape may entail demand increases lasting as long as several decades. The experience of the first decade of the 2000s, which witnessed a boom in several populous emerging market countries, most famously China, fits within this pattern. That said, these positive cross-commodity price correlations do not rule out supply-side explanations for commodity supercycles. Technological improvements in how one kind of metal is mined or produced, for instance, may also ultimately spill over into supply trends for related commodities in parallel ways, which could also underlie the correlations in the price data.

Robust demand growth for a particular commodity is typically a necessary but insufficient ingredient of lasting commodity booms. Supply-side factors also matter in at least three ways.[29] For one thing, the project lead

---

[26] *Global Economic Prospects 2009: Commodities at the Crossroads* (Washington, DC: The World Bank, 2009): 52–57.

[27] Ibid., 55.

[28] John T. Cuddington and Daniel Jerrett, "Super Cycles in Real Metals Prices?," *IMF Staff Papers* 55 no. 4 (2008), 541–565.

[29] David Humphreys, "The Great Metals Boom: A Retrospective," *Resource Policy* 35 no. 1 (March 2010), 1–13.

times necessary to add new production capacity may prove longer than anticipated. Tighter regulations in recent decades, partly in the form of stricter environmental permitting, may have contributed to a recent rise in lead times. A dearth of skilled labor can also prove a roadblock to the expansion of capacity in the mining and petroleum industries after long slumps in the industry, as long-term low prices tend to mean fewer young workers train to enter the industry, as job openings are fewer. This phenomenon is generally truer in minerals and oil extraction than in agriculture, given that the relative speed of the planting-to-planting cycle makes crop production respond more quickly to changes in price than is the case for more price-inelastic commodities.[30] Although likely an unrepresentative example, one analysis of fifty-four major base and precious metals deposits around the Pacific Rim, conducted in 1995, found that 27.5 years passed on average between successfully locating a base metals deposit and eventual cash flow generation. Gold deposits took an even-longer twenty-nine years on average.[31] These timelines are not representative of all projects in the industry. Where minerals caches have already been located or production has already been in place, lead times will be shorter. Still, these sorts of figures show the unreliability of counting on a sub-decadal timeline for bringing all new capacity on-stream for some commodity sectors. They are not limited to minerals alone. Protracted oil price cycles stem in part from the same long implementation lags for discovery, exploration, and capital investment experienced in the metals industry.

A sustained rise in the cost of finding and developing new production capacity may also contribute to price booms. When the marginal cost of production rises, the price of the commodity must increase to induce investors to build new capacity. In the case of the commodities boom of the 2000s, the marginal cost of producing metals, for example, grew substantially. A *Financial Times* article, "Metals: Seam Stress," bore witness to that fact in October 2010:

It is becoming harder to reach the best deposits. With Chilean and North American copper veins, as well as Indonesian tin, on the wane, miners are forced to turn to countries such as Mongolia, Afghanistan and Congo. "There's no doubt that the best resources in the first world have been developed," says Evy Hambro, head of natural resources at BlackRock, one of the sector's largest institutional investors.

---

[30] "Commodity Price Swings and Commodity Exporters," in *World Economic Outlook: Growth Resuming, Dangers Remain*, World Economic and Financial Surveys (Washington, DC: International Monetary Fund, April 2012).

[31] Graham A. Davis and Michael Samis, "Using Real Options to Manage and Value Exploration," *Society of Economic Geologists Special Publication* 12, no. 14 (2006): 274.

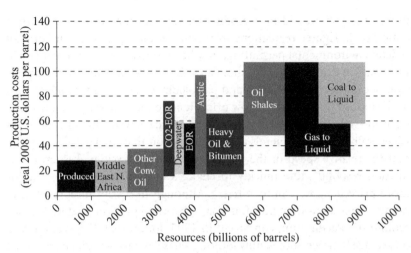

Figure 7. Long-Term Oil Supply Cost Curve as of 2008. *Source:* International Energy Agency

"The remaining best deposits to be discovered are in challenging locations – be they politically or physically challenging.[32]

Part of this increase stemmed from the fact that in a commodities boom, the cost of the goods and services needed to boost production also moves higher, as those industries struggle with output capacity constraints of their own. Another element of the marginal cost increase for base metals has been the boom in small-scale Chinese production, which tends to lie at the top of the production curve. This feature of China's newfound prominence in metals markets has received less attention than has the boom in the country's appetite for metals, but it has also had a significant effect on prices, particularly given rising costs of electricity for industrial use in the Middle Kingdom.[33] Prices can fall below the marginal cost of supply for periods of time, but that occurrence tends to be fleeting. Deliveries to the market can come from inventories, so that even if high-cost production folds, the market can remain well supplied and thus act as a weight on prices.

For some commodities, notably oil, barriers to entry in fields with the lowest cost of production – onshore Saudi Arabia and other low-cost Middle Eastern and North African fields – by OPEC member countries boost

[32] "Rebasing Our Commodity Index," *Economist*, October 28, 2010.
[33] Michael Elliott, Anjani Agrawal, Carlos Assis, Bob Stall, Pierre Mangers, and Angie Beifus, *Global Steel 2013: A New World, a New Strategy* (Ernst & Young, 2013): 22–27.

the global price of the marginal barrel, as does curtailing production in these same fields for the sake of imposing a price floor to enhance producer revenues. A jump in global oil demand of over 10 mb/d between 2001 and 2010 to 87.4 mb/d pushed the marginal barrel produced to heavy Canadian oil and North American oil shale.[34] The cost of producing these liquids dwarfs that supplied by OPEC, which can be produced for as little as $5 per barrel, according to the Energy Policy Information Center. As long as the marginal barrel is supplied at such a cost and spare production capacity worldwide stays in short supply relative to historical norms, spot market prices can remain far above their longer-term historical average.

A third mechanism that can spur a boom is demand growth that catches producers by surprise. If the public or private sector underestimates the scale of the capacity additions required to bring spare capacity levels back to historical norms, then increases in consumption can have jarring effects on prices.[35] This kind of surprise demand shock has generally come about for one of two reasons over the past two centuries: (1) the economic maturation of a large, populous country or region; or (2) the outbreak or aftermath of a large-scale war, which inevitably entails a giant rebuilding effort as well. These events can provide a demand-side stimulus that catches industry unprepared and leaves it playing catch-up for years to come.[36] Building out capacity is in itself not a straightforward feat; it is often complicated by the two obstacles noted earlier: longer-than-expected project lead times and increases in the marginal cost of new production. There are several examples of this kind of large, unexpected demand shock over the past fifty years. China's economic rise played a leading role in the spike in the consumption of raw materials on a vast scale. China's swelling middle class is prompting ever greater demand for durable consumer goods, whereas Beijing is laboring to construct public infrastructure, from roads to electrical wires to sewage systems. World War II and its aftermath also provided a similar kind of jolt to raw materials markets. The takeoff from wartime demand continued after the armistice, as the reconstruction effort in Japan

[34] BP, *BP Statistical Review of World Energy 2011* (London: BP, June 2011).

[35] See Goldman Sachs, "Underinvestment in Commodities Means Markets Will Be Tighter, Sooner," CEO Confidential, Issue 2002/05 (April 2002).

[36] Colin A. Carter, Gordon C. Rausser, and Aaron Smith, "Commodity Booms and Busts," *Annual Review of Resource Economics* vol 3 (October 2011), 87–118, "Characteristics of the Current Commodity Boom," in *Global Economic Prospects 2009: Commodities at the Crossroads* (Washington, DC: The World Bank, 2009).

and Europe proved a further materials-intensive post-conflict phase that kept prices on a secular upswing.

DIRECTIONAL PRICE TRENDS OVER THE VERY LONG RUN

Research on primary commodity price trends that peers as far back into the past as possible supports the conclusion that these prices have generally fallen (or at most remain stagnant) over the long sweep of history.[37] Although prices can rise steeply for years or even decades, making the window of time over which data are sampled crucial, looking at price trends over the longest span of time possible – many decades or as far back as data exist, which is nearly five centuries – suggests that these goods have gotten cheaper over time once inflation is factored in. Raul Prebisch and Hans Singer documented in 1950 the tendency for the price of primary commodities to decline relative to manufactured goods over time, drawing on earlier work by Charles Kindleberger on this long-term deterioration in the terms of trade of raw goods.[38]

Several arguments have been put forward in an attempt to explain this finding. These include the low income elasticity of demand for commodities, which causes their real prices to fall relative to finished goods as the world becomes wealthier; that manufacturing has become less input-intensive over time, thanks to technological innovation, meaning relatively less demand for raw materials compared to finished goods; and superior productivity growth in the agricultural and mining sectors, which has tended to lower prices for their output in relative terms.[39] Other scholars cite a long-term decline in transportation costs and relative quality differentials as a contributing factor. Because these costs constitute a larger share of the final cost of these goods, the fact that transportation has gotten significantly cheaper over time has had a disproportionately deflationary effect on them versus manufactured goods.[40] Moreover, the quality of raw materials delivered

---

[37] David I. Harvey, Neil M. Kellard, Jakob B. Madsen, and Mark E. Wohar, "The Prebisch-Singer Hypothesis: Four Centuries of Evidence," *Review of Economics and Statistics* 92 no. 4 (May 2010): 367–377.

[38] Raúl Prebisch, "The Economic Development of Latin America and Its Principal Problems," (New York: United Nations Department of Economic Affairs), 1950. Hans Singer, "The Distribution of Gains between Investing and Borrowing Countries," *American Economic Review* 40, no. 2 (1950), 473–485.

[39] John O'Connor and David Orsmond, "The Recent Rise in Commodity Prices: A Long-Run Perspective," Reserve Bank of Australia Bulletin, April 2007, 1–2.

[40] David Sapsford, "Primary Commodity Prices and Terms of Trade," *Economic Record* 66 no. 4 (December 1990): 342–356.

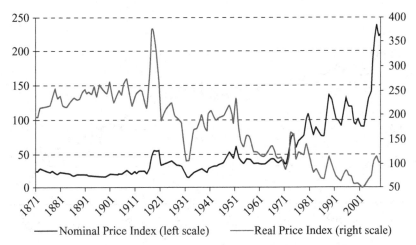

———Nominal Price Index (left scale)   ———Real Price Index (right scale)

Figure 8. *Economist* Industrial-Commodity Price Index in Real and Nominal Terms (1871–2010). *Note:* Shiller's historical inflation data can be accessed at http://www.econ. yale.edu/~shiller/data.htm (accessed October 2012). *Source: Economist,* Shiller (2012), U.S. Bureau of Labor Statistics

to the marketplace has not changed significantly over the centuries, while the quality of manufactured goods has many times over. The difficulty of holding this quality differential constant in constructing long-term prices indices also possibly contributes to the relative decline of real commodity prices.[41]

These two graphs depict long-term real price trends for commodities. Figure 8 shows the Economist commodity-price index in real and nominal terms; Figure 9 contains an index created by four scholars led by David Harvey of the University of Nottingham (referred to here as the Harvey index).[42] The Economist industrial commodities index was first published

[41] Marian Radetzki, *A Handbook of Primary Commodities in the Global Economy* (Cambridge and New York: Cambridge University Press, 2008): 75–76.

[42] For details regarding the *Economist* commodity index, see "Markets & Data," *Economist,* http://www.economist.com/markets-data (accessed October 2012). For a good overview of how the index's component commodities and their weightings index have evolved over time, see "Appendix: The Economist's Industrial Commodity-Price Index" from Paul Cashin and C. John McDermott, "The Long-Run Behavior of Commodity Prices: Small Trends and Big Variability," *IMF Staff Papers* 49 no. 2, International Monetary Fund (2002). For the so-called Harvey index, see David I. Harvey, Neil M. Kellard, Jakob B. Madsen, and Mark E. Wohar, "The Prebisch-Singer Hypothesis: Four Centuries of Evidence," *Review of Economics and Statistics* 92, no. 2 (May 2010), 367–377.

Figure 9. Logarithm of Index of Real Commodity Prices Based on Harvey et al. (1650–2005). *Note*: This index was constructed by Harry Bloch and David Sapsford for "Innovation, Real Primary Commodity Prices and Business Cycles," Paper presented at the 13th conference of the International Joseph A. Schumpeter Society, Aalborg, Denmark, June 21–24, 2010. See pages 2–3. It is derived from the data compiled by Harvey et al. (David I. Harvey, Neil M. Kellard, Jakob B. Madsen, and Mark E. Wohar, "The Prebisch-Singer Hypothesis: Four Centuries of Evidence," *Review of Economics and Statistics* 92, no. 2 (May 2010), 367–377. *Source*: Bloch and Sapsford (2010)

in 1864 and the underlying data stretch back to 1845.[43] It is deflated here using U.S. consumer price index data since 1871, which is used in the Case-Shiller historical home price index.[44] The industrial commodity index is a better reflection of long-term trends in nonrenewable resource prices than the all-commodity index, which also includes food prices, so this analysis focuses on the former index.[45] The commodities included in the industrials

---

[43] Although the nominal index stretches back to 1845, data before 1857 are incomplete and data between 1857 and 1861 reflect January prices only. Only figures from 1862 onward, which represent averages of the underlying monthly figures, are used here.

[44] Shiller explains his methodology in compiling the historical CPI data set that starts in January 1871: "The CPI-U (Consumer Price Index-All Urban Consumers) published by the U.S. Bureau of Labor Statistics begins in 1913; for years before 1913 I spliced to the CPI Warren and Pearson's price index, by multiplying it by the ratio of the indexes in January 1913. December 1999 and January 2000 values for the CPI are extrapolated." ("Online Data Robert Shiller," Homepage of Robert J. Shiller. http://www.econ.yale.edu/~shiller/data.htm (accessed October 2012). The data have been brought current to 2011 using recent Bureau of Labor Statistics figures.

[45] Most studies of long-run trends in commodity prices make use of the Grilli-Yang index of raw materials prices (Enzo Grilli and Maw Cheng Yang, "Primary Commodity Prices, Manufactured Goods Prices, and the Terms of Trade of Developing Countries: What the

index, as well as their relative weightings, have changed over time, with the current weightings reflecting the value of world imports from 2004 to 2006.[46] The Harvey index is composed of a sample of global prices for twenty-five commodities over the period from 1650 to 2005. Prices for some of the goods, such as crude oil, are only available for a subset of the period shown given that they were not actively bought and sold in modern form until after the start of the index. As a result, the index is a compilation of various sub-indices, with prices denominated in British pounds, a currency that has remained in circulation over the entire period.[47] The average price of each good is calculated across major industrialized countries in a common currency and then added to an unweighted index. Nominal prices are deflated using an unweighted manufacturing value-added price index.

Both indices support the notion that raw materials prices have deteriorated relative to manufactured goods over very long stretches of time. The *Economist* industrial commodity-price index shows average annual compound growth of −0.4% between 1871 and 2012. The index fell to roughly half its original value over that period, notwithstanding the sizeable post-2000 upturn in real prices. The general directional trend in the data does not change materially regardless of whether the data are deflated using the U.S. consumer price index (CPI) or the GDP deflator.[48] The Harvey index

Long Run Shows," *The World Bank Economic Review* 2 no. 1 (1988): 1–47). Rather than use that data set, however, I opt instead for the Economist industrials index, for the reasons outlined in Paul Cashin and C. John McDermott, "The Long-Run Behavior of Commodity Prices: Small Trends and Big Variability," *IMF Staff Papers* 49 no. 2, International Monetary Fund (2002). As they note, the latter index includes four additional decades' worth of data. Regardless, given the high degree of correlation between the two data sets – 0.85 in Cashin and McDermott's extension of the Grilli-Yang data from 1900 to 1999 – means that using either index should allow for substantially similar results.

[46] For the current weightings, see "Economist Commodity Price Index: Weights in the Index," *Economist*, http://media.economist.com/media/pdf/Weights2005.pdf (accessed October 2012).

[47] Twelve of the commodity price data sets begin in the seventeenth century (beef, coal, cotton, gold, lamb, lead, rice, silver, sugar, tea, wheat, and wool), three the following century (coffee, tobacco, and pig iron), eight in the nineteenth century (aluminum, cocoa, copper, hide, nickel, crude oil, tin, and zinc), and two in the year 1900 (banana and jute).

[48] See the *Economist* industrial commodity price index since 1845, for example, in "Commodities: Crowded Out," *Economist*, September 24, 2011, which is adjusted by the U.S. GDP deflator. As of the start of 2012, the index stands at roughly half its 1845 value in real terms. For a discussion of which deflator to use when assessing long-term commodity price trends, see John T. Cuddington, "Calculating Long-Term Trends in the Real Prices of Primary Commodities: Deflator Adjustment and the Prebisch-Singer Hypothesis," Working Paper, August 29, 2007 (updated September 14, 2007).

shows a broadly similar downward trajectory over an even longer time period. Adjusted for inflation, eleven of the twenty-five commodities display a statistically significant drop in prices if structural breaks are included (eight of the twenty-five do if they are not). None shows a significant upward trend in price over the past three and a half centuries.[49]

The declining price trend underscores one of the fundamental aspects of non-renewable resource economics, which appears to fly in the face of reason: despite growing demand for exhaustible natural resources like oil and precious metals over the centuries, and that these substances are limited – in an ultimate, physical sense – market forces have tended to make them cheaper over long periods of time. The Malthusian paradigm of human welfare being limited by absolute scarcity constraints, doomed to resource depletion and hence a perpetual increase in prices as long as population growth continues unabated, is not the empirical story of history when it comes to these tradable raw materials. Real prices of natural resources tend to trend lower over time, despite rising rates of production.

There are at least four flaws with the depletionist paradigm.[50] Consider the case of crude oil. First, the view assumes that conventional oil resources are a fixed quantity, which fails to take into account the role of investment in expanding the existing stock. Implicit in the view is the error of ignoring the productive potential of unconventional oil resources to expand global supply. Second, it assumes that future demand will grow without constraint. Mainstream economic thought would argue that a variety of forces (in addition to the price mechanism) would temper demand should supply become increasingly scarce, among them environment and supply security concerns, sales taxes on petroleum products in net-consumer nations, and other unspecified forces. Third, it ignores basic market mechanisms. A worsening shortage would tend to increase costs of production and market prices, which would simultaneously temper the quantity of oil demanded and boost the quantity supplied. Fourth, advances in technology, induced by higher prices, allow for the development of more efficient processes for growing, finding, or refining raw materials.

---

[49] See David I. Harvey, Neil M. Kellard, Jakob B. Madsen, and Mark E. Wohar, "The Prebisch-Singer Hypothesis: Four Centuries of Evidence," *Review of Economics and Statistics* 92, no. 2 (May 2010), 367–377: 376.

[50] M. A. Adelman, "Mineral Depletion, with Special Reference to Petroleum," *Review of Economics and Statistics* 72 no. 1 (February 1990): 1–10; Richard L. Gordon, "IAEE Convention Speech: Energy, Exhaustion, Environmentalism, and Etatism," *The Energy Journal* 15 no. 1 (1994): 1–16; Peter J. McCabe, "Energy Resources – Cornucopia or Empty Barrel?," *AAPG Bulletin* 82 no. 11 (November 1998).

The length of the window over which price data is studied can have a decisive impact on whether the data show a net declining or inclining trend. The longer the window, the more certain one can be a declining real price trend will be found. By the same token, shorter windows typically give undue weight to the large cyclical fluctuations that occur around the declining long-term trend. If the sampling window is not long enough, those studies whose time series data end right after the conclusion of the 1970s or 2000s commodities booms are more likely to find an uptrend, whereas those that extend into the 1980s bust are more likely to find a downtrend.[51]

The fact that the real prices of exhaustible resources as a group do not tend to increase over the course of history casts doubt on the intuitive yet bleak notion that the price of a natural resource necessarily increases as it is used up. The classic story about this debate is of the bet that Julian Simon, a resource economist at the University of Maryland, made with Paul Ehrlich, a Stanford biologist, in September 1980. Ehrlich's 1968 *The Population Bomb*, which sold 3 million copies, held that rising population growth amid depleting resources was leading inexorably to "a substantial increase in the world death rate," which, "at this late date," nothing could prevent.[52] Simon disagreed. He offered a $10,000 bet to anyone who would wager that "the cost of non-government-controlled raw materials (including grain and oil) will not rise in the long run." His only stipulation was that inflation be accounted for and the time horizon had to be longer than one year. Simon went as far as allowing anyone who accepted his offer to choose which commodities to track.

Ehrlich was the first to accept, alongside his colleagues, Berkeley's John P. Holdren and John Harte of the Lawrence Berkeley Laboratory. One report tells the rest of the story this way:

Ehrlich and his colleagues picked five metals that they thought would undergo big price rises: chromium, copper, nickel, tin, and tungsten. Then, on paper, they bought $200 worth of each, for a total bet of $1000 using the prices on September 29, 1980, as an index. They designated September 29, 1990, 10 years hence, as the payoff date. If the inflation-adjusted prices of the various metals rose in the interim, Simon would pay Ehrlich the combined difference; if the prices fell, Ehrlich et al. would pay Simon.

Then they sat back and waited.

Between 1980 and 1990, the world's population grew by more than 800 million, the largest increase in one decade in all of history. But by September 1990, without

---

[51] Jeffrey A. Frankel, "The Natural Resource Curse: A Survey," NBER Working Paper No. 15836 (National Bureau of Economic Research, March 2010).

[52] Paul R. Ehrlich, *The Population Bomb* (New York: Ballentine Books, 1986).

Table 1. *Winner of the Bet Each Year between 1981 and 2004*

1981: Simon	1990: Simon	1999: Ehrlich
1982: Simon	1991: Simon	2000: Ehrlich
1983: Simon	1992: Simon	2001: Ehrlich
1984: Simon	1993: Simon	2002: Ehrlich
1985: Ehrlich	1994: Ehrlich	2003: Ehrlich
1986: Ehrlich	1995: Ehrlich	2004: Ehrlich
1987: Simon	1996: Ehrlich	2005: Ehrlich
1988: Simon	1997: Ehrlich	2006: Ehrlich
1989: Simon	1998: Ehrlich	2007: Ehrlich

Source: Kodrosky (2010)

a single exception, the price of each of Ehrlich's selected metals had fallen, and in some cases had dropped through the floor. Chrome, which had sold for $3.90 a pound in 1980, was down to $3.70 in 1990. Tin, which was $8.72 a pound in 1980, was down to $3.88 a decade later.

Which is how it came to pass that in October 1990, Paul Ehrlich mailed Julian Simon a check for $576.07.[53]

Although demand for the commodities in question grew over that time period – a fact that Simon had likely assumed would be the case – the inflation-adjusted prices of these five metals fell. If Simon and Ehrlich had repeated this wager but extended the time horizon over the longest period possible – centuries rather than one decade – the same result would have held, research shows.[54] Simon's money would have again been safe.

While this classic story is a useful illustration of this counterintuitive aspect of commodity price behavior over the long term, on closer examination, it can also be profoundly misleading. Simon was right about the direction commodity prices tend to go over the very long term. But ten years is not the very long term. Indeed, had he made the same bet in another year, rather than 1980, Simon well could have lost. As Paul Kedrosky points out, his big win was also highly dependent on the wager's start date. The time period of the bet is shaded in the Figure 10.

Kedrosky shows that had the bet been started in any given year in the 1980s, Simon would have beaten Ehrlich eight out of ten times. But his look would have changed in the 1990s. Had the wager been initiated in a given

---

[53] Ed Regis, "The Doomslayer," *Wired*, February 1997.
[54] David I. Harvey, Neil M. Kellard, Jakob B. Madsen, and Mark E. Wohar, "The Prebisch-Singer Hypothesis: Four Centuries of Evidence," *Review of Economics and Statistics* 92, no. 2 (May 2010).

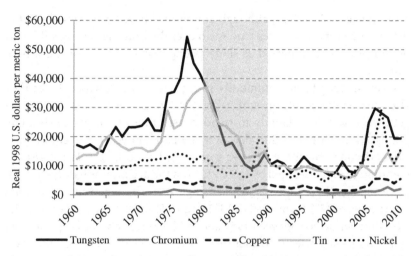

Figure 10. Inflation-Adjusted Commodity Prices for the Five Simon-Ehrlich Metals. *Source:* U.S. Geological Survey

year in that decade, Ehrlich would have won six out of the ten years, or 60% of the time. And Simon's luck would have completely run dry in the 2000s. In all ten of the 2000s, Ehrlich would have been the victor, with the inflation-adjusted price of the basket of the five metals higher than it had been ten years earlier.[55] So with doomsday gambling, as in comedy, timing is everything.

SHORT- AND LONG-TERM VARIABILITY IN REAL COMMODITY PRICES

This retrospective look at Simon and Ehrlich's 1980 wager raises a crucial point about the nature of commodity prices, which is that price variability is large relative to the gradual downward trend discussed earlier. While the slight downward march in most commodities has held true over a very long window, over shorter time periods, such price behavior has frequently and emphatically not been the case. Large and persistent price moves, both upward and downward, characterize commodities prices over the long haul and dominates the long-term trend in terms of its economic and statistical

---

[55] Paul Kedrosky, "Relitigating the Simon/Ehrlich Bet," *Infectious Greed: Finance and the Money Culture by Paul Kedrosky*, February 18 2010, http://paul.kedrosky.com/.

significance.[56] Therefore, although Simon may have been right about the direction commodity prices tend to go over the centuries, being willing to bet on prices over a period as short as one year was more or less a pure gamble.

Over the long term, commodity prices may trend downward, but they also experience sizeable upward swings that can last years, even decades. To get a sense for this variability-to-trend, consider the results of an IMF study published in 2001. It found that over the past 140 years, real commodity prices declined by about 1% per year, as indicated by the *Economist* all-commodity index deflated by U.S.CPI.[57] But the decline was hardly smooth; prices changed by as much as 50% in a single year. The largest annual declines in prices were 37% from 1930 to 1931 and 1974 to 1975, just larger than the 34% drop witnessed between 1951 and 1952. Conversely, the largest annual spike was 49% between 1972 and 1973 – just two years prior to the largest year-on-year drop in 1974–1975. In second place was a 33% annual rise between 1916 and 1917. Between 1862 and 1999, more than 5% of annual price movements, as reflected by the index, were in excess of 20%.

Prices have gone through distinct chapters over time, which historical events can play a role in beginning and ending. A 2001 IMF study, for instance, identified a structural break in the index after World War I, with a steepening secular price decline after that event. While the overall decline over the 140-year period averaged 1.3% per year, for the period from 1917

---

[56] Walter C. Labys, Eugene Kouassi, and Michel Terraza, "Short-Term Cycles in Primary Commodity Prices," *The Developing Economies* 38 no. 3 (September 2000): 330–342; Paul Cashin, C. John McDermott, and Alasdair Scott, "Booms and Slumps in World Commodity Prices," IMF Working Papers 99/155 (International Monetary Fund, November 1999); and Paul Cashin and C. John McDermott, "The Long-Run Behavior of Commodity Prices: Small Trends and Big Variability," Working Paper 01/68, International Monetary Fund (2001).

[57] The CPI used is Robert Schiller's extrapolation of the U.S. Bureau of Labor Statistics data, which begin in 1913. The longest running U.S. GDP deflator data series, provided by the U.S. Bureau of Economic Analysis, goes back only as far as 1929, so in this case this particular CPI dataset, which extends as far back as 1871, is preferable. Shiller details the methodology behind the construction of his consumer price index since 1871 at http://www.econ.yale.edu/~shiller/data.htm. As he describes, "The CPI-U (Consumer Price Index-All Urban Consumers) published by the U.S. Bureau of Labor Statistics begins in 1913; for years before 1913 1 spliced to the CPI Warren and Pearson's price index, by multiplying it by the ratio of the indexes in January 1913. See George F. Warren and Frank A. Pearson, *Gold and Prices* (New York: John Wiley and Sons, 1935). Data are from their table 1, pp. 11–14. For the Plots, I have multiplied the inflation-corrected series by a constant so that their value in January 2000 equals their nominal value, i.e., so that all prices are effectively in January 2000 dollars."

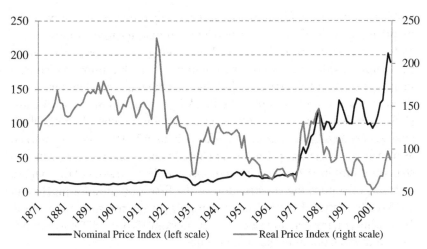

Figure 11. Real and Nominal *Economist* All-Commodity Indices (1871–2008). *Source: The Economist*

to 1999, the average annual price decline was a larger 2.3%.[58] Other studies found a somewhat similar result, although they put the break a bit later, such as in the 1930s or after World War II, even though none meets a high degree of statistical confidence.[59] Sometimes these changes come in a particular market – say, gold, or wheat – rather than to the entire class. Harvey and his coauthors find that six markets show this kind of structural break: crude oil in 1875, hide in 1905, wheat in 1938, both sugar and tobacco in 1951, and jute in 1960.[60] The authors argue that the extraordinary wave of technological progress in and around the twentieth century, particularly in terms of resource extraction and infrastructure development, may be the reason why these breaks are concentrated within an eighty-five-year period.

These sorts of breaks in long-term price patterns can come about for different reasons, as two examples illustrate. Jute, a natural fiber used for

[58] Paul Cashin and C. John McDermott, "The Long-Run Behavior of Commodity Prices: Small Trends and Big Variability," Working Paper 01/68, International Monetary Fund (2001).

[59] John T. Cuddington and Carlos M. Urzua, "Trends and Cycles in the Net Barter Terms of Trade: A New Approach," *Economic Journal* 99, no. 396 (June 1989), 426–442; John T. Cuddington, "Long-run Trends in 26 Primary Commodity Prices: A Disaggregated Look at the Prebisch-Singer Hypothesis," *Journal of Development Economics* 39, no. 2 (1992), 207–227.

[60] David I. Harvey, Neil M. Kellard, Jakob B. Madsen, and Mark E. Wohar, "The Prebisch-Singer Hypothesis: Four Centuries of Evidence," *The Review of Economics and Statistics* 92, no. 2 (May 2010), 367–377.

making coarse fabrics for industrial and clothing purposes, is one example. Its price began to fall more swiftly relative to manufactured goods than it had in past centuries in the 1960s, likely owing to the popularization of petroleum-based synthetics during the mid-twentieth century, which permanently undercut demand for jute by introducing a popular substitute. Crude oil is a second example. The break in the data found in 1875 comports with that found by a study by Eyal Dvir and Kenneth Rogoff, which analyzes crude oil prices from 1865 through 2009.[61] The crude oil market, as measured by average prices in the United States, underwent a profound structural shift in 1878 on both the supply and demand sides of the market. In terms of supply, the construction of the first long-distance pipeline in 1878–1879 shattered the railroad monopoly on the transportation of oil. Meanwhile, on the demand side, the period from 1861 to 1878 corresponds to an industrial boom in the United States.

The differences that exist across these individual markets underscore the fact that price trends can vary considerably across individual commodities. Thus, while commodity indices can be useful in portraying the behavior of commodities as a class, they risk masking the degree of idiosyncrasy that can exist from one commodity to another. Indices allow for generalization. Such generalization can be useful in understanding aggregate trends but misleading if the aggregate trend read onto specific markets, where it may be inapplicable. The example of crude oil again helps illustrate this point.

Figure 12 depicts annual average oil prices from 1861 through 2010 in both nominal and 2010-equivalent U.S. dollars, using data from the *BP Statistical Review of World Energy 2012*. In inflation-adjusted terms, world benchmark crude prices hit an all-time high of $111 in 1864 before trending downward sharply over the ensuing three decades, at which point it decreased gradually until the 1970s. Since the 1970s, however, oil prices have been anything but downward-trending. Instead, after spiking briefly to $97.46 in 1980, they shot up to an even higher $98.50 in 2010. No downtrend is evident in this market; three distinct "epochs" in crude oil prices, as Dvir and Rogoff call them, have existed over the market's relatively short history (in comparison to other commodities, such as tea or gold).[62]

---

[61] Eyal Dvir and Kenneth S. Rogoff, "Three Epochs of Oil," NBER Working Paper No. 14927 (National Bureau of Economic Research, April 2009).

[62] This price series is based on three sets of crude oil prices. The prices for the years 1861–1944 is based on U.S. average spot prices, while 1945–1983 is based on Arabian Light prices as posted at Ras Tanura, and 1984–2010 is the Brent dated price. Eyal Dvir and Kenneth S. Rogoff, "Three Epochs of Oil," NBER Working Paper No. 14927, National Bureau of Economic Research (April 2009).

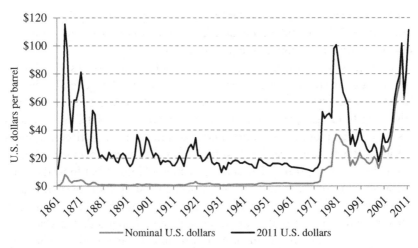

Figure 12. Real and Nominal World Benchmark Crude Oil Prices (1861–2011). *Source:* BP Statistical Review of World Energy 2012

Crude oil prices illustrate the fact that although commodity prices may be trending downward over the centuries, individual commodities, such as crude oil, may not follow that trajectory. In the case of oil, fundamental changes to the supply side of the market, as well as cycles on the demand side of the equation, have been the primary cause, as Dvir and Rogoff argue. In 1933–1934, for example, U.S. federal and state agencies, most notably the Texas Railroad Commission, began to regulate domestic oil production. They did so in an attempt to rein in the rampant overproduction, which posed an existential threat to U.S. oil producers. By mandating that domestic production stay below capacity (though adjusting it from time to time based on market demand), the U.S. government kept prices stable. Prices and volatility hit lows over the next four decades not seen before or since that time.

By the early 1970s, the tide turned yet again. The newly formed Organization of Petroleum Exporting Countries (OPEC) controlled much of the world's most cheaply exploitable sources of oil. But rather than ensuring low, stable oil prices in the world market, OPEC has been effective at stabilizing the market only for stretches and generally prefers higher prices. Its ascent restructured global supply by restricting access to the lion's share of the world's most easily exploitable oil reserves and by rationing production within the territories of its member countries. Spare oil production capacity in the United States also evaporated in the early 1970s, eliminating Washington's ability to provide a domestically regulated buffer against fundamental, unforeseen changes in the market. Thus, a new epoch of oil prices emerged around 1973 that is still underway, featuring on average sharply higher and more volatile prices than in the preceding four decades.

How does one reconcile these periods of prolonged increases in real commodities prices with the slight centuries-long decline that generally characterizes them? Ultimately, the most empirically satisfying way to understand the long-term real price behavior of commodities to date, as a class, is as experiencing dominant short- and medium-term oscillations around a series of longer-term averages that have tended to slope downward slightly over the very long run.[63] The success of Julian Simon's bet hinged on the dependability of the long-term trend in manifesting itself over medium-term cycles – in his case, ten years. But short-run instability in prices, driven by the low elasticities of both supply and demand that characterize many commodities, not to mention unpredictable interruptions in supply, can easily dislodge longer-term trends over briefer intervals. Furthermore, turning points in the business cycle can lead to significant deviations from longer-term price trends, certainly from any real price decline over the centuries. Still, this short- and medium-term price volatility takes place within the broader secular landscape that often leads to prices for a particular commodity hovering within a long-term range, as seismic shifts in the global market structure for the good prove a persistent force in shaping prices.

The high degree of short-run instability in commodity markets should be enough to give any gambler pause before betting that commodity prices will move in one direction or another over a ten-year period.

By way of example, U.S. rubber prices rose from $0.94 per kilogram in 1992 to $1.51 in 1995 before falling to $0.79 in 1999. Cotton prices slid from $1.71 per kilogram in 1991 to $1.25 in 1993 and then climbed to $1.79 three years later before crashing to $1.20 in 1999. Nickel prices spiked by more than 200% to $13,831 per metric ton between 1986 and 1988 before backsliding to $8,614 in 1990. Copper saw wild fluctuations in the ten years starting in 1986, increasing from $1,609 per metric ton to $2,876 in 1989 before retreating to $1,742 in 1994.[64]

What are the implications of the long-term price trends discussed in this chapter for those who are impacted by whether commodity prices rise or fall? The pronounced cyclicality of commodities prices is a more useful

---

[63] Jeffrey A. Frankel, "The Natural Resource Curse: A Survey," Faculty Research Working Paper Series, Harvard University (February 2010): 9.

[64] See World Bank Commodity Price Data (Pink Sheet), available at www.data.worldbank .org.

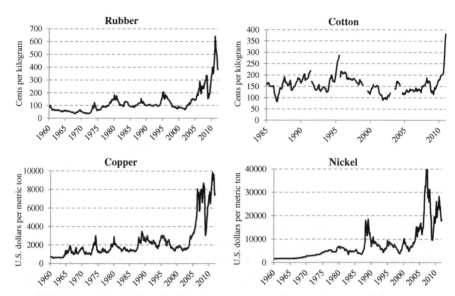

Figure 13. Nominal Historical Prices of Rubber, Cotton, Copper, and Nickel. *Source*: World Bank

guide to anticipating the short- and medium-term trajectory these markets than any centuries-long trend. Simon was right that real commodity prices tend to go down over the course of centuries, but that time horizon is far different from that of most policymakers and investors. In terms of the economic development of countries that rely heavily on exporting primary commodities and the economic health of industrial countries buffeted by volatility in the oil market, understanding the cyclical drivers and nature of these markets is a first step toward crafting policy that can mitigate the damage of a sudden change in prices. Moreover, the alluring but wrongheaded logics that often find a voice in discussion about commodity markets – namely, that real prices are all but assured to grind higher over time as the best exhaustible resource deposits are used up and that a supposedly stable marginal cost of production ensures a more or less hard floor to prices – have not held true over the course of history. Neither notion is well-supported by economic theory.

3

Volatility in Global Food Markets

The four fault lines that define the commodity trade, outlined in Chapter 1, converge in the volatility seen in global foods markets over the past decade. Although in real terms still far below long-term historical averages, recent food prices, having trended higher over that period, constitute a reversal of the generally declining prices that had prevailed since the mid-1970s. The economic consequences for rich and poor countries, not to mention net exporting versus net importing countries, differ markedly. Among the world's poor, evidence suggests problematically high food costs can weigh on educational attainment in the rising generation with long-term negative consequences for economic productivity.[1] Rising prices also present an acute inflationary threat in emerging economies, given that food represents a larger share of household expenditures, which can also weigh on economic growth. Many analysts have argued that severe food cost escalation can contribute to escalating political unrest, which they see as being a contributing factor in the ongoing upheaval in the Middle East and North Africa.[2]

Yet the food market is another sphere in which a misdiagnosis of the problem can worsen it. Although financial market speculation is often cited as the root cause of high or unpredictable food prices, that explanation obscures more than it reveals. Fundamental forces of supply and demand

---

[1] For a discussion of the impact of high food and fuel prices on developing countries, see the report from the IMF's 2014 *International Conference on Food Price Volatility: Causes and Challenges*, available at http://www.imf.org/external/np/seminars/eng/2014/food/ (accessed May 2015).

[2] Clemens Breisinger, Olivier Ecker, and Perrihan Al-Riffai, "Economics of the Arab Awakening: From Revolution to Transformation and Food Security," IFPRI Policy Brief 18 (May 2011); Rami Zurayk, *Food, Farming, and Freedom: Sowing the Arab Spring* (Charlottesville, VA: Just World Books, 2011).

in these markets, compounded by macroeconomic trends (secular trends in the U.S. dollar and a falling real interest rate environment in the G10), domestic price controls, and at times nationalistic trade policy by major exporters, are better supported by the econometric evidence as spurring the volatility. The food markets are an arena in which the structurally opposing interests of net importing and exporting countries can hinder cooperation among trade partners, pitting sovereign states and their national champions against private-sector enterprises and limiting the scope for international agreements that could increase the resiliency of these markets in times of severe market stress.

THE ONSET AND IMPLICATIONS OF THE GLOBAL FOOD CRISIS

Among the most dramatic storylines of the mid-2000s commodities boom was the sizeable leap in the price of food and agricultural products in the world market. "Across the World a Crisis is Unfolding at Alarming Speed," read an April 2008 headline. "Climate change, China's increasing consumption and the dash for biofuels are causing food shortages and rocketing prices – sparking riots in cities from the Caribbean to the Far East."[3] The prices of basic food commodities – corn, rice, soybeans, and others – on the international market were on a tear. Yet this was not a crisis that was affecting all corners of the globe equally. The rising cost of imported food was felt especially keenly in some emerging market countries, threatening the health of the poorest, while going almost unnoticed by more affluent consumers in the developed world. So deep was the disparity in the effect of the boom, in fact, that one writer asked in an earnestly titled piece, "Could the Global Food Crisis Impact America?"[4]

Dozens of world leaders sounded the alarm. "The next few weeks are critical for addressing the food crisis. For two billion people, rising food prices are now a matter of daily struggle, sacrifice, and, for too many, even survival," World Bank President Robert Zoellick said in late April 2008. United Nations Secretary General Ban Ki-moon voiced similar concern. The food crisis was an "unprecedented challenge" with "multiple effects on the vulnerable." In the United Nations' judgment, it was the worst problem that the U.N. World Food Program had experienced in its forty-five-year history,

---

[3] Robin McKie and Heather Steward, "Hunger. Strikes. Riots. The Food Crisis Bites," *The Guardian*, April 12, 2008.

[4] Saeed Shabazz, "Could the Global Food Crisis Impact America?," FinalCall.com, April 30, 2008.

Figure 14. UN Food Price Index (January 1990–June 2012). *Note:* Note that 2002–2004 set equal to 100. *Source:* Food and Agriculture Organization of the United Nations (as of 12/6/2012)

"threatening to plunge more than 100 million people on every continent into hunger."[5] Meanwhile, U.S. President George W. Bush, under pressure to tackle the crisis, called for Congress to authorize $770 million for food aid and other measures meant to help "improve the ability of the developing world to feed itself."[6]

The global economic crises caused the market to collapse in the latter half of 2008, sending one food index down by more than one-third from peak to trough.[7] But the collapse in food prices proved momentary. By 2011, food prices had catapulted back to – and even surpassed – their 2008 highs. Once again, accounts in the popular press about what was behind the rebound in food prices, and what it might mean for governments and human welfare, were front page news.

An article in *Foreign Policy* magazine, "The Great Food Crisis," published in January 2011, captured the spirit of the coverage:

As the new year begins, the price of wheat is setting an all-time high in the United Kingdom. Food riots are spreading across Algeria. Russia is importing grain to sustain its cattle herds until spring grazing begins. India is wrestling with an

[5] Marc Wolfensberger, "Ban Ki-Moon to Chair UN Task Force on Food Crisis," *Bloomberg*, April 29, 2008.

[6] Missy Ryan and Tabassum Zakaria, "Bush proposes $770 million For World Food Crisis," *Reuters*, May 1, 2008.

[7] See Food and Agriculture Organization of the United Nations, "FAO Food Price Index."

18-percent annual food inflation rate, sparking protests. China is looking abroad for potentially massive quantities of wheat and corn. The Mexican government is buying corn futures to avoid unmanageable tortilla price rises. And on January 5, the U.N. Food and Agricultural organization announced that its food price index for December hit an all-time high.[8]

For the second time in just five years, food commodities were indeed on a roar, at least relative to the two decades prior. Corn, rice, wheat, and soybean prices tripled in price between the fall of 2005 and summer of 2008.[9] The U.N. FAO index of real food prices, which tracks a number of goods (meats, dairies, cereals, oilseeds, and sugar), shot upward by 57% over the eighteen months beginning in January 2007. After a second enormous leap in 2011, they have since retreated yet again.

Of all the trends in commodity markets since 2000, perhaps none has posed a more immediate threat to human welfare than the persistent climb in international food prices. Unlike other, more arcane financial markets, the global market for food has a human dimension that imbues what would be otherwise arcane market gyrations with a palpable urgency. Written as food prices were soaring to their highest levels in decades in April 2008, one account of the so-called food crisis conveys a sense of the havoc that the "silent tsunami" in food markets was wreaking:

A wave of food-price inflation is moving through the world, leaving riots and shaken governments in its wake. For the first time in 30 years, food protests are erupting in many places at once. Bangladesh is in turmoil; even China is worried. Elsewhere, the food crisis of 2008 will test the assertion of Amartya Sen, an Indian economist, that famines do not happen in democracies. Famine traditionally means mass starvation. The measures of today's crisis are misery and malnutrition. The middle classes in poor countries are giving up health care and cutting out meat so they can eat three meals a day. The middling poor, those on $2 a day, are pulling children from school and cutting back on vegetables so they can still afford rice. Those on $1 a day are cutting back on meat, vegetables and one or two meals, so they can afford one bowl. The desperate – those on 50 cents a day – face disaster.[10]

As the author notes, the very poor, particularly in the developing world, are the ones hit the hardest by high food prices. Food makes up a larger share of their meager spending. Unlike in the United States, where even the poorest households spend only 16% of their income on food, those in developing countries often devote the majority of their budgets on food.

[8] Lester Brown, "The Great Food Crisis of 2011," *Foreign Policy*, January 10, 2011.
[9] Colin A. Carter, Gordon C. Rausser, and Aaron Smith, "The Food Price Boom and Bust," *Gianni Foundation of Agricultural Economics* (2009): 2–4.
[10] "The Silent Tsunami," *The Economist*, April 17, 2008.

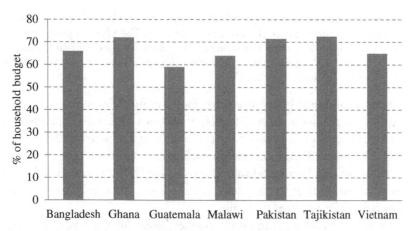

Figure 15. Percentage of Household Budget Spent on Food by Country in 2008. *Source:* Food and Agriculture Organization of the United Nations

Figure 15 depicts the percentage of household incomes used to buy food in many of the world's poorest countries. In Nigeria and Ghana, the figure is higher than 70%.[11]

The malign effects of sudden jumps in food prices are a challenge for economic policymaking. Elevated prices for food, marked by extreme volatility, pose a threat to the still-anemic U.S. and global economies. They underpin inflation, which in turn tends toward a tightening in monetary policy that slows economic growth. Economies that lack credible monetary policy and where food accounts for a large percentage of consumer spending, depend heavily on food commodity exports, or face rising prices for related goods are especially at risk of rising inflation.[12] Food also accounts for a much larger share of the basket of goods used to compute the consumer price index (CPI) in developing countries, which means high food prices have a larger effect on headline inflation. Inflationary pressure in the developing world can also spread to developed economies. Pricier exports from China, for example, can filter into consumer price levels in the United States.

Other economic effects of high food prices, such as on a country's balance of payments, exchange rate, and budgetary position vary significantly by country. Net exporters of these goods benefit when prices rise, just as net importers lose, at least in the short-to-medium term. Taking a longer-term

[11] "Editorial: The World Food Crisis," *New York Times*, April 10, 2008.

[12] "Is Inflation Back? Commodity Prices and Inflation," in *World Economic Outlook: Financial Stress, Downturns, and Recoveries* (Washington, DC: International Monetary Fund, October 2008): 83.

view, high prices can actually benefit importers if they stimulate domestic investment in food production, thus buoying their own agricultural industry. In terms of a country's current account balance, high prices also heighten the pain to those countries that rely heavily on food imports, even though they are a boon to those that export a large share of their production. However, changes in a country's terms of trade can help offset this dynamic. If other, non-food commodities that a country exports see their prices rise faster than the food it imports, the jump in food prices matter less to its balance of payments. Those countries that devote a greater portion of their national budgets to maintaining food subsidies also tend to fare especially badly when prices rise in the world market. Trying to keep prices stable via subsidies becomes more expensive for an importer as prices elsewhere rise. Even exporters that subsidize domestic food prices can be hurt by higher prices by means of lost opportunities elsewhere. The fiscal price of providing subsidized food can mean less spending elsewhere, such as on vital infrastructure and public education.[13]

Domestic instability can also result from high food prices. One 2008 news report argued that "food riots have erupted in countries all along the equator" in response to rising prices. "In Haiti, protesters chanting 'We're hungry' forced the prime minister to resign; 24 people were killed in riots in Cameroon; Egypt's president ordered the army to start baking bread; the Philippines made hoarding rice punishable by life imprisonment." Many analysts attributed the outbreak of the so-called Arab Spring in early 2011 as due in part to the rising cost of food. In fact, many observers, notably Joachim von Braun, the erstwhile director of the International Food Policy Research Institute, had predicted just a few years earlier that "world agriculture [had] entered a new, unsustainable, and politically risky period."[14]

Volatile food prices – even if short-lived – can cause enduring harm. A study by the United Nations Food and Agriculture Organization identifies three social and economic costs from volatile food prices, even if they are not unusually high.[15] First, jarring dislocations in food prices can lead to what development economists call "poverty traps." In this scenario, a

---

[13] Food and Agriculture Organization, *The State of Food Insecurity in the World: How Does International Price Volatility Affect Domestic Economies and Food Security?* (Rome, Italy: Food and Agriculture Organization of the United Nations, 2011): 14.

[14] "The New Face of Hunger," *The Economist*, April 17, 2008.

[15] Food and Agriculture Organization of the United Nations, *The State of Food Insecurity in the World: How Does International Price Volatility Affect Domestic Economies and Food Security?* (Rome, Italy: Food and Agriculture Organization of the United Nations, 2011): 19–20.

short period of unusually high or low prices can have long-lasting negative effects. For example, high food prices can mean poorer nutrition for the poorest children, permanently impairing their physical and cognitive development, and hence later productivity in the economy. Likewise, expensive food may force families to sell assets to make up for the loss of discretionary income. In both cases, a temporary reduction in the welfare of the poor, as they struggle to cope with unforeseen expenses, has long-term implications. Second, agricultural price volatility can discourage poor farmers from making investments that will enhance productivity down the road. Instead, they tend to adopt a "low risk, low return" approach, focusing only on short-term survival. Scarce access to credit exacerbates this problem for farmers in many parts of the world. Third, volatile food prices "reduce the ability of prices to function as signals that guide resource allocation." The harder time investors have trying to ascertain where prices might be headed, the worse they tend to fare at steering capital into those sectors of the economy that could grow, but for the infusion of cash. The extent to which food prices are unpredictable – as opposed to volatile but foreseeable (as in the case of highly seasonal prices, for example) – also matters. The more unpredictable these fluctuations in price, the fiercer their negative repercussions. Although volatile or less predictable prices may have benefits for a select few, the economic costs they impose tend to outweigh any benefits.[16]

Food prices quoted in the news media are generally those on the international market, but domestic prices can vary significantly. National governments tend to shun trade in food much more than in manufactured goods, for instance, out of concerns about supply security, domestic stability, and economic disruption. The amount of food that crosses international borders is far smaller than for oil or coal, for example. Trade policies, such as import duties, export taxes, and non-tariff barriers can all decouple prices in a given country from international prices, as can domestic policies like price supports. Other considerations – such as exchange rate dynamics, domestic market structure, the geography of final consumption good processing, and domestic market infrastructure – can also affect the degree to which prices on the international market pass through to a given domestic market. During the tumultuous price swings of 2006 through 2009, regional and

---

[16] Food and Agriculture Organization of the United Nations, *The State of Food Insecurity in the World: How Does International Price Volatility Affect Domestic Economies and Food Security?* (Rome, Italy: Food and Agriculture Organization of the United Nations, 2011): 18.

local food markets varied enormously in the speed and extent to which trends in the international market touched them.[17]

An example from December 2010 underscores how radically food price swings in a given country, measured in the local currency, can diverge from those in the global market or even in a neighboring country. That month, inflation-adjusted prices on the world market were nearly 20% higher than a year earlier, as measured by the U.N. Real Food Price Index. They had been on a tear, up 33% in the past six months alone. Yet the local price of food in a handful of countries had actually fallen year-over-year. South Africa, India, and Egypt had each seen prices decline by as much as 7% since December 2009. Food prices in other countries had fallen even more steeply, down 8% in Ghana and an astounding 23% in Uganda. Two reasons likely account for much of the disparity. Among the most important were likely exchange rate fluctuations and domestic harvest robustness. The depreciation of the U.S. dollar against a country's currency more than offset a rise in the dollar price of food. In Uganda, the value of the shilling, the national currency, rose by 19% against the dollar between December 2009 and 2010. Also, because policy commonly impedes cross-border trade in food, bountiful harvests in one country can depress domestic prices below the world market.[18]

THE PRICE SPIKES OF 2008 AND 2011

There is no doubt that the prices of various food commodities have reached record high levels in recent years – but only in nominal terms.

As Figure 16 illustrates, the international price of major cereals like rice, corn, and wheat in the summer of 2008 were higher than any other time over the prior half-century in current U.S. dollar terms. By late 2011, the price of some goods, such as corn (not to mention nonagricultural food commodities, such as beef), had surpassed even their 2008 levels. Judging by the World Bank's nominal food price index, the surge in prices in 2008 was broad-based, not limited to grains or oilseeds. Even during their nadir in the aftermath of the Great Recession, nominal food prices were 50% higher than they had been even in November 1974, the next-highest measures ever recorded. Prices did not stop climbing with the 2008 boom. By February

---

[17] Food and Agriculture Organization et al., *Price Volatility in Food and Agricultural Markets: Policy Responses, Report prepared for the G20*, (London: OECD, June 2, 2011): 8–9.

[18] "Food Prices," *The Economist*, June 8, 2011, http://www.economist.com/blogs/dailychart/2011/06/inflation (accessed September 2011).

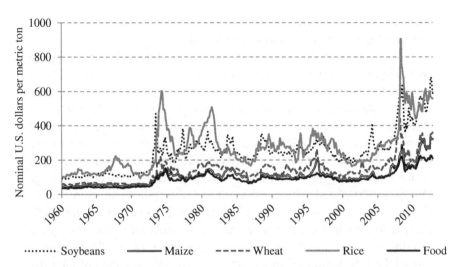

Figure 16. Monthly Commodity Prices in Nominal U.S. Dollars (1960–2012). *Source*: World Bank

2011, they had rebounded to stand shoulder-to-shoulder with their summer of 2008 highs.

When adjusted for inflation, however, the data paint a much different picture of the 2008 boom in food prices. Figure 17 depicts an index of the

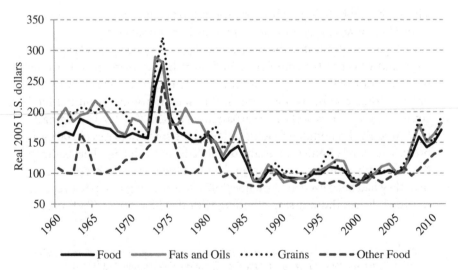

Figure 17. Annual World Bank Commodity Price Indices in Real 2005 U.S. Dollars (1960–2012). *Note*: The year 2005 set equal to 100. *Source*: World Bank

real price of food commodities, broken down by category, between 1960 and 2011.

As the graph shows, food in real terms was still cheaper at the height of the 2008 and 2011 booms than it had been thirty years prior. And it was nowhere near as expensive as it had been in the mid-to-late 1970s. Indeed, at the height of the 1973–1974 explosion in prices, food was nearly four times as expensive as it was during much of the 2000s. It had trended sharply lower over the ensuing three decades, only to gradually climb at the start of the 2000s. The surge in prices in global food markets was far shy of what occurred in the 1970s. In real terms, buyers on international markets enjoyed far lower prices during even the highest points of the post-2000 than they had between 1960 and 1985.

How did food prices in the post-2000s boom years compare to long-term trends? Two researchers at the International Monetary Fund, who tracked food prices since the turn of the twentieth century, found that real food prices are actually near their lowest levels in more than a hundred years.[19] One of the reasons why the spike in food prices between 2006 and 2008 was so disruptive was because consumers had grown accostomed to relatively cheap food. Low prices had also discouraged investment in food production, as it had for other commodities, such as crude oil.

As Figure 18 shows, food prices adjusted for inflation in the late 1980s and 1990s were actually lower than they had been even during the depths of the Great Depression. Even after the uptrend in prices that began around 2000, food prices were still more than 20% below their historical average. So while food prices were indeed high relative to the prior two decades, and had risen quite quickly between 2006 and 2008, they were nowhere near as high as they had been during nearly all of the twentieth century.

That is not to say that the food price booms of 2008 and 2011 was not impactful. Relative price shifts, in addition to absolute price levels, carry economic implications. Inflation is a relative measure. Price volatility can carry malign consequences for capital investment and consumer spend-ing, as discussed earlier (though certainly the base from which prices rise matters as well). When viewed in relative terms, the 2007–2008 and 2010–2011 increases were the largest since the mid-1970s. Yet, over the course of the twentieth century, real food prices had seen sustained relative upward movement on numerous occassions that surpassed that of the post-2000s, including the early 1920s, 1933–1937, and immediately following World

---

[19] Thomas Helbling and Shaun Roache, "Rising Prices on the Menu," *Finance and Develop-ment* 48 no. 1, (March 2011): 24–25.

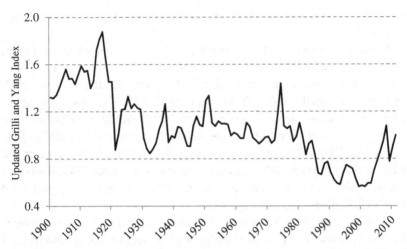

Figure 18. Real Annual Food Price Index (1900–2011). *Sources:* Sourced from Grilli and Yang data in Excel, deflated by an index of manufactured goods' unit values. See also Enzo Grilli and Maw Cheng Yang, 1988. "Primary Commodity Prices, Manufactured Goods Prices, and the Terms of Trade of Developing Countries: What the Long Run Shows," *The World Bank Economic Review* 2 no. 1 (1988):1–47; and Stephan Pfaffenzeller, Paul Newbold, and Anthony Rayner, "A Short Note on Updating the Grilli and Yang Commodity Price Index," *World Bank Economic Review* 21 no. 1 (2007), 151–163. Natural logarithm of an index.

War II. By the same token, the crashes following many of the twentieth century booms were frequently longer than the boom that preceded them.[20]

Two other aspects of price behavior in the 2008 food boom were notable, as Headey and Fan note.[21] First, the boom was not limited to food, but involved a broad range of primary commodities, from food to fuel. In constant 2000 U.S. dollars, according to World Bank data, staple food crop prices rose by 102% between 2004 and 2008, with non-staple crops rising a shallower 58%. Energy prices were likewise up – 183% for crude oil and 82% for coal, for instance. Metals and minerals likewise rose 119%, while fertilizers leaped by 379%. As the data show, however, commodities varied

[20] Paul Cashin and C. John McDermott, "The Long-Run Behavior of Commodity Prices: Small Trends and Big Variability," Working Paper 01/68, International Monetary Fund (2001); "Characteristics of the Current Commodity Boom," in *Global Economic Prospects 2009: Commodities at the Crossroads* (Washington, DC: The World Bank, 2009), 53–56.

[21] Derek Headey and Shenggen Fan, "Anatomy of a Crisis: The Causes and Consequences of Surging Food Prices," *Agricultural Economics* 39, no. s1 (2008), 376–377.

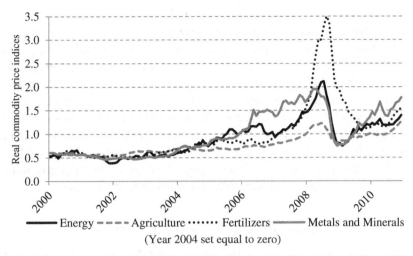

Figure 19. Real Monthly Commodity Price Indices in Real U.S. Dollars (2000–2011). *Note*: Index based on nominal U.S. dollar prices adjusted by the U.S. Consumer Price Index. *Source*: World Bank; U.S. Department of Labor

significantly in the magnitude of their gains. Some, such as seafood, saw much smaller increases (+18%).

A second, related observation is that food commodities differed in the timing of their upward moves, as did other commodities. Metals prices as a class began to their take-off in 2004, while many other commodity prices remained largely dormant, but failed to match the gains of in energy and fertilers, for example, in 2007–2008. Even within grains, upward growth differed significantly. Corn and wheat experienced their greatest relative boom years before 2008, while three-quarters of rice's upswing occurred in 2008 alone.

The contours of the 2005–2008 food price boom shared common elements with that of the early 1970s, which peaked in 1974, but also differed in several ways.[22] One similarity was that the price surge extended across various commodities, from food to energy. But there were several important differences. In the 1970s boom, the timing of the surge across commodity families was not as closely synchronized as it was in the more recent one. Raw agricultural prdouctions, quickly followed by food goods, jumped before energy prices did. Also, during the past decade's boom, metals prices

[22] Colin A. Carter, Gordon C. Rausser, and Aaron Smith, "Commodity Booms and Busts," *Annual Review of Resource Economics* vol 3 (October 2011), 87–118.

were among the biggest movers upward, and tended to rise in advance of the other classes of commodities, whereas cereals, vegetable oils, and energies eclipsed metals' gains in 1973–1974.[23] The jump in nominal grains prices in 1973 is likely related to the entrance of the Soviet Union into the global grain market. The opening of the country's economy that year created a new source of demand.[24] Moreover, livestock, and later soft commodities (such as sugar and cotton), saw large gains between 1973 and 1975, but were more peripheral in 2000s. Another difference between the two episodes was in their ending: The 2008 boom ended in a dramatic crash in the second half of that year, encompassing a diverse range of commodities. By contrast, the bust of the mid-1970s was generally less synchronized and slower.

DRIVERS OF THE FOOD PRICE BOOM

What were the drivers and mechanisms behind the boom in international food prices between 2006 and 2008? Many explanations gained a degree of credence at the time as concerned parties, from developing country officials to World Bank economists, struggled to make sense of rapidly rising prices. Now, with the benefit of hindsight, econometric analyses suggest that some of the explanations do not hold water, while others appear persuasive. All in all, a number of supply and demand factors, coupled with macroeconomic effects, combined to create what the executive director of the United Nations World Food Program, Josette Sheeran, aptly termed a "perfect storm" hitting global food markets.[25]

THE POPULAR MYTHS

Of the explanations for rising food prices broadcast widely in the news media, perhaps the most widely circulated was that soaring Chinese and Indian demand for food lay at the heart of the trend.[26] According to this

---

[23] Some datasets show metals prices rising more strongly than do others. Carter et al. (2011) base their judgment on data from the International Monetary Fund and the Commodity Research Bureau, deflated by the U.S. CPI. Cooper and Lawrence (1975), making use of the Economist index of industrial metals, show a steeper rise in metals prices relative to food and other agricultural prices. See Carter et al. (2011); Richard N. Cooper and Richard Z. Lawrence, "The 1972–1975 Commodity Boom," *Brooking Papers on Economic Activity*, 3.

[24] I owe thanks to an anonymous reviewer for this insight.

[25] Edmund Sanders and Tracy Wilkinson, "U.N. Food Aid Costlier as Need Soars," *Los Angeles Times*, April 1, 2008.

[26] See for instance "Fixing The Food Crisis," CBSNews.com, February 11, 2009.

argument, the ascent of these two Asian countries' urban middle classes, now hungrier for meat and other high-calorie food, was placing untold strain on world agriculture supplies. These stories often implied that China and India were importing increasing amounts of food for domestic consumption, just as they were for crude oil, which was leading to pushing up food prices around the globe.

But the evidence suggests this argument was simplistic. China and India had long been largely self-sufficient in food. They were generally minor players in the international market, with net trade less than 1% of production and use.[27] Neither country's trade patterns had spilled over into global markets in a dramatic way. China was generally a net exporter of corn, rice, and wheat.[28] Its grain production exceeded its consumption throughout the height of the price boom by a healthy margin.[29] China imported less wheat from 2000–2007 (33.8 million metric tons) than it had in the eight years prior (40.3 million metric tons). The story for India is broadly similar. Indian imports of corn and wheat had been negligible during the boom years, and it was a net exporter of rice.[30] The country had sent away more grain than it had consumed nearly every year between 1990 and 2008.[31]

The exception to China's general food self-sufficiency was in the soybean market. Unlike it did in grains, the country had maintained only minimal stocks of soybeans. Lacking sizeable domestic inventories, imports were the primary means of satisfying rising demand. Chinese imports of soybeans quadrupled between 2001 and 2008. However, China's rising soybean imports cannot be the major cause of the broader increase across grains and oilseeds that took place. Chinese soybean imports had actually begun to increase in the early to mid-1990s, a decade before food prices took off. Although Asian demand for soybeans did likely affect global markets (emerging market economies gradually increased their imports from 20.4 million tons in the mid-1990s to 33.4 million tons in 2008), that fact

[27] Philip C. Abbott, Christopher Hurt, and Wallace E. Tyner, "What's Driving Food Prices in 2011?," Farm Foundation Issue Report (July 2011): 13.

[28] Colin A. Carter, Gordon C. Rausser, and Aaron Smith, "The Food Price Boom and Bust," *Giannini Foundation of Agricultural Economics* (2009): 2–4.

[29] Daryll E. Ray, "USDA Top Officials versus USDA Data," *Policy Pennings no. 409. Institute of Agriculture at the University of Tennessee*, May 30, 2008.

[30] Derek Headey and Shenggen Fan, "Anatomy of a Crisis: The Causes and Consequences of Surging Food Prices," *Agricultural Economics* 39, no. s1 (2008): 377.

[31] Daryll E. Ray, "USDA Top Officials Versus USDA Data," *Policy Pennings no. 409. Institute of Agriculture at the University of Tennessee*, May 30, 2008.

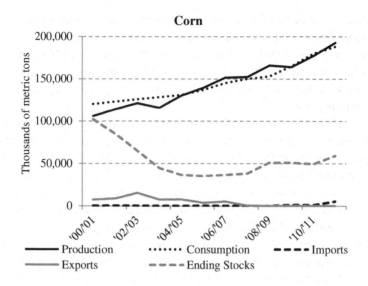

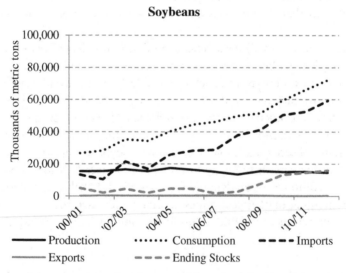

Figure 20. Chinese Supply Utilization for Grains and Soybeans (2000–2011). *Source:* USDA

cannot account for much broader price increases in global grain and oilseed prices between 2006 and 2008.[32]

---

[32] Derek Headey and Shenggen Fan, "Anatomy of a Crisis: The Causes and Consequences of Surging Food Prices," *Agricultural Economics* 39, no. s1 (2008): 377.

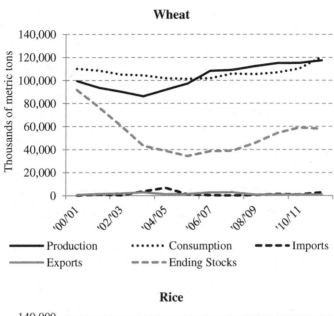

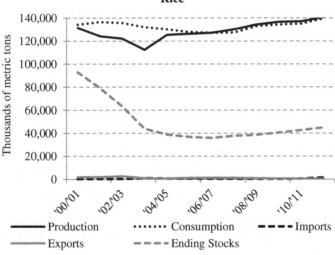

Figure 20 (*continued*)

That said, factors within China likely helped spur the rise in food prices through indirect channels. Soaring oil demand in the Middle Kingdom played a leading role in pushing oil prices higher between 2003 and 2008. High oil prices tend to raise food prices by increasing input costs, as in fertilizer, as well as for planting, harvesting, and marketing the final goods.

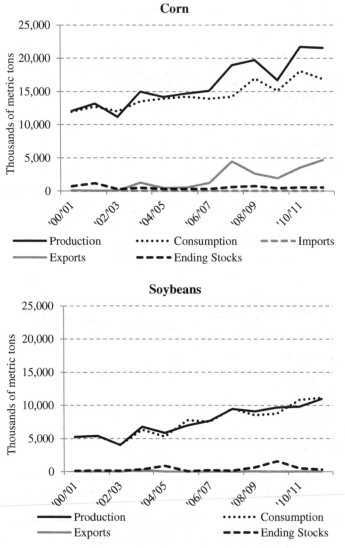

Figure 21. Indian Supply Utilization for Grains and Soybeans (2000–2011). *Source*: USDA

(This dynamic is described in more detail later.) China's climbing imports of iron ore, which placed an increasingly large burden on dry carrier and port infrastructure, may have also contributed to higher imported food prices by increasing transportation costs. In addition, China drew down its enormous cereal inventories beginning in the 1990s after Chinese officials judged them to be inefficiently high. Had market participants interpreted those

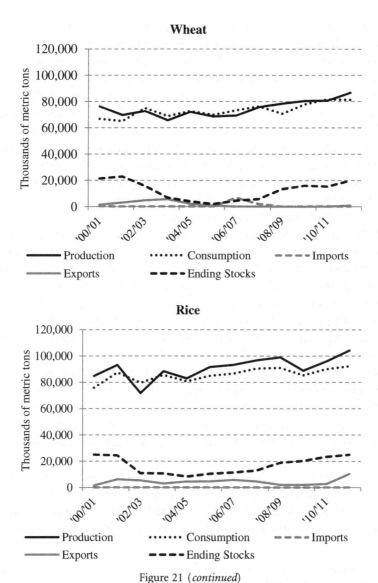

Figure 21 (*continued*)

drawdowns as a bullish signal, they might have helped spur the price boom. But many analysts are skeptical that was the case, given the country's long history in self-sufficiency in most major grains. Moreover, many countries saw their food inventories shrink in the years prior to 2008, not just China.[33]

---

[33] Christopher L. Gilbert, "How to Understand High Food Prices," Discussion Paper No. 23, Dipartimento di Economia at the Università degli Studi di Trento (2008): 15–16.

Other ways of looking at trends in emerging markets underscore their limited role in the price surge. Growth in Chinese and Indian food consumption was lower from 2002–2008 than it had been from 1995–2001, whether measured by annual average percentage growth or in absolute terms. Developing and high-income countries accounted for similar shares of the growth in global cereal consumption (+6%) in the three years preceding the boom (2003–2005) as they did during it (2006–2008). Although developing countries' imports grew slightly faster than those of high-income countries during these years, the former actually increased exports by nearly 30%, while exports from high income countries barely moved. Net imports by developing countries increased by 4 million tons of food compared to 6 million tons to high-income countries.[34]

Still, rising food prices did reflect a broader-based climb in demand from emerging markets and rising income levels there, spurred by economic growth. Demand for food oils, such as soybean oil and palm oil, grew by close to 10% in the 2006–2007 crop year, underpinned by emerging markets.[35] Not only was the quantity of food demanded increasing, but the quality was also improving. The global diet was turning to higher protein food and feed, as well as fattier, more oil-rich food, as a result of consumption trends among the world's developing economies.[36]

Another common explanation for the rise in retail food prices was speculation in commodities markets, especially by financial firms. Proponents of this theory noted, correctly, that noncommercial participation in futures markets (that is, buying and selling by traders not exposed to commodity price movements through their normal business activities, as commercial producers and consumers are) had risen alongside food prices. Some commentators extrapolated from these concurrent events that there was a causal link, with the inflow of speculative capital responsible for a price gain far beyond what market fundamentals justified.[37] They frequently cited the popularization of commodity index funds, which allow investors to gain

[34] John Baffes, "Going against the Grain on the Post-2005 Commodity Price Boom," International Economic Bulletin, Carnegie Endowment for International Peace, April 19, 2012.

[35] "Is Inflation Back? Commodity Prices and Inflation," in *World Economic Outlook: Financial Stress, Downturns, and Recoveries* (Washington, DC: International Monetary Fund, October 2008): 97.

[36] Ibid., 96.

[37] See, for instance, U.S. Senate Committee on Homeland Security and Governmental Affairs, *Testimony of Michael W. Masters*, hearing on "Financial Speculation in Commodity Markets: Are Institutional Investors and Hedge Funds Contributing to Food and Energy Price Inflation?," May 20, 2008.

exposure to a basket of commodities without holding the underlying physical good, as a root cause of high food prices. This debate is explored in
detail in the next chapter. Suffice it to say, there is little discernible evidence
that excessive speculation in financial markets was a significant driver of the
general uptrend in food prices during the mid-2000s.[38] However, irrational
exuberance in the market may well have caused prices to overshoot what
fundamentals alone would have warranted at the zenith of the boom during
the summer of 2008 and the crash in early 2009.

If Chinese import demand was only part of the equation, what other factors help explain the sustained rise in food prices in the mid-2000s? Answer-
ing this question requires distinguishing between those forces that affected
food goods in isolation (say, wheat or corn) versus those that were capable
of lifting the entire class. Because food prices rose generally, yet with varying
strength among the individual commodities, a more complete explanation
should encompass those forces that would have been bullish for agricultural goods broadly as well as those that were more commodity-specific.
In terms of broader forces capable of stimulating prices, macroeconomic
forces (the depreciation of the U.S. dollar as well as low real interest rates)
and oil prices all appear to have played a significant role, So too did some
commodity-specific factors, included rising demand for crops to be used as
biofuels, inclement weather, and export restrictions.

GENERAL FACTORS

The depreciation of the U.S. dollar (or simply "dollars" going forward)
against other major currencies was one reason food prices rose on the global
market. Because food is typically priced in dollars on the international market, a decline in the value of the dollar relative to other currencies means
that the price of the good in dollars must rise proportionately to maintain its
value. This denomination effect is likely the most direct and high-frequency
way that fluctuations in the dollar affect global commodity prices.[39] There
are other channels as well, some of which feed into prices more quickly

[38] For a good overview of the scholarship, see Scott H. Irwin and Dwight R. Sanders, "The
Impact of Index Funds in Commodity Futures Markets: A Systems Approach," *Journal
of Alternative Investments* 14 (2011), 40–49. Another excellent source, with an empha-
sis on oil markets, is Bassam Fattouh, Lutz Kilian, and Lavan Mahadeva, "The Role of
Speculation in Oil Markets: What Have We Learned So Far?," Working Paper, June 30,
2012.
[39] Edward L. Morse and Daniel P. Ahn, "The Oil-Gold-Dollar Trinity," Citi Commodities
Strategy, September 2, 2011.

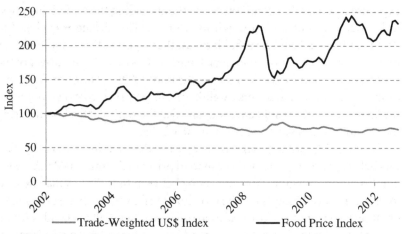

Year 2002 set equal to 100

Figure 22. Food Prices Relative to a Trade-Weighted U.S. Dollar Index (2002–2012). *Source*: Federal Reserve Bank of St. Louis

than others. One is related to purchasing power and market price. A depreciating dollar can raise demand by making dollar-denominated commodities less expensive for non-dollar consumers, while weighing on supply by cutting into nondollar profits, which can depress investment. It can also lead to greater investor demand for real assets, including commodities, which can bid up prices all along the supply chain, as money flows into nondollar assets and investors seek defense against the risk of inflation.[40]

What do data show about the effect of the simplest of these channels – the U.S. dollar as numeraire – on food prices? Between January 2002 and June 2008, the value of the dollar relative to the Euro declined by roughly 35%. It underwent a similarly significant drop (−26%) against the USDA's basket of currencies weighed according to U.S. bulk agricultural exports over that time. The difference between the two figures likely stems from the fact that some importers of U.S. agricultural products, such as China, peg their currencies to the U.S. dollar. Assuming an elasticity of 0.75 between the real trade-weighted exchange rate and an index of food prices, a World Bank analysis judges that the decline in the dollar was responsible for about 20% of the rise in dollar-denominated food prices.[41]

[40] International Monetary Fund, *World Economic Outlook: Housing and the Business Cycle* (Washington, DC: International Monetary Fund, April 2008): 48–49.
[41] Donald Mitchell, "A Note on Rising Food Prices," *Policy Research Working Paper 4682*, Development Prospects Group (Washington, DC, The World Bank, 2008): 15.

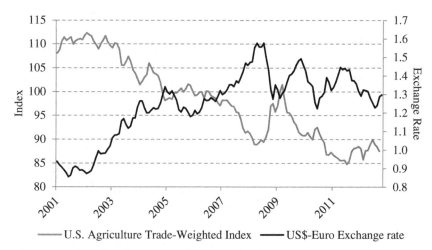

Figure 23. Bilateral Exchange Rates (2001–2012). *Source*: USDA; Federal Reserve Bank of St. Louis

Food prices not priced in U.S. dollars sidestepped the worst of the price increase from 2006 through 2008. The disparity between the rise of major grains, for instance, nominally priced in Euros versus U.S. dollars is striking. Corn prices rose 101% in U.S. dollars, but only 66% in Euros; soybeans rose +116% in dollars and +78% in Euros; and rice rose +38% in dollars and +14% in Euros. A similar pattern was visible for oil, gold, and other major commodities.

The downtrend in the value of the U.S. dollar did not occur in isolation, however. Low real U.S. interest rates were likely one of the causes of the boom in commodity prices, particularly from 2007 through mid-2008. In theory, low interest rates can boost prices in various ways. As a 2008 IMF study notes: "Many commodity prices have traditionally been more flexible than either wages or prices for other goods, and therefore they tend to respond faster to such monetary policy impulses, with some scope for short-term price overshooting."[42] Low rates can increase demand for, and reduce the supply of, storable commodities through at least three channels. They lower the incentive for producing commodities as quickly as possible, whether in terms of pumping oil or logging timber, although this likely applies more to those goods that are easy to keep in the ground, such as oil and metals, rather than to food. Lower interest rates also reduce the cost of carrying

---

[42] "Is Inflation Back? Commodity Prices and Inflation," in *World Economic Outlook: Financial Stress, Downturns, and Recoveries* (Washington, DC: International Monetary Fund, October 2008): 87.

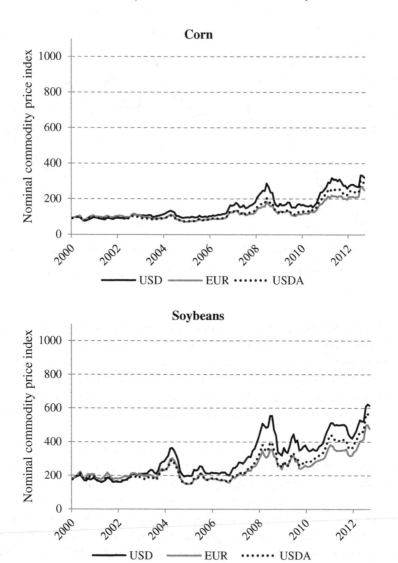

Figure 24. Selected Commodity Price Indices in Various Currencies (2000–2012). *Source*: International Monetary Fund; USDA

physical inventories, and they encourage shifts out of money market instruments and into commodity-linked securities, as investors seek higher yield.[43]

---

[43] See Jeffrey A. Frankel, "Expectations and Commodity Price Dynamics: The Overshooting Model," *American Journal of Agricultural Economics* 68, no. 2 (1986), 344–348; and Jeffrey

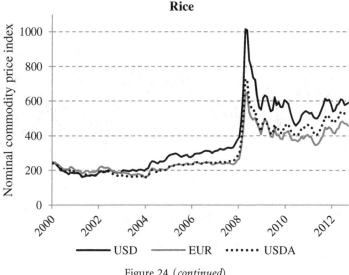

Figure 24 (*continued*)

This third mechanism is not necessarily inconsistent with the view that financial market speculation, by itself, is the primary driver of major commodity price trends. Lower interest rates are likely to raise investors' inflation expectations. That can lead to greater bidding for assets in the food-related supply chain, from planting to harvesting to marketing, which puts upward pressure on prices. There can also be feedback loops among interest rates, inflation expectations, dollar strength, investor demand, and food prices. For example, low interest rates are generally positive for economic growth expectations, increasing market forecasts of future commodity demand, which can feed back into prices immediately. Similarly, low U.S. rates put downward pressure on the dollar relative to other currencies, which can increase dollar-denominated commodity prices via numeraire effects. That said, credit conditions during the financial crises tilted against the economics of storage, whether in grains or crude oil, which may have eaxcersbated the crash of 2008 and 2009. Most empirical studies find that lower real interest rates do in fact spur higher commodity prices, though some economists do not see a clear relationship.[44]

A. Frankel, "The Effect of Monetary Policy on Real Commodity Prices," in *Asset Prices and Monetary Policy*, edited by John Y. Campbell (Chicago and London: University of Chicago Press, 2008), 291–327.

[44] See Q. Farooq Akram, "Commodity Prices, Interest Rates, and the Dollar," Working Paper 12/2008 (Oslo, Norway: Norges Bank, August 2008); Jeffrey A. Frankel, "The Effect of

Figure 25. Ten-Year U.S. Treasury Indexed Security, Constant Maturity. *Source:* Federal Reserve Bank of St. Louis

The 2006–2008 food price boom likely stemmed in part from low U.S. real interest rates. Sorting through the mechanisms is difficult, though. U.S. rates appear to have accommodated the deterioration in the value of the dollar over these years, particularly after mid-2007. Food prices leaped in the fall of 2007, around the same time that the U.S. Federal Reserve lowered rates, coinciding with a sharp drop in the dollar. The European Central Bank did not follow suit until the summer of 2008.

Inflation expectations also increased appreciably between 2005 and mid-2007, as evidenced by the yield on Treasury inflation-protected securities, which may have heightened demand for commodity-related real assets. The fact that commodities were not the only assets that boomed during these years – real estate and equities did as well – suggests that lax monetary policy had spilled over into asset prices.[45]

High oil prices appear to have played a major part in raising food prices as well. Oil prices rose at an astounding pace between 2005 and mid-2008, with front-month Brent crude catapulting from $40 a barrel at the start of 2005 to more than $140 three and half years later. Adjusted for inflation,

Monetary Policy on Real Commodity Prices," in *Asset Prices and Monetary Policy*, edited by John Y. Campbell (Chicago and London: University of Chicago Press, 2008), 291–327; Helyette Geman, *Commodities and Commodity Derivatives: Modeling and Pricing for Agriculturals, Metals and Energy* (London: John Wiley & Sons, 2005): 120.

[45] Christopher L. Gilbert, "How to Understand High Food Prices," Discussion Paper No. 23, Dipartimento di Economia at the Università degli Studi di Trento (2008): 17.

Figure 26. Front-Month ICE Brent Crude Oil Futures (2004–2008). *Source*: Bloomberg

world crude oil prices in 2008 were the highest they had been since 1864, on an average annual basis.[46] Although food production in the emerging world requires relatively little hydrocarbon energy, that is not the case in the United States, which is the dominant producer and exporter of grains. More than any other energy source, food production requires energy, both for making the stuff (including electricity for water supply) and then for transporting it. Unfortunately for consumers, oil prices outpaced other energy sources in their mid-2000s climb.

Record-high oil prices pushed food higher in at least two ways.[47] First, crude oil is required for making fertilizer, the price of which nearly tripled between mid-2006 and 2008, and other food-related chemicals. Fertilizer costs represent a full third of total operating costs for wheat and corn. Headey and Fan (2008) find that higher oil prices led to an increase in corn prices of about 8%, of soybean prices by 11%, and wheat prices by 20%. Second, higher oil prices make food more expensive by increasing the cost of transportation, both in the production process itself and in getting food to consumers. Taken together, the result of higher production and transport costs for U.S. grown corn, soybeans, and wheat likely raised U.S. export prices by 15–20% between 2002 and 2007, according to a World

---

[46] BP, *BP Statistical Review of World Energy 2009* (London: BP, June 2009).

[47] Derek Headey and Shenggen Fan, "Anatomy of a Crisis: The Causes and Consequences of Surging Food Prices," *Agricultural Economics* 39, no. s1 (2008): 381.

Bank study.[48] Similarly, an IMF study calculated that pass-through effects from higher energy costs accounted for roughly 20% of the rise in the price of major grains and oilseeds from 2006 through mid-2008.[49]

This array of forces were likely the leading causes of the explosion in food prices between late 2007 and mid-2008, as several University of California economists argue.[50] They point to two reasons why these generalized factors were more consequential than commodity-specific causes. First, nearly all commodity prices rose and fell more or less in unison in 2008, including grains, oilseeds, and softs (e.g., cotton, coffee, and cocoa). Livestock was the only exception to this trend. Second, the spike in food prices was broad enough to include energy (such as natural gas and crude oil) and metals (such as copper, gold, and aluminum). All of these goods rocketed higher in late 2007 into 2008, only to plummet to a fraction of their previous value by early 2009. That kind of synchronicity suggests common drivers, not commodity-specific ones, were particularly impactful.

CROP-SPECIFIC FACTORS

While the forces already discussed put upward pressure on food commodities as a class, other factors – increased biofuels production, disruptive weather, slower yield growth, and export restrictions – placed additional strain on some food markets, to varying degrees. Yet, in some cases, tightness in one market spilled over into others through what economics call substitution and complementarity effects, which caused high prices in one market to raise those of substitute goods.

High oil prices raised food prices in another, less direct way than the previous section mentioned: by increasing demand for biofuels and shifting crop utilization from food to fuel. Biofuels are liquid fuels and blending components produced from organic non-fossil material, which are used as supplements in transportation fuels. During the 2000s, demand from biofuels producers for agricultural goods used to make biofuels – notably corn and some oilseeds – soared. This rapid growth stemmed from a combination of high prices for other energy sources and government policy support, especially in advanced economies, in the form of biofuel mandates,

---

[48] Donald Mitchell, "A Note on Rising Food Prices," *Policy Research Working Paper 4682*, Development Prospects Group (Washington, DC, The World Bank, 2008): 5–6.

[49] "Is Inflation Back? Commodity Prices and Inflation," in *World Economic Outlook: Financial Stress, Downturns, and Recoveries* (Washington, DC: International Monetary Fund, October 2008): 98.

[50] Colin A. Carter, Gordon C. Rausser, and Aaron Smith, "The Food Price Boom and Bust," Giannini Foundation of Agricultural Economics (2009): 2.

government subsidies, and tariff protection. These policies played a role in drawing down corn and oilseed inventories in the United States and Europe. Several economists judged biofuels demand as responsible for the largest share of the food price increase in the mid-2000s.[51]

Demand for corn-based ethanol in the United States, spurred by mandates in the Energy Policy Act of 2005, may have been the single largest demand-side pressure on grain prices, according to some estimates.[52] No less than 70% of the global increase in corn production between 2004 and 2007 went into ethanol production. The United States is the world's dominant corn supplier, providing 40% of production and more than 60% of all exports. It is also the largest producer of corn-based ethanol. During the 2008 crop year, more than 30% of the country's corn production went toward ethanol rather than food – more than double the percentage just three years earlier. Global corn production did rise between 2006 and 2008 to meet this rising demand for ethanol, but not quickly enough. A 2008 IMF report estimated that biofuels demand accounted for 25% to 45% of the increase in international corn prices leading up to 2008.[53] The Energy Policy Act of 2005, which raised the amount of biofuels that must be mixed with U.S. gasoline, likely began to move markets as soon as 2006, given the long lead times involved in building ethanol plants and planning for future years' production. One study concludes that ethanol production accounted for most of the doubling in corn prices between the fall of 2005 and 2006.[54]

Demand for oilseeds used in biodiesel production and other industrial processes also increased sharply. European biofuels generally take the form of biodiesel. About one-third of the increase in global vegetable oil

[51] See for example, Donald Mitchell, "A Note on Rising Food Prices," *Policy Research Working Paper 4682*, Development Prospects Group (Washington, DC, The World Bank, 2008); Philip C. Abbott, Christopher Hurt, and Wallace E. Tyner, "What's Driving Food Prices?," *Farm Foundation Issue Report* (July 2008).

[52] See Philip C. Abbott, Christopher Hurt, and Wallace E. Tyner, "What's Driving Food Prices?," Farm Foundation Issue Report (July 2008); Derek Headey and Shenggen Fan, "Anatomy of a Crisis: The Causes and Consequences of Surging Food Prices," *Agricultural Economics* 39, no. s1 (2008), 375–391; Donald Mitchell, "A Note on Rising Food Prices," *Policy Research Working Paper 4682*, Development Prospects Group (Washington, DC, The World Bank, 2008); Randy Schnepf, *High Agricultural Commodity Prices: What Are the Issues?*, CRS Report for Congress (Washington, DC: Congressional Research Service, 2008).

[53] "Is Inflation Back? Commodity Prices and Inflation," in *World Economic Outlook: Financial Stress, Downturns, and Recoveries* (Washington, DC: International Monetary Fund, October 2008): 97.

[54] Colin A. Carter, Gordon C. Rausser, and Aaron Smith, "The Food Price Boom and Bust," Giannini Foundation of Agricultural Economics (2009): 3.

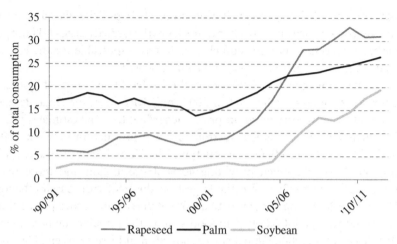

Figure 27. Industrial Use of Oils as a Percentage of Global Consumption (1990–2011). *Source:* USDA

consumption from 2004 to 2007 came from biodiesel demand. The share of global vegetable oil produced funneled into industrial uses swelled from 14.4% in 2004 to 18.7% in 2007.[55] By 2008, 20% of all rapeseed demand was eaten up by biodiesel demand, even though rapeseed is only a small player in the edible oils market.[56] The industrial share of world soybean demand climbed from 3% in 2004 to nearly 15% by 2008.[57] Imports of vegetable oil into the European Union and the United States grew quickly between 2000 and 2007 in tandem with biodiesel production. EU-27 imports increased from 4.4 to 6.9 million tons, while U.S. imports were up from 1.7 to 2.9 million tons over the same time frame.[58]

Biofuels spurred higher prices in other foods through indirect channels as well. As prices rose for biofuels-related crops, such as corn and soybeans, farmers devoted more and more acreage to producing them. Switching came at the expense of other crops, whose prices rose. This dynamic – known as the substitution effect – caused price gains in those crops directly affected by

[55] Donald Mitchell, "A Note on Rising Food Prices," *Policy Research Working Paper 4682,* Development Prospects Group (Washington, DC, The World Bank, 2008): 7–8.

[56] "Is Inflation Back? Commodity Prices and Inflation," in *World Economic Outlook: Financial Stress, Downturns, and Recoveries* (Washington, DC: International Monetary Fund, October 2008): 97–98.

[57] Philip C. Abbott, Christopher Hurt, and Wallace E. Tyner, "What's Driving Food Prices in 2011?," Farm Foundation Issue Report (July 2011): 4.

[58] Donald Mitchell, "A Note on Rising Food Prices," *Policy Research Working Paper 4682,* Development Prospects Group (Washington, DC, The World Bank, 2008): 8.

rising biofuels demand to spill over into those with which they compete for acreage. Thus, a price hike for one good can spark a more generalized bull market. In the United States, for instance, farmers increased the amount of land they devoted to corn by 23% in 2007. As a result, area for soybeans fell 16%, cutting into production and sparking a price rise of around 75% between April 2007 and April 2008, according to one estimate.[59] A second way that biofuels demand led to higher food prices was by increasing the cost of livestock feed, which passed through to meat prices.[60] Many agricultural commodities are complementary goods: a change in the price of one good that is used to produce another can alter that market as well. As an example, more than 70% of the cost of raising a pig is feeding it, so a jump in the price of corn can quickly affect the price of pork.[61] All told, one study concludes that biofuel demand comprised 60% to 70% of the rise in corn prices and as much as 40% for soybeans over that time frame. Via substitution effects, biofuels likely caused the price of wheat and rice to jump by around 25%.[62]

Bad weather may have been partly to blame for higher prices, but it was likely only a minor factor, except for in the wheat market. Weather as an explanation of the boom is more tempting than it is accurate. Droughts in Australia, one of the top five wheat exporters in the world, in 2006 and 2007 did cause wheat production in the country to slip 50% to 60% below trend in those years. The European Union and Ukraine both had modestly disappointing production in 2007. Global wheat production fell by 4.5% in 2006, followed by a weak 2% rebound in 2007. But looking at these weather-induced declines in isolation exaggerates their likely impact on the grain market. After dipping by 1.3% in 2006, global grain production rose by 4.7% in 2007. Output declines in Australia and other countries in 2007 were more than offset by bumper crops in Argentina, Kazakhstan, Russia, and the United States. Production shortfalls are endemic in agricultural markets, particularly wheat. The decline in global wheat production experienced in 2007, as a percentage of global supply, was less than half the size of the one in 2000–2001. Much larger shortfalls from trends in wheat production in the United States and Australia were also not uncommon in the preceding

[59] Ibid., 10.
[60] Christopher L. Gilbert, "How to Understand High Food Prices," Discussion Paper No. 23, Dipartimento di Economia at the Università degli Studi di Trento (2008): 11–14.
[61] Colin A. Carter, Gordon C. Rausser, and Aaron Smith, "Commodity Booms and Busts," *Annual Review of Resource Economics* vol 3 (October 2011), 87–118.
[62] Derek Headey and Shenggen Fan, "Anatomy of a Crisis: The Causes and Consequences of Surging Food Prices," *Agricultural Economics* 39, no. s1 (2008): 380.

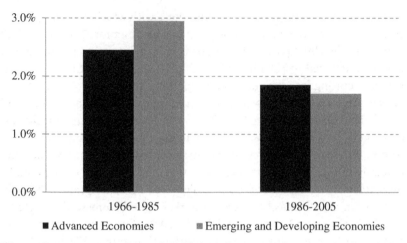

Figure 28. Average Annual Cereal Yield Growth in Agriculture, Pre- and Post-1985. *Source:* International Monetary Fund

two decades. Still, with inventories low, bad weather in crucial exporting countries, particularly for wheat, did not help matters.[63]

A slowdown in the rate of growth of cereal yields in the decades before the boom in world food prices had helped set the stage. Crop yield is a measure of agricultural productivity, the output generated per unit area of cultivated land. Cereal yields did grow in the two decades prior to 2005, at a rate of just under 2% in advanced economies and roughly 1.5% in emerging and developing economies on an average annual basis (see Figure 28). This productivity growth allowed for the decline in real food prices that occurred from around 1975 to 2000. But that was well short of what they had done between 1966 and 1985, when annual yield growth in both areas had averaged 2.5% and close to 3%, respectively. Rice and wheat were among the crops whose yields had slowed, while those for corn and soybeans largely stagnated. Some analysts attributed this long-term decline in cereal yields to two forces. One was a slowdown in public investment in agricultural research.[64] The second was protectionist

[63] Donald Mitchell, "A Note on Rising Food Prices," *Policy Research Working Paper 4682*, Development Prospects Group (Washington, DC: The World Bank, 2008): 13–14; Derek Headey and Shenggen Fan, "Anatomy of a Crisis: The Causes and Consequences of Surging Food Prices," *Agricultural Economics* 39, no. s1 (2008): 379.

[64] Philip C. Abbott, Christopher Hurt, and Wallace E. Tyner, "What's Driving Food Prices in 2011?," Farm Foundation Issue Report (July 2011): 32.

policies in developed countries and widespread food subsidies in developing ones.[65]

Lower yield growth tends to raise food prices. To begin with, slower yield growth means that more land must be tilled to generate the same amount of output. Bringing additional farmland into production requires new investment, which factors into higher prices. Not all land is equally productive; some acres are higher quality than others. There are also geographical limits, which are particularly stiff in the short-term, to bringing new farmland online. As IMF economists point out, these factors can cause lower yield growth to lead to higher food prices in two ways.[66] First, the difficulty of bringing new land into production quickly, in the face of geographic and land-quality constraints, means that yields can dip. Devoting more land to one crop can mean less is available for others, unless total acreage in production grows sufficiently. Second, farmers open up land that is increasingly marginal as demand rises. The incentive to plant and harvest new acreage, especially when it might be less productive land, comes only through higher prices.

Restrictive trade policies, including temporary export bans imposed by several countries, were also a significant factor in tightening some food markets and hence raising prices. Some scholars deemed these trade restrictions to have been the second more important factor, after higher energy costs, on the food price boom between 2006 and 2008.[67] These policies – among which export bans were only one form, though the most severe – represented an effort by net food importing and exporting countries to stabilize their domestic markets, seeking to protect their economies and national populations against the malign economic effects of higher prices in international markets. The temptation for governments to adopt emergency measures to intervene in food markets gained urgency as prices shot upward in 2007 through mid-2008. These sorts of protectionist measures are a common occurrence during food price surges. They are essentially a collective action problem: each country, seeking to ensure domestic price stability for critical food commodities, exacerbates the instability of the global market.[68]

---

[65] "Is Inflation Back? Commodity Prices and Inflation," in *World Economic Outlook: Financial Stress, Downturns, and Recoveries* (Washington, DC: International Monetary Fund, October 2008): 96.

[66] Thomas Helbling and Shaun Roache, "Rising Prices on the Menu," *Finance and Development* 48 (March 2011), 24–27.

[67] Ibid., 26.

[68] D. Gale Johnson, "World Agriculture, Commodity Policy, and Price Variability," *Agricultural Economics* 57, no. 5 (1975), 823–828.

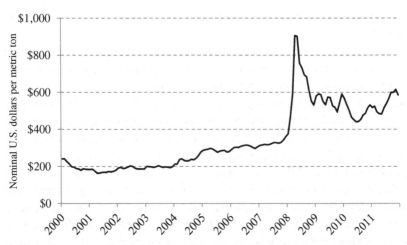

Figure 29. Nominal Monthly Price of Thai 5% White Rice (2000–2011). *Source:* The description provided by the World Bank Commodity Price Data is as follows: "Rice (Thailand), 5% broken, white rice (WR), milled, indicative price based on weekly surveys of export transactions, government standard, f.o.b. Bangkok." See "World Bank Commodity Price Data (Pink Sheet)."

Exporters can respond in several ways via trade policy to a jump in food commodities prices, as can importers.[69] Their decisions, even if meant as defensive measures, can have real and potentially highly disruptive effects beyond their borders. Fearful that domestic prices may rise, exporting countries may raise export tariffs and taxes or lower subsidies. This tactic helps block more of what it produces from going elsewhere, but it takes much-needed supplies off the global market, pushing prices up further. Importing countries, meanwhile, may reduce import restrictions or increase subsidies to avoid a harmful rise in domestic prices. Although in normal times reducing an import tariff would remove an impediment to an efficient global market, during a price spike, it can amplify the price hike in international markets by raising demand for imports.

Of all the food markets, rice was the one most affected by sudden national changes in trade policy, which were partly responsible for prices rising from around $329 per metric ton in October 2007 to more than $907 per metric ton by April 2008 (see Figure 29). After watching rice prices rise approximately 50% in real terms between the fall of 2005 and 2007, the Indian government banned rice exports below $425 per ton in October

[69] Will Martin, "Export Restrictions and Price Insulation During Commodity Price Booms," Policy Research Working Paper 5645, *Development Research Group, Agriculture and Rural Development Team* (Washington, DC: The World Bank, 2011): 3–7.

2007. By February 2008, India had proscribed all rice exports. By then, rising prices had prompted a domino-like series of export restrictions and outright bans across Egypt, Cambodia, and Vietnam. The Philippines undertook extraordinary precautionary buying, matching their total 2007 purchases in the first four months of 2008 alone. The upward surge finally broke in early summer, after Japan released 200,000 tons of rice to the Philippines. The market cooled, and trade restrictions were gradually removed. Like rice, the wheat market also underwent trade-policy inflicted turmoil, as did soybean oil and palm oil though to a lesser degree.[70]

The rice market is especially vulnerable to policy-related disruptions because the volume traded on the world market is very small relative to total production. How much were these trade policy changes in the rice market responsible for the 127% increase in the world price of rice between 2005 and 2008? According to one study, more than 45% of that price jump is explained by "changes in border restrictions that countries used in an attempt to insulate themselves from the initial increases in price." That number is slightly larger than 50% over 2008 alone. For wheat, the next-most affected food commodity after rice, these policy disruptions explain 29% of the 114% surge in prices.[71]

The tumult in agricultural prices over the past decade was on a scale not seen in the preceding quarter-century. In a sense, however, the boom was a rebound toward the long-term mean from the 1990s and early 2000s, when food was cheaper even after adjusting for inflation than at any time in the previous century. Food prices at the height of the 2008 boom were still only a fraction of what they had been in the 1973–1974 crisis, but the market dislocation was enough to reawaken old fears among policymakers and analysts about the threat of severe inflation in the price of consumer staples.

CONCLUSION

Extinguishing the volatility in food markets is neither possible nor desirable, yet public policy can make the difference between hardship and outright

---

[70] Derek Headey and Shenggen Fan, "Anatomy of a Crisis: The Causes and Consequences of Surging Food Prices," *Agricultural Economics* 39, no. s1 (2008): 379; "Is Inflation Back? Commodity Prices and Inflation," in *World Economic Outlook: Financial Stress, Downturns, and Recoveries* (Washington, DC: International Monetary Fund, October 2008): 98. Also Raja M, "Asia Faces Growing Rice Crisis," *Asia Times Online*, February 14, 2008, www.atimes.com (accessed May 2015).

[71] Will Martin, "Export Restrictions and Price Insulation During Commodity Price Booms," Policy Research Working Paper 5645, *Development Research Group, Agriculture and Rural Development Team* (Washington, DC: The World Bank, 2011): 10.

famine. Making global food markets more transparent is likely one part of the answer. Improving ways of tracking and disseminated information about where supply and demand portends a looming problem, particularly in the developing world, is crucial. Removing impediments to free trade would help the smooth functioning of world food markets, and yet there is little likelihood that these flaws in the trading system will be remedied anytime soon, given the inherent interest of national governments to use strategic trade policy to stop a spike in the world food market from entering its borders.[72] Over the longer term, increased public and nonprofit spending on agricultural research could likely help spur growth in agricultural productivity and increase aggregate food output, a success experienced decades ago in the Green Revolution, a technology-driven boom in crop yields that began in the mid-twentieth century thanks largely to public and nonprofit investment.[73]

---

[72] See Food and Agriculture Organization of the United Nations, "The 2007–08 Rice Price Crisis," Policy Brief 13, February 2011, which discusses this idea in more depth.

[73] Nienke Beintema and Howard Elliott, "Setting Meaningful Investment Targets in Agricultural Research and Development: Challenges, Opportunities and Fiscal Realities," Food and Agriculture Organization of the United Nations, Paper prepared for the FAO Expert Meeting on "How to Feed the World in 2050," June 24–26, 2009, Rome, Italy: 2.

4

Commodity Markets and Financial Speculation

The so-called financialization process that has occurred in commodities markets over the past three decades has given rise to intense public debate over whether the proliferation of commodity-backed securities and increasing presence of financial market participants has caused prices for these goods to rise and fall beyond their fair value, harming producers' and consumers' abilities to hedge their risks – the use for which forward grain markets were invented centuries ago – and hurting the businesses and consumers who would benefit from more stable, less unpredictable prices. The debate is a contentious one, and hardly new. For centuries, traders in commodity markets have raised suspicion among public officials and drawn the ire of consumers, who have questioned whether these market participants are playing a productive role or profiting at the expense of others. The launching of electronic futures trading and the proliferation of commodity-linked derivatives products over the past decade have intensified these concerns. It is true that broad, persistent increases in the prices of a host of commodities have occurred concurrently with a rise in commodity trading volumes and commodity holdings among investors. But is there a causal relationship between the two phenomena – in other words, are financial speculators pushing up prices? Or is the relationship between the two trends more nuanced and uncertain? The answer to these questions is critical for regulating energy markets and ensuring that market prices reflect fair value for producers and consumers alike.

A host of research explores the role and effect of financial speculators (that is, those who trade commodity-linked securities but do not produce, consume, or take delivery of the underlying good) on commodity prices. The lack of comprehensive, reliable data about the flow of goods and money within the world's commodity markets poses an enormous challenge to the ability of these studies to yield definitive conclusions. That said, some policy-relevant insights have emerged. There is little credible evidence that excessive financial speculation is systematically causing commodity prices to diverge significantly from what economic fundamentals would justify. Moreover, theoretical models and empirical data make clear the vital role that well-regulated speculation plays in commodity markets by enhancing price discovery, improving liquidity, allowing producers and consumers to hedge their market risk, and helping prices respond to fluctuations in supply, demand, and inventories. Overly aggressive or poorly conceived regulations risk stifling this essential risk-taking role of speculative buyers and sellers. That said, commodity markets, like all markets, should be supervised to prevent manipulation, fraud, and abuse. The largest scope for improving commodity markets lies in increasing the transparency of the physical market – that is, the actual goods as they move from production through transport and storage on their way to the end user. The relatively opaque nature of commodity markets, as opposed to those for equities, for instance, exacerbates the already-volatile nature of these markets. Data about production, consumption, inventory holdings, and trade flows worldwide leaves much to be desired in terms of reliability, affordability, and timeliness. The problem is particularly acute as it relates to market conditions in countries outside the Organization for Economic Cooperation and Development.

THE DEBATE OVER SPECULATORS IN COMMODITY MARKETS

Worry among U.S. policymakers over whether commodity traders were contributing to high gasoline problems was feverish in the spring of 2012. Gas prices in the United States had risen 20% over the first quarter of the year. As they did, public pressure mounted for elected officials to help ease the pain at the pump. In March, a group of House and Senate Democrats sent a letter to the Commodity Futures Trading Commission (CFTC) chiding federal regulators for not doing enough to end "excessive oil speculation" in the market.[1] A week later, President Barack Obama asked Attorney General Eric Holder to "pay attention to potential speculation in the oil markets" and reconstitute a task force to investigate whether Wall Street was artificially driving up oil prices.[2]

When prices continued to rise in April, close to breaching $4 per gallon on average nationwide, President Obama announced further measures

---

[1] Ben Geman, "Dems Blame Wall Street For High Gas Prices, Urge CFTC Action," E2 Wire, *The Hill*, March 3, 2012, http://www.thehill.com (accessed October 2012).

[2] Nick Snow, "Obama Cites Bottlenecks, Speculation as Possible Gasoline Price Factors," *Oil and Gas Journal*, March 7, 2012, http://www.ogj.com/.

intended to curb speculation. In a Rose Garden speech on April 17, he said:

We can't afford a situation where speculators artificially manipulate markets by buying up oil, creating the perception of a shortage, and driving prices higher – only to flip the oil for a quick profit. We can't afford a situation where some speculators can reap millions, while millions of American families get the short end of the stick. That's not the way the market should work. And for anyone who thinks this cannot happen, just think back to how Enron traders manipulated the price of electricity to reap huge profits at everybody else's expense.

U.S. policymakers, he argued, should be "doing everything we can to ensure that an irresponsible few aren't able to hurt consumers by illegally manipulating or rigging the energy markets for their own gain." The President then outlined a five-part plan to "strengthen oversight of energy markets." These steps included: (1) increasing the surveillance and enforcement staff at the CFTC; (2) providing the CFTC with additional funding for information technology upgrades to better monitor market activity; (3) significantly upping criminal and civil penalties for manipulating energy markets; (4) empowering the CFTC to raise margin requirements in oil futures markets; and (5) expanding expert access to CFTC data on trading in energy markets to better understanding investor behavior and its effect on prices.[3]

President Obama is not the first U.S. president, let alone the first U.S. elected official, to suggest that oil companies and traders might be fleecing consumers. Ever since the days of Rockefeller, the world's largest oil companies have been objects of suspicion. Ida Tarbell's exposé on Standard Oil, first published in 1902, decried the "open disregard for decent ethical business practices" in the oil market that had made Rockefeller the richest man in the world. The accusation – that Standard "never played fair," at the expense of the American working class – contributed to fostering a distrust among American people of oil companies and oil markets that persists to this day, more than a century later.[4] While in office, Presidents Theodore Roosevelt and Jimmy Carter both denounced oil companies for obscene profits.[5] In

---

[3] Office of the Press Secretary, "Remarks by the President on Increasing Oversight on Manipulation in Oil Markets," The White House, April 17, 2012. See also Office of the Press Secretary, "Fact Sheet: Increasing Oversight and Cracking Down on Manipulation in Oil Markets," The White House, April 17, 2012, http://www.whitehouse.gov/.

[4] PBS, "People and Events: Ida Tarbell, 1857–1944," American Experience: The Rockefellers, http://www.pbs.org/wgbh/amex/rockefellers/peopleevents/p_tarbell.html.

[5] See William L. Anderson, "Profits Do Not Cause High Prices," Mises Daily, Ludwig von Mises Institute, May 24, 2004; Thomas Sowell, "The 'Progressive' Legacy," *The National Review*, February 14, 2012.

2006, Republican Congressional leaders called on then-President Bush to direct the U.S. attorney general and the Federal Trade Commission to investigate whether spiking gasoline prices were indeed a result of a "change in market conditions" or more troublingly, of "price gouging." Similar calls from Congressional leaders were repeated throughout 2007 and 2008 as oil prices spiked.[6]

For decades, Americans placed more blame on oil companies for rising gas prices than other possible culprits. According to an April 2012 CNN/ORC poll, a larger number of Americans thought U.S. oil companies deserved "a great deal of blame" (61%) for consumers' pain at the pump than foreign oil producers, Western tensions with Iran, the Obama Administration, or Republicans in Congress.[7] The same poll found that 90% of Americans consider oil companies at least partially to blame for high oil prices, the highest of any group.[8] These attitudes echo Americans' views during the energy crises of the 1970s. In a 1974 poll, 67% of respondents accused oil companies of being "very responsible" for the energy crisis – making them the single largest perceived cause – followed by government planners (58%), President Nixon (40%), and politics in the Middle East (20%).[9] That is remarkable, given that the proximate cause of the extraordinary gasoline prices at the time was the Arab oil embargo.

Suspicion (or outright condemnation) of speculators among U.S. policymakers and the American public predates the 1970s. As one historian observes,

Even before the rise of organized commodity exchanges, popular sentiment has, at best, been openly suspicious, but generally, openly hostile to the person of the speculator. Coming in between the producer and ultimate consumer, the role of the speculator – carrying with it sufficient price margins – has always been judged by physiocratic standards: productive of nothing, deserving of nothing.[10]

Today's rhetoric about speculators is actually less charged than what it was in the distant past. Then, as now, the opprobrium cut across the political spectrum. Vladimir Lenin once declared that "as long as we fail to treat

---

[6]   See, for example, David Goldman, "Democrats: Close Speculation Loophole," *CNNMoney*, May 8, 2008.
[7]   See "Energy," PollingReport.com, April 2012 (accessed October 2012).
[8]   Christian Houser, "Poll: Americans blame oil companies for high gas prices," WCPO.com, April 4, 2012 (accessed October 2012).
[9]   Louise Cook, "Oil Firms Get Most Blame in Poll on Energy Crisis," *St. Petersburg Times*, March 5, 1974.
[10] David S. Jacks, "Populists versus Theorists: Futures Markets and the Volatility of Prices," *Explorations in Economic History* 44, no. 2 (April 2007): 343.

speculators the way they deserve – with a bullet in the head – we will not get anywhere at all." He was not alone. Decades earlier, Abraham Lincoln said that "for my part, I wish every one of them [speculators] had his devilish head shot off." In the United States, political outcry over the perceived abuses on speculators was at its zenith in the decades after the Civil War, when many commodities began to be traded on futures markets. Newspapers carried stories describing these exchanges as "an engine of wrong and oppression" held captive by a "den of speculators" that were liable to inflict "gradual misery and ruin . . . upon all classes."[11] Judging by the eighteenth-century writings of Adam Smith, however, these accusations were nothing new. He compared public fears over speculation in English grain markets to "popular terrors and suspicions of witchcraft."[12]

The debate over the effect of speculators on oil markets took a new turn in the early 2000s, as prices began to push upward with surprising ferocity. Spot West Texas Intermediate (WTI) crude oil cost barely $18 a barrel in December 2001. By 2006, it had quadrupled. But that was only the beginning. In July 2008, spot prices had catapulted to $145 a barrel, before collapsing with astounding force to just $34 in February 2009.

Spot prices were not the only parts of the market that witnessed back-breaking volatility. During much of the time between 2003 and 2008, long-dated crude oil futures displayed volatility that was similar to the fluctuations at the front-end of the forward curve. That level of volatility in long-term prices is a radical departure from the 1990s. As Bassam Fattouh and Pasquale Scaramozzino point out, even major geopolitical events (such as the 1990–1991 Gulf War, the 1998 Asian financial crisis, or the U.S.-led invasion of Iraq in 2003), which often jostled near-term oil futures, were not enough to dislodge long-term oil prices from the $20–22 range. But around 2002, that price stability in distant futures contracts disappeared. No longer did near-dated prices reliably revert to the longer-term anchor.[13]

To some observers, these astounding dislocations in the oil market suggested that forces other than economic fundamentals must be driving prices. Instead, they attributed them to the increased presence of financial

---

[11] All quoted in David S. Jacks, "Populists versus Theorists: Futures Markets and the Volatility of Prices," *Explorations in Economic History* 44, no. 2 (April 2007): 343–344.

[12] Adam Smith, *An Inquiry into the Nature and Causes of the Wealth of Nations*, 5th ed. (London: Methuen & Co. Ltd., 1904).

[13] Bassam Fattouh and Pasquale Scaramozzino, "Uncertainty, Expectations, and Fundamentals: Whatever Happened to Long-Term Oil Prices?," The Oxford Institute for Energy Studies (March 2011): 1–2.

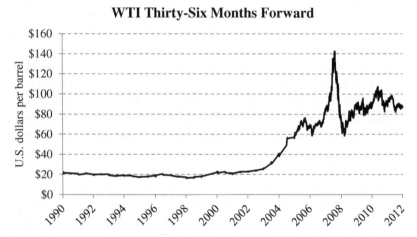

Figure 31. NYMEX Crude Oil Prices for Delivery One- and Thirty-Six Months Forward. *Source:* Bloomberg (as of 12/13/12)

investors – or speculators, loosely speaking – in oil futures markets. They noted that spot prices were rising around the same time that investors were becoming more involved in oil futures markets. They reasoned that high and rising oil prices were being driven by the increased prominence of investor money into futures markets. Among the first to propose this idea were two hedge fund managers, George Soros and Michael Masters, while testifying to Congress in 2008. As they saw it – and in a formulation that would become the assumed truth in popular discourse and for some policymakers – the link was simple: hedge funds and other investors put money into futures markets, bidding prices higher, which then fed back into higher spot prices, causing retail prices for things like gasoline, diesel, and heating oil to rise.[14]

It is true that a flood of investor capital began to flow into these markets around 2003, a dynamic many commentators refer to as the "financialization" of the oil market. In the mid-2000s, institutional investors – for example, pension funds, insurance companies, hedge funds, and foundations – began to allocate a portion of their portfolios to commodity futures (and other derivatives), eventually pouring tens of billions of dollars into these markets.[15] Investors were attracted to the recent gains in spot commodity prices, especially compared to the equities crash in 2000, not to mention promising new research touting the investment properties of commodities futures. These studies argued that a basket of commodity futures displayed a negative correlation to equities (and hence diversification properties),[16] minimal positive co-movement with each other,[17] the potential for long-term "equity-like" returns,[18] and positive correlation to inflation (including unexpected inflation).[19]

Between 2001 and 2012, aggregate trading volumes of WTI and Brent futures on the NYMEX and ICE swelled by about six-fold.[20] CFTC data reveal that the share of non-commercial activity in oil futures markets has likewise jumped from 21% of total open interest in 2000 to 50% by 2008.[21]

---

[14] Bassam Fattouh, Lutz Kilian, and Lavan Mahadeva, "The Role of Speculation in Oil Markets: What Have We Learned So Far?," Working Paper, June 30, 2012.

[15] "Report of the Working Group on the Volatility of Oil Prices," Centre de traduction MINEIE et MBCPFP, Ministère de l'Économie, de l'Industrie et de l'Emploi, February 2010.

[16] Robert Greer, "The Nature of Commodity Index Returns," *Journal of Alternative Investments* 3, no. 1 (2000), 45–52.

[17] Claude B. Erb and Campbell R. Harvey, "The Tactical and Strategic Value of Commodity Futures," NBER Working Paper No. 11222, National Bureau of Economic Research (March 2005).

[18] Gary Gorton and K. Geert Rouwenhorst, "Facts and Fantasies about Commodity Futures," *Financial Analysts Journal* 62, no. 2 (March/April 2006), 47–68.

[19] Ibid.

[20] Aakash Doshi et al., "Commodity Flows: Week Ending July 31st 2012," Citi Research: Commodities, August 6, 2012. Note that these data do not capture OTC trading activity.

[21] Bahattin Büyükşahin et al., "Fundamentals, Trader Activity and Derivative Pricing," EFA 2009 Bergen Meetings Paper, December 4, 2008. Cited in Daniel O'Sullivan, *Petromania: Black Gold, Paper Barrels and Oil Price Bubbles* (London: Harriman House, 2009), 100. Many experts believe that if over-the-counter (OTC) trading activity were included in these figures, both trading volume in oil futures as well as noncommercial interest as a percentage of total open interest would be significantly higher than these figures suggest.

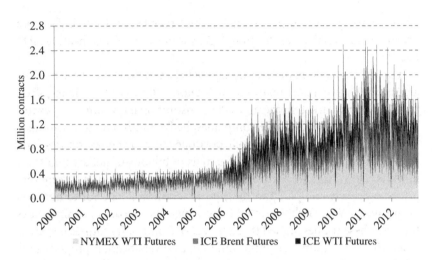

Figure 32. WTI and Brent Futures Aggregate Trading Volumes (2000–2012). *Source:* Citi Research; Bloomberg

Many analysts, policymakers, and others have argued that this financialization process has altered the oil futures market in important ways over the past decade. The simplest and most popular claim is that that the growing presence of speculative capital is making oil prices higher and more volatile for everyday consumers than economic fundamentals justify. As a blogger at *New York Times* Dealbook put it, critics feel that the oil market has devolved

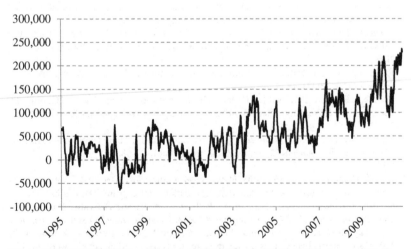

Figure 33. NYMEX WTI Non-Commercial Net Length (1995–2011). *Source:* U.S. Commodity Futures Trading Commission

into a "virtual casino where the consumer always loses."[22] But the debate extends beyond price levels. Bassam Fattouh and two coauthors summarize these views nicely:

The financialization of oil futures markets has been held responsible for a variety of phenomena including changes in price volatility, increased co-movement between oil futures prices and other financial asset and commodity prices, a breakdown of the statistical relationship between oil inventories and the price of oil, and in increased influence of the decisions of financial investors such as swap dealers, hedge funds and commodity index traders on the oil futures price. Most importantly, there is a perception that oil futures markets no longer adequately perform their function of price discovery and risk transfer.[23]

The scholars also note that some experts have linked changes in risk premia in oil futures contracts in recent years.[24]

The most widely cited articulation of the view that the financialization of the oil market has caused prices to decouple from economic fundamentals came from Michael Masters, a hedge fund manager, in his testimony before the U.S. Senate's Committee on Homeland Security and Government Affairs in May 2008. Masters declared "unequivocal[ly]" that investors, especially index funds, are "contributing to food and energy price inflation." As he saw it, commodity supplies were "ample," and yet prices were rising. Why? A "demand shock," he argued, stemming from "a new category of participants in commodities futures markets: institutional investors" using "buy-and-hold" strategies in futures markets for the first time. He laid most of the blame at the feet of index investors because "*they never sell.*" This kind of speculation, he asserted, "provide[s] no benefit to futures markets" but "inflict[s] a tremendous cost upon society." Masters suggested that speculators had in effect "stockpiled, via futures markets, 1.1 billion barrels of petroleum effectively adding eight times as much oil to their own stockpile as the United States has added to the Strategic Petroleum Reserve over the last five years." He called on the CFTC to tighten its regulation of commodities markets before prices "rise higher still."[25]

---

[22] Cyrus Sanati, "Sewing the Energy Loopholes Shut," *Dealbook*, NYTimes.com, May 30, 2008 (accessed October 2012).

[23] Bassam Fattouh, Lutz Kilian, and Lavan Mahadeva, "The Role of Speculation in Oil Markets: What Have We Learned So Far?," Working Paper (June 30, 2012): 1.

[24] Ibid., 20–23.

[25] U.S. Senate Committee on Homeland Security and Governmental Affairs, *Testimony of Michael W. Masters*, Hearing on "Financial Speculation in Commodity Markets: Are Institutional Investors and Hedge Funds Contributing to Food and Energy Price Inflation?," May 20, 2008.

The debate over speculators and oil prices is far from academic, carrying important implications for policymakers and consumers alike, which are summarized in the next chapter. Elevated prices for oil, marked by extreme volatility, pose risks to the U.S. and global economy. They leave consumers with higher bills for staples, such as food, gasoline, and heating oil. They hit the poorest segments of the country's population the hardest, and underpin inflation, which in turn tends toward a tightening in monetary policy that puts the brakes on economic growth. Unemployment in the United States tends to increase when higher energy prices lead businesses to reshuffle their operations. Given that painfully high energy prices can drag on economic activity, market activity that pushes prices higher than is justified might mean the difference between growth and recession.

Dramatic changes in oil prices can cause other problems as well. They heighten the degree of uncertainty in the marketplace, which discourages businesses from investing in long-term projects and hiring new employees, especially in the industries most affected by these price swings, such as manufacturing, transportation, agriculture, and natural resource extraction. Price uncertainty also hinders the development and commercialization of renewable energy and energy efficiency technology.

Numerous scholarly studies have sought to determine what impact, if any, increased speculative activity by financial investors in the oil market has on prices. Beginning around 2006, as oil prices began to rise steeply, the issue took on increasing urgency for regulatory officials worldwide. A lack of data about global oil trade flows, off-exchange trade activity, and publicly available disaggregated CFTC data makes the risk of erroneous conclusions high.[26] It may be that better data available in the future will help answer the question with more precision than is possible today or will challenge recent scholarly findings. Still, with that caveat in mind, what does the evidence show so far?

WHAT IS SPECULATION?

The imprecision with which the term "speculation" is often used in the mass media is one reason why the current debates often generates more

---

[26] For an excellent discussion of how limited publicly available data about energy markets can be problematic for regulators and market participants alike, see Daniel P. Ahn, "Improving Energy Market Regulation: Domestic and International Issues," CGS/IIGG Working Paper, New York, NY: Council on Foreign Relations, 2011.

heat than light. What is speculation? One scholar offers a useful definition, noting that the term can be construed broadly or narrowly:

> In the context of commodities and in the broadest sense, it involves all actions that aim at profiting from a move in commodity price. Buying a futures contract on the exchange, or prematurely filling a half-full automobile tank, both in anticipation of an impending price rise, can be classified as speculative activity, even though the latter action is undertaken by a commodity consumer (the car driver). A narrower definition, in which the speculators have no intrinsic interest in the commodity as such, is common. According to the Shorter Oxford English Dictionary, speculators buy and sell "in order to profit by the rise or fall in the market value, as distinct from regular trading or investment."[27]

As this definition notes, and as most other scholarship reinforces, the common denominator to speculative activity broadly construed is that the buyer (or seller) is seeking to profit from taking a position. Whether the purchaser of a commodity like gasoline is the end user (a car owner) or an intermediary (a trader) who puts the oil into storage or does not take delivery, he is still a speculator in the broader sense of the term. Kilian and Murphy argue that from the standpoint of economic theory there are four ways to speculate: by buying oil and then holding it, or by buying an oil futures contract, with the intent to sell it later at a profit (or take the opposite tack, selling oil or taking a short position).[28] Most of the political criticism that has been leveled against speculators over the past decade has targeted those who fit within the narrower definition: traders who take short-term positions in the financial markets seeking to profit from price movements but do not engage in physical moving or storing the stuff. Michael Masters' much-maligned "index speculators," for example, would fit in this category.

This narrow definition of speculation still encompasses a wide variety of phenomena, however. One of the most common is precautionary buying by companies that rely on a ready supply of oil. Naturally these buyers fear a future supply disruption. If they believe that prices are about to rise or a disruption is around the corner, they might buy oil (or purchase the option to buy it later), a move known as precautionary buying. This sort of buying can cause oil prices to rise or fall temporarily, but it serves an economically important function. As one author explains:

---

[27] Marian Radetzki, *A Handbook of Primary Commodities in the Global Economy* (Cambridge and New York: Cambridge University Press, 2008): 100.

[28] Lutz Kilian and Dan Murphy, "The Role of Inventories and Speculative Trading in the Global Market for Crude Oil," Centre for Economic Policy Research (March 2010): 18.

This type of speculation . . . acts as a form of insurance, both for the imperiled companies and for the economy more generally. It lowers the risk of an extreme spike in prices later on – or worse still, a dire shortage of gasoline – by tempering demand and calling forth more supplies. Facing uncertainty, companies are wise to rush to secure oil that they can use in the future. If businesses did not pad their inventories, a disruption could mean catastrophe for them and their customers. Moreover, the relatively gradual rise in prices that cautionary buying prompts is far easier on the economy than the alternative: prices flying through the roof in an oil market caught completely flatfooted by an unforeseen interruption to trade.[29]

Precautionary buying, though broadly speaking an act of speculation, is essential to a well-functioning market.

The critical distinction between speculation and manipulation is often lost in popular debate. They are not the same. The CFTC attempts to delineate the two practices by defining speculation as "any planned operation, transaction, or practice that causes or maintains an artificial price." Manipulating the market, on the other hand, consists of cornering or squeezing a market, as well as making "unusually large purchases or sales of a commodity or security in a short period of time in order to distort prices, and putting out false information in order to distort prices."[30] While all manipulation in the oil market could be called speculation, the reverse is not true: speculation is not necessarily manipulative. It is equally true that the increased presence of speculative money (that is to say, capital employed in the oil market by those without a legitimate need for hedging physical exposure) in commodity markets is not evidence that market manipulation is proliferating. Regulators have uncovered isolated instances of manipulation in commodity markets, as they have in other markets.[31] Weeding out this illegal behavior is essential, and regulators should continue to police the market carefully to guard against such criminal activity. Still, given the sheer size of the world oil trade, executing the kind of conspiracy to raise

---

[29] Blake Clayton, "In Defense of Oil Speculators," ForeignAffairs.com, April 9, 2012 (accessed October 2012).

[30] According to the CFTC Glossary, cornering the market means "(1) securing such relative control of a commodity that its price can be manipulated, that is, can be controlled by the creator of the corner; or (2) in the extreme situation, obtaining contracts requiring the delivery of more commodities than are available for delivery." Squeezing the market refers to "a market situation in which the lack of supplies tends to force shorts to cover their positions by offset at higher prices." U.S. Commodity Futures Trading Commission, "CFTC Glossary," http://www.cftc.gov/ (accessed August 2012).

[31] See, for example, U.S. Commodity Futures Trading Commission, "Federal Court Orders $14 Million in Fines and Disgorgement Stemming from CFTC Charges against Optiver and Others for Manipulation of NYMEX Crude Oil, Heating Oil, and Gasoline Futures Contracts and Making False Statements," Press Release, April 19, 2012.

prices via futures markets manipulation, which popular rhetoric often suggests is occurring, "would be exceedingly difficult to pull off, and there is no evidence that anything like it" has been responsible for recent energy woes.[32]

Typically, critics of speculators are referring to those who buy and sell commodity-linked securities without having an intrinsic exposure to the price of the underlying physical commodity, as so-called hedgers do. These hedgers (often referred to as "commercial" investors by the CFTC) use commodity derivatives to manage the price risk inherent in their businesses, such as trucking or farming. By contrast, speculators (at least in this definition) are neither producing the actual commodity nor taking delivery of them in service of a larger enterprising. Instead, the profits generated from buying and selling in these markets is the crux of their business. Critics of financial speculators in commodity markets charge that their activity is economically and socially worthless, costly to consumers, and unfair to hedgers. Joseph P. Kennedy articulated this perspective well in an April 2012 *New York Times* op-ed, "The High Cost of Gambling on Oil":

But there are factors contributing to the high price of oil that we can do something about. Chief among them is the effect of "pure" speculators – investors who buy and sell oil futures but never take physical possession of actual barrels of oil. These middlemen add little value and lots of cost as they bid up the price of oil in pursuit of financial gain. They should be banned from the world's commodity exchanges, which could drive down the price of oil by as much as 40 percent and the price of gasoline by as much as $1 a gallon.[33]

In his view, the markets do more harm than good. Excluding them from these markets would leave everyone else better off.

This argument has at least two problems. First, it is far harder to distinguish between speculators and hedgers than it would first appear. Some trading houses, for example, play an important role in efficiently allocating physical commodities worldwide, moving and storing them in a vast supply chain. They typically speculate in both paper and physical markets. Moreover, even those firms the CFTC would define as "commercial" (in other words, nonspeculative) often make speculative trades on the future price of oil in search of greater profits, not less risk. Second, speculative trading is a vital part of a functioning commodity market. Even those who have stressed

[32] Blake Clayton, "In Defense of Oil Speculators," ForeignAffairs.com, April 9, 2012 (accessed October 2012).
[33] Joseph P. Kennedy II, "The High Cost of Gambling on Oil," *New York Times*, April 10, 2012.

the need for prudent regulation of commodity markets, such as Commissioner Bart Chilton of the CFTC, recognize that speculators provide the liquidity in these markets that is vital for them to function effectively as a means of hedging risk by producers and consumers.[34]

Why are speculators necessary in futures markets? For oil producers and consumers to be able to hedge their exposure to price fluctuations, they need a counterparty to trade with who is willing to assume their risk. Speculators frequently fill this gap. By taking the other side of a trade, speculators allow producers and consumers to take on their risk at a lower cost than they could without them (if they could at all). If companies choose to contract with one another directly, rather than through a speculator acting as an intermediary, they are free to do so. Were intermediaries banned from the market, however, companies that would like to minimize their risk by buying or selling oil in advance would frequently be stymied.[35] The amount of damage an oil producer or consumer could suffer by losing out on the ability to hedge is sizeable. As oil prices trended upward between 1998 and 2008, Southwest Airlines saved more than $3.5 billion thanks to hedging in the oil market, while many of its peers that did not hedge suffered.[36] Trading with so-called pure speculators almost certainly enabled it to rack up that magnitude of savings, though there is no public data on who the company's counterparties were.[37]

Thus, in assuming a hedger's risk, speculators perform the economically useful function of enabling a wide variety of businesses to manage their risk at a lower cost than they could otherwise. Econometric evidence suggests that as the quantity of speculative capital in oil futures markets has increased over the past decade, the market price of risk has fallen, markets have become better integrated thanks to lower transaction costs and improved physical arbitrage, and prices have become more efficient.[38] All of these outcomes make for a better functioning, more useful oil market.

---

[34] Commissioner Bart Chilton, "Speculators and Commodity Prices – Redux," U.S. Commodity Futures Trading Commission, February 24, 2012, http://cftc.gov/PressRoom/SpeechesTestimony/chiltonstatement022412 (accessed October 2012).

[35] Ronald D. Ripple, "Comment: Futures Trading: What is Excessive?," *Oil and Gas Journal* 106, no. 22 (June 9, 2008), 15.

[36] Associated Press, "Airlines Hedge Against Soaring Fuel Costs," June 30, 2008.

[37] Portions of this paragraph are taken from a post the author wrote on his blog at the Council on Foreign Relations (Blake Clayton, "An Anti-Speculative Frenzy," *Energy, Security, and Climate*, CFR.org, April 12, 2012, accessed October 2012).

[38] Craig Pirrong, *Commodity Price Dynamics: A Structural Approach* (New York, NY: Cambridge University Press, 2012); Bahattin Büyükşahin, Michael S. Haigh, Jeffrey H. Harris, James A. Overdahl, and Michel A. Robe, "Fundamentals, Trader Activity and Derivative Pricing," EFA 2009 Bergen Meetings Paper, December 4, 2008.

For many policymakers, speculation in oil futures markets is not necessarily a bad thing – it is *excessive* speculation that is the real worry. In the words of Senator Bernie Sanders of Vermont: "Millions of American consumers are hurting as a result of excessive speculation on the oil futures market and the future of our economy hangs in the balance. . . . The CFTC has the power to stop this excessive speculation, but has been dragging its feet."[39] Just as the term "speculation" defies easy identification, however, it is difficult to gauge when speculation has become "excessive." Economists have suggested two definitions of excessive speculation: (1) when it is beyond what is required for the oil market to function properly, and (2) when it serves the interest of certain market participants but does not optimize aggregate welfare. As one study puts it, this type of speculation may be "beneficial from the private point of view, but would not be beneficial from the social planner's point of view."[40] A conspiracy by the world's largest oil companies to hoard oil, for example, may enrich them temporarily, but society would likely be worse off, given the large number of consumers who might be hurt by higher prices.

Yet determining whether speculation is excessive is not always straightforward. When commentators suggest that speculation has become excessive in recent years, they tend base their argument on at least one of three observations. First, they attempt to link excessive speculation to the historical profitability of trading in oil futures markets. They cite "obscene profits" by speculators, implying that they are unfairly exploiting the system. But analyzing historical returns to speculative traders offers no real insight into whether their activity is economically harmful. Indeed, one could argue that extraordinary returns imply that the market is in need of more speculative activity, which would winnow away economic rents.[41] For these markets to function, speculators need a sufficiently high return to justify the risk they run as middlemen.

Second, some analysts have argued that the ratio of open interest or daily trading volume on oil futures exchanges to the actual rate of U.S. oil production or consumption is too high, which they believe implies that speculation has reached excessive levels. They calculate that oil futures trading volumes on the NYMEX has averaged between three and fifteen

---

[39] Office of Senator Bernie Sanders, "Stop Excessive Oil Speculation," Press Release, March 21, 2012, http://www.sanders.senate.gov/newsroom/ (accessed May 2012).

[40] Bassam Fattouh, Lutz Kilian, and Lavan Mahadeva, "The Role of Speculation in Oil Markets: What Have We Learned So Far?," Working Paper, July 30, 2012: 3.

[41] As Hilary Till writes in the *Financial Times*, "technically, an excess of speculation is economically necessary for a well-functioning market."

times the size of actual world demand in recent years.[42] But, as Ronald Ripple of Macquarie University shows, these findings are based on a flawed methodology. He points out that open interest is a measurement taken at a single point in time, whereas daily production and consumption measure a flow rate, making direct comparisons between the two an apples-to-oranges measure. Moreover, comparisons of trading volume for a given futures contract often overlook the fact that contracts often extend over many months. Once these analytical errors are corrected for, it becomes apparent that daily trading volume is only a fraction of daily global oil production. The average ratio of daily futures trading activity to consumption was likely closer to 50% for oil in 2007–2008. Additionally, on the question of whether excessive trading is occurring, the data from 2007 imply fewer than one trade per day for front-month contracts, the most active, relative to open interest. That number does not imply harmfully high levels of trading activity.[43]

A third barometer of excessive speculation is the so-called Speculative "T" index, devised by Holbrook Working. It measures the level of speculation in a market relative to the minimum amount necessary to meet demand from would-be commercial hedgers. The T index ratio is calculated as the "amount by which speculation exceeds commercial hedging needs, divided by commercial open interest."[44] Working observed that the primary economic function of a commodity futures market is to help commercial participants manage their risk through hedging. Speculators play an essential role in allowing them to do that cheaply and effectively. Beyond the role they play facilitating hedging activity by other parties, market liquidity lets hedgers make informed judgments about future prices that are needed to manage their risk exposure. It provides them with an informed view of market sentiment. The question, however, becomes how much speculative activity is useful, and when does it become detrimental to the hedgers?

One way to answer this question is to gauge recent levels of speculation against historical norms. By that metric, Hilary Till of the EDHEC Risk Institute finds that speculative trading on NYMEX WTI oil futures and options between 2006 and 2009 was not excessive. Instead, it was within the historical norms for other commodity markets. The T index oscillated

[42] Mohsin S. Khan, "The 2008 Oil Price 'Bubble,'" Policy Brief PB09–19, Peterson Institute for International Economics (August 2009).

[43] Ronald D. Ripple, "Comment: Futures Trading: What is Excessive?," *Oil and Gas Journal* 106, no. 22 (June 9, 2008), 15; Ron Alquist and Olivier Gervais, "The Role of Financial Speculation in Driving the Price of Crude Oil," Bank of Canada Discussion Paper/Document d'analyse 2011–2016 (July 2011): 4.

[44] Hilary Till, "Speculation in Oil Futures Not Excessive," *Financial Times* December 6, 2009.

between 1.2 and 1.7 for that market, very close to what other commodity markets have done since 1947.[45] A study by Buyuksahin and Robe, which makes use of nonpublic CFTC data, finds that although excess speculation across commodities did increase by a factor of four between 2000 and 2010, it was still generally lower than what was found in twentieth-century U.S. agricultural futures markets.[46] Fluctuations in the Speculative T index do not correlate with changes in the price of oil. Working's index suggests that the ratio of speculators to hedgers in the market at the end of 2010, when spot WTI was roughly $90 per barrel, was lower than they were in mid-2003 with oil at around $30 per barrel.[47]

THE EFFECT OF FINANCIALIZATION ON THE OIL FUTURES MARKET

The growing presence of the financial sector in oil trading, beginning around 2003, has led many to fear that financial firms are responsible for the sharp rise in oil prices since that time.[48] This conjecture is understandable, given that the two trends appear to correlate. With the so-called financialization of the market has come a rise in the trading volumes in WTI and Brent futures contracts as well as in net open interest in oil futures among non-commercial firms (i.e., traders not involved in the production, processing,

---

[45] Hillary Till, "Has There Been Excessive Speculation in the US Oil Futures Markets?," EDHEC-Risk Institute, November 2009. In her *Financial Times* write-up, Till notes that if futures are considered without options – arguing a less complete way to analyze the market, given that commercial participants use options as well to hedge – then the index "would potentially show excessive speculation in the US oil futures market." She also stresses that "the study is restricted to the Nymex oil futures markets, so we cannot say there was not excessive speculation through other venues." Notwithstanding, her bottom line conclusion is that "based on traditional speculative metrics, the balance of outright speculators in the Nymex oil futures markets does not appear excessive relative to commercial hedging needs over the past three-and-4-half years."

[46] Bahattin Büyükşahin and Michel A. Robe, "Speculators, Commodities and Cross-Market Linkages," Working Paper (February 12, 2011): 15.

[47] Ron Alquist and Olivier Gervais, "The Role of Financial Speculation in Driving the Price of Crude Oil," Bank of Canada Discussion Paper/Document d'analyse 2011–6 (July 2011): 6.

[48] Several studies present evidence that financial investors became more involved in oil futures markets around 2003. See, for instance, the working paper by James D. Hamilton and Jing Cynthia Wu, "Risk Premia in Crude Oil Futures Prices," September 14, 2011; Ke Tang and Wei Xiong, "Index Investment and Financialization of Commodities," Working Paper, September 2009 (revised March 2011); and Ron Alquist and Lutz Kilian, "What Do We Learn from the Price of Crude Oil Futures?," CEPR Discussion Papers DP6548, Center for Economic Policy Research (November 2007).

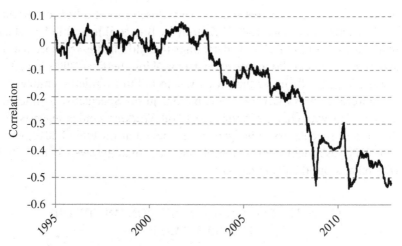

Figure 34. One-Year Rolling Correlations between U.S. Dollar Spot Index and WTI Front Month (1995–2012). *Source*: Bloomberg (as of 12/10/2012)

or merchandising of oil). These trends are indisputable. Yet there is no conclusive evidence that this trading activity has *caused* retail oil prices to move away from what economic fundamentals would justify. That said, the influx of financial market traders into oil futures markets does appear to have altered price behavior and risk premia in certain ways.

One effect of the increased participation of financial investors in oil futures markets appears to be stronger correlations between oil futures prices and other asset classes. This trend has been evident in the relationship between crude oil prices and the U.S. dollar. Historically, the relationship between front-month WTI prices and the U.S. dollar (proxied by the DXY index) has been weak. Simple one-year correlations of daily returns tended not to exceed +/−0.1. Around 2004, however, the correlation moved into sharply negative territory, staying within a 0.4–0.5 range since 2008. An analysis by LCM Commodities on the impact of dollar returns on WTI returns shows a similar pattern. Whereas the relationship was not strong between 1987 and 2003, between 2004 and 2012 daily returns of the DXY index have been statistically significant in explaining front-month crude prices at a 1% confidence level.[49]

[49] Daniel P. Ahn, Edward L. Morse, and Edward Kott, "LCM Commodities Special Report: Sound FX," March 26, 2009. See also Q. Farooq Akram, "Commodity Prices, Interest Rates, and the Dollar," *Energy Economics* 31, no. 6 (2009), 838–851.

Figure 35. Return Correlation between SP-GSCI and S&P Stock Index (1994–2012). *Source:* Bloomberg (as of 12/10/12)

Oil futures prices have also begun to display greater co-movement with equities prices. In 2008, several studies found that conditional correlations between equity indices and commodities futures prices over the past two decades were at most very small and particularly low when stock markets were at their most volatile. Rolling cross-correlations of returns fluctuated around zero between 1992 and 2008, as Buyuksahin and his colleagues show.[50] These findings contravene the notion that the financialization of commodity markets in the mid-2000s was the driving force behind the strong positive correlation that has existed since early 2008.[51]

In a 2010 study, Silvennoinen and Thorp find that conditional correlations between individual commodity futures and U.S. stocks rose from close to zero in the 1990s to 0.5 by 2009. These correlations were particularly pronounced during times of heightened equity market volatility.[52] A similar study, which is particularly notable because it draws on confidential CFTC trading data, corroborates these findings. It notes that cross-market trading

---

[50] James Chong and Joëlle Miffre, "Conditional Return Correlations between Commodity Futures and Traditional Assets," EDHEC Risk and Asset Management Research Centre Working Paper (April 2008); Bahattin Büyükşahin, Michael S. Haigh, and Michel A. Robe, "Commodities and Equities: Ever a 'Market of One'?," *Journal of Alternative Investments* 12, no. 3 (Winter 2010), 76–95.

[51] See "Buttonwood: We all fall down," *The Economist*, March 8, 2007 (accessed May 2012).

[52] Annastiina Silvennoinen and Susan Thorp, "Financialization, Crisis and Commodity Correlation Dynamics," Quantitative Finance Research Centre, Research Paper 267, January 2010.

activity (that is, market participants who trade in both commodity and equity futures) has soared from less than 20% of total commodity open interest in 2001 to 40–47% since mid-2005. It finds that equity-commodity co-movements are strongest when financial markets are under the greatest stress and for shorter-dated maturities. Driving these co-movements appear to be trading specifically by hedge funds (as opposed to index funds, swap dealers, commercial traders, or some other class of market participant) that trade across equities and commodities, though their influence is lower when financial markets are under stress.[53]

The increase of speculative capital in commodity futures markets also appears to coincide with an increase in the degree of co-movement among different commodities.

Figure 36 depicts the one-year rolling correlations of crude oil futures returns between 1985 and 2010 with those for a variety of other commodities, like soybeans, cotton, cattle, and copper. All four of these commodity pairs tended to show return correlations that fluctuated between +/−0.2 until around 2003, when they rose to between 0.4 and 0.6 in a statistically significant departure from the historical norm. Tang and Zong attribute this trend to the rise of investable commodity indices. Assets under management in these vehicles grew from around $15 billion in 2003 to more than $200 billion by 2008. They observe that these cross-commodity co-movements are strongest for those goods that are included in these major commodity indices. A study by Silvennoinen and Thorp also finds that crude oil futures returns have become much more closely correlated with those of other commodities in the mid-2000s, especially grains and oilseeds. They conclude that the influence of common macroeconomic factors that drive these markets, coupled with environmental policy calling for greater production of biofuels, has tightened the linkages between futures prices for agricultural commodities and oil. A 2014 Citigroup report finds that energy prices lie at the heart of the price behavior of all other commodities, due to the energy intensity of the processes involved in their production.[54]

Another apparent consequence of the financialization of the oil market has been a change in oil futures risk premia. In a 2011 study, Hamilton and Wu find that as the volume of commodity futures trading began to

[53] Bahattin Büyükşahin and Michel A. Robe, "Speculators, Commodities and Cross-Market Linkages," Working Paper, February 12, 2011, http://www.cftc.org (accessed May 2012).

[54] Annastiina Silvennoinen and Susan Thorp, "Financialization, Crisis and Commodity Correlation Dynamics," Quantitative Finance Research Centre, Research Paper 267, January 2010; Interview with Edward L. Morse, 2015.

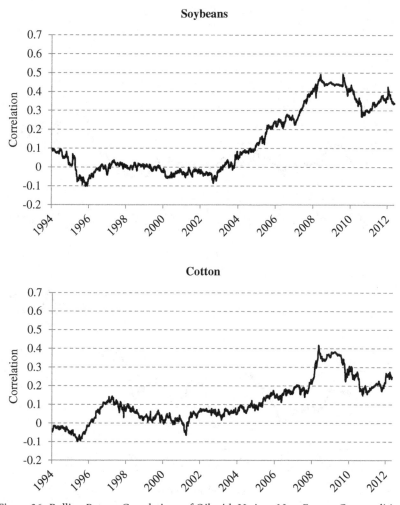

Figure 36. Rolling Return Correlations of Oil with Various Non-Energy Commodities (1994–2012). *Source:* Bloomberg (as of 12/10/12)

swell in the mid-2000s, the compensation to taking a long position in near-dated contracts "decreased substantially" and became more volatile after 2005. They suggest that increased buying pressure from financial investors, particularly via index funds, "may have been a factor" in this secular change. The relative abundance of financial investors as natural counterparties for commercial hedgers reduced the premium that speculators had typically received prior to that time for the risk they assumed. Whereas the risk premium on the two-month futures contract stayed in positive territory

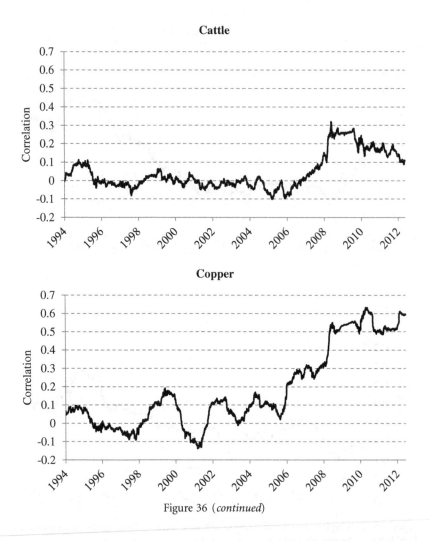

Figure 36 (*continued*)

between 1990 and 2005, based on their model, it has oscillated wildly in the ensuing years and been sharply negative when the forward curve was backwardated.[55]

Some evidence suggests that buying and selling in the oil futures market by index funds may subtly affect the term structure of the forward curve. Index funds work by taking (typically long) positions in a basket of commodity futures. Because some of these futures expire in the next month, they need

[55] James D. Hamilton and Jing Cynthia Wu, "Risk Premia in Crude Oil Futures Prices," Working Paper, September 14, 2011.

to be rolled forward to maintain exposure. This process requires closing the maturing contract and replicating the position in a contract that is further from expiration. In a 2011 study, Yiqun Mou finds that this rolling of futures contracts "exerts large and time-varying price pressure on the relative prices of the contracts involved in the rolling in the largest commodity markets," such as oil.[56] Using the Standard and Poor's/Goldman Sachs Commodity Index, he documents two trading strategies that exploit its mechanical rolling process to yield excess returns. The larger the amount of index fund capital in the market, and likewise the smaller the amount of arbitrage capital, the greater the profitability of this trading strategy.

Policymakers have rightly asked whether the growth of index fund trading in oil futures has distorted prices for everyday consumers. Most analysis concludes that financial investment flows in the oil market tend to chase price movements rather than cause or predict them.[57] It suggests that speculators react to changes in market conditions, and not the other way around. In other words, when economic fundamentals change, reflected in prices, financial investment tends to change accordingly. This finding is crucial because it points to an oil futures market in which even a large increase in investment flows has not fundamentally disrupted the ability of these markets to help determine a fair spot price for oil. It describes a market in which fundamentals are still in charge, rather than, as some critics have suggested, a casino where speculative investors push prices to and fro as they please. Corroborating these findings are several studies that find no statistically significant relationship between speculative open interest in oil futures with their returns, realized volatility, and implied volatility.[58] One 2011 study does find evidence that investment flows "may induce prices to drift away from 'fundamental' values" and significantly affect futures prices.[59] Several analysts have criticized the methodology and data on which this argument

---

[56] Yiqun Mou, "Limits to Arbitrage and Commodity Index Investment: Front-Running the Goldman Roll," Working Paper, Columbia University School of Business, November 19, 2010.

[57] See, for example, Bahattin Büyükşahin and Jeffrey H. Harris, "Do Speculators Drive Crude Oil Futures Prices?," *The Energy Journal* 32, no. 2 (2011), 167–202; Celso Brunetti and Bahattin Büyükşahin, "Is Speculation Destabilizing?," Working Paper, April 22, 2009; and Celso Brunetti, Bahattin Büyükşahin, and Jeffrey H. Harris, "Speculators, Prices and Market Volatility," Working Paper (January 6, 2011).

[58] Scott H. Irwin and Dwight R. Sanders, "The Impact of Index Funds in Commodity Futures Markets: A Systems Approach," *Journal of Alternative Investments* 14:1 (2011), 40–49; Hans R. Stoll and Robert E. Whaley, "Commodity Index Investing and Commodity Futures Prices," *Journal of Applied Finance* 20 (2010), 7–46.

[59] Kenneth J. Singleton, "Investor Flows and the 2008 Boom/Bust in Oil Prices," Working Paper, Stanford University School of Business, May 23, 2012.

was made.[60] They argue that the study does not differentiate between index investment that causes prices to change in unjustified ways (according to the whim of the speculator, in other words) or whether it comes in response to exogenous changes in economic conditions to which index investors are simply responding.

IS SPECULATION A BAD THING?

The critical questions that government regulators should be asking is, do these changes in oil and other commodity markets (stronger cross-asset correlations in futures markets, for example) leave society as a whole worse of? Do they result in a market that is less economically beneficial and socially fair, or are they merely a reflection of an evolving market? If the changes in price behavior and risk premia do not have any significant implications for anyone besides commodity traders, they need not prompt tightening regulation. But are they a sign of a market gone wrong? Finally, on a different but related note, are there types of commodity-linked securitized products, such as exchange traded funds (or ETFs), which cater largely to retail investors, that could arguably be deemed not appropriate for this type of customer?

To begin with, the increased co-movement between oil futures and other asset classes (or within commodities as a class) is not necessarily evidence that more financial speculation has caused prices to detach from what economic fundamentals justify. This is true for three reasons. First, the most careful research suggests that the general trajectory of oil prices between 2003 and 2008, which countless analysts have described as a speculative bubble, was supported by developments in supply and demand. Stagnant growth in non-OPEC production and only tepid growth in OPEC production capacity winnowed away spare production capacity globally, which contributed to prices racing higher. Hamilton argues that "the two key ingredients needed" to conclude that speculation caused the oil shock of 2007–2008 are "a low price elasticity of demand, and the failure of physical production to increase." Yet a "fundamentals-based explanation of the same phenomenon" would require the same things. His econometric analysis suggests that those two factors, "rather than speculation per se, should be construed as the primary cause of the oil shock of 2007–8. Certainly

---

[60] See Bassam Fattouh, Lutz Kilian, and Lavan Mahadeva, "The Role of Speculation in Oil Markets: What Have We Learned So Far?," Working Paper (June 30, 2012), for a summary of this debate.

the casual conclusion one might have drawn from . . . hearing some of the accounts of speculation – that it was all just a mistake and prices should have stayed at $50/barrel . . . would be profoundly in error."[61]

Second, because oil prices share some of the same drivers as equities and the U.S. dollar, there is a rational basis for their prices to show a significant degree of correlation. For example, market expectations of a stronger economy should make for higher corporate profits and greater demand for oil, a net plus for both stocks and oil. Likewise, the U.S. dollar and oil are inextricably linked through numerous channels, the most obvious and perhaps most determinative of which, at least on a short-term basis, is that world oil prices are denominated in U.S. dollars. Strong co-movement between oil futures and other asset classes is not proof that speculators are moving oil prices in a way that economic fundamentals do not justify.

Third, prices for non-exchange-traded commodities rose more quickly than crude oil prices did between 2006 and 2008, though crude oil fell more sharply beginning in the summer of 2008. Moreover, some commodities not traded on a futures exchange saw much more violent volatility between 2000 and 2010 than oil did. Their prices fluctuated by more than 2,000% from trough-to-peak over that time frame, while crude oil moved only 663%. If financial speculators in commodity exchanges were ultimately responsible for exaggerating price movements, one might expect prices on the exchange to be higher and more volatile than those not traded on a futures exchange, but that did not happen. One illustration of this principle is the Onion Futures Act of 1958, which banned futures trading in onions in the United States. The goal of the law was to make the market less volatile by taking Wall Street, so to speak, out of the market. But what has happened since? Onion prices have been higher and more volatile after the ban than before it. The "moneyed interests" that farmers had decried for disrupting the market likely helped stabilize prices, not disrupt them.[62]

The sharp divide between U.S. natural gas and crude oil prices helps illustrate why an increase in the presence of financial investors in energy futures markets does not mean that prices will be higher or more volatile. CFTC data from the spring of 2012 shows that non-hedging parties held a larger share of natural gas futures contracts (60%) on the NYMEX than

[61] James D. Hamilton, "Causes and Consequences of the Oil Shock of 2007–08," Brookings Papers on Economic Activity (Spring 2009): 240; James L. Smith, "World Oil: Market or Mayhem?," *Journal of Economic Perspectives* 23, no. 3 (2009), 145–164.

[62] International Energy Agency, "Monthly Oil Report," *Oil Market Report: 15 March 2011*, March 15, 2011: 44–45. Also "The Onion Ringer," *Wall Street Journal*, July 8, 2008.

they did for WTI crude oil (47%).[63] And yet natural gas prices were at their lowest levels in a decade. The pronounced difference in supply-and-demand fundamentals in the markets for these two energy goods justified those historic lows. A dramatic increase in shale gas production in the United States has boosted gas supplies, while still-weak economic growth and unusually warm winter weather had glutted the North American market. This surfeit of gas, in the words of James Hamilton, put "irresistible downward pressure on the price of natural gas, a reality that completely swamps any purported effect that commodity index buying could conceivably have."[64]

Moreover, the claim that financial investment is causing a change in how futures prices behave does not necessarily imply that they are having the same effect on spot or retail prices. Some analysts have argued that higher futures prices tend to feed back into higher spot prices, principally as a result of the fact that forward contracts often use futures prices as a reference price. Yet, as a 2012 study concludes, there is no "compelling evidence that oil futures prices help forecast the spot price of oil."[65] Put another way, the "distinction between hedging and speculative trading in the futures market is not important because neither one exerts any significant effect on current oil prices." Futures market speculators could in theory raise spot prices if they provide incentive for physical traders to amass large inventories or curb current production. Likewise, if physical traders or producers believe that speculative traders are liable to alter spot prices, they might change their own behavior with regard to inventories, production, or bidding in the spot market. But no evidence exists that anything like this has prompted the chronically high oil prices of the past decade.[66]

Like any other market, the oil market is not immune to periodic bouts of immoderation and irrational exuberance, which may lead prices to diverge from fundamentals for a time. Neither commodity nor any other market always functions perfectly. Even some analysts who have been deeply skeptical about sweeping indictments of financial speculators in futures markets agree on this point. Hamilton, writing in 2009, finds it "hard to deny that the price rose too high in July 2008, and that this miscalculation was influenced in part by the flow of investment dollars into commodity futures

---

[63] Blake Clayton, "In Defense of Oil Speculators," ForeignAffairs.com, April 9, 2012.

[64] James D. Hamilton, "Fundamentals, Speculation, and Oil Prices," Econbrowser, August 28, 2011, http://www.econbrowser.com/ (accessed May 2012).

[65] Cited in Bassam Fattouh, Lutz Kilian, and Lavan Mahadeva, "The Role of Speculation in Oil Markets: What Have We Learned So Far?," Working Paper (June 30, 2012): 13.

[66] James L. Smith, "World Oil: Market or Mayhem?," *Journal of Economic Perspectives* 23, no. 3 (2009), 145–164.

contracts."[67] Front-month WTI prices had catapulted from $96 per barrel to $145 between January and July that year. Edward Morse detected anomalous behavior in the back end of the forward curve in May 2008. Normally, tight market conditions in the present correspond to lower prices for oil for delivery far out into the future, in part to provide incentive for producers and storers of oil to get it onto the market right away. For part of May and June 2008, however, futures prices showed the exact opposite. The further out into the future the contract, the more expensive oil prices became. In a May 29, 2008 report, *Oil.com*, Morse wrote:

What has been striking about the rise in the back end of the curve over the first three weeks of the month has been – at least until last Friday – nearly a complete lack of interest by producers in selling oil forward. In the past, producer selling would have slowed or impeded the upward price drive. In its absence, retail investors, hearing a growing number of reports about "peak oil," continued to buy at higher and higher strike prices, indicating that there is no necessary physical ceiling to the market.

Meanwhile, a number of banks and well-known investors publicized their views that the long run was also going to be tight for oil markets. For some of these analysts/investors, the reason for higher prices had to do with the need to trigger an adequate supply and demand response; for others, it was because they believed peak oil had arrived and, in their opinion, Saudi Arabia could no longer raise its output.[68]

Arguing that economic fundamentals rather than financial speculation tend to drive oil prices does not mean that there are not instances in which excessive buying or selling by speculators may not be occurring.

Data about even the most basic aspects of the global oil trade – such as supply, demand, and commercial inventories – is woefully incomplete, which problematizes scholarly attempts at pinpointing the effect of speculative investment by non-commercial participants on the market. Data from official sources, such as the IEA or the EIA, are frequently at odds. The lack of transparency in the market has gotten worse over the past decade, as emerging market countries, which rarely keep or publish thorough oil data, have assumed a bigger role in the market. Yet econometric models that try to link speculation and prices often gloss over these severe data limitations.[69]

---

[67] James D. Hamilton, "Causes and Consequences of the Oil Shock of 2007–08," Brookings Papers on Economic Activity (Spring 2009): 240.

[68] Edward Morse and Michael Waldron, "Oil Dot-com," Lehman Brothers Energy Special Report, May 29, 2008.

[69] Philip K. Verleger Jr., "Exercises in Random Numbers: A Review of Economic Studies Purporting to Demonstrate the Impact of Speculation on Oil Prices," March 2009, www.pkverlegerllc.com/ (accessed May 2012).

With that caveat, what do these models show? Kilian and Murphy do not find any evidence for the notion that speculation was responsible for driving the oil price boom from 2003 through mid-2008.[70] Indeed, as Kilian notes, the "academic literature on this subject is virtually unanimous that financial speculation played no independent role" in that long-term price increase.[71] Some scholars disagree. Among the most notable are Juvenal and Petrella, whose study published by the Federal Research Bank of St. Louis in 2011 was widely cited in the popular press and by U.S. policymakers. Using adjusted versions of Kilian and Murphy's structural autoregressive model, they conclude that speculation was the second most important driver of the increase in oil prices between 2004 and 2008, second only to global demand growth. Yet this finding is based on evidence that is shaky at best, and their model, methodology, and interpretations have come under fire. Kilian describes their conclusion that the financialization of commodity markets played a major role in raising spot prices between 2003 and 2008 as an "overreach."[72]

Has the increased presence of financial speculators in commodities markets been a good or bad thing? For investors who enjoyed the diversification that commodities as an asset class could provide, the financialization of the market may have worn away that benefit during moments of high financial-market volatility.[73] On the other side of the argument, many of the most sophisticated analyses suggest that an increase in financial speculation has improved the functioning of the oil market. Greater liquidity in crude oil futures markets appears to have helped reduce price inefficiencies across different geographies and crude types.[74] It also seems to have aided price discovery in energy-related derivatives markets, which improves the functionality and efficiency of those markets for commercial hedgers.[75] Pirrong argues that in a controlled theoretical environment – which he stresses the

---

[70] Bassam Fattouh, Lutz Kilian, and Lavan Mahadeva, "The Role of Speculation in Oil Markets: What Have We Learned So Far?," Working Paper (June 30, 2012): 15–18.

[71] Lutz Kilian, "Guest Contribution: Oil Price Spike Exacerbated by Wall Street Speculation?," Econbrowser, July 25, 2012, http://www.econbrowser.com/ (accessed October 2012).

[72] See Lutz Kilian, "Guest Contribution: Oil Price Spike Exacerbated by Wall Street Speculation?," Econbrowser, July 25, 2012, http://www.econbrowser.com (accessed October 2012).

[73] Bahattin Büyükşahin and Michel A. Robe, "Speculators, Commodities and Cross-Market Linkages," Working Paper (February 12, 2011).

[74] Bassam Fattouh, "The Dynamics of Crude Oil Price Differentials," *Energy Economics* 32, no. 2 (2010), 334–342.

[75] Bahattin Büyükşahin, Michael S. Haigh, and Michel A. Robe, "Fundamentals, Trader Activity and Derivative Pricing," EFA 2009 Bergen Meetings Paper, December 4, 2008.

real-world oil market is not – greater speculation reduces the market price of risk. Because that reduction makes holding or hedging inventories less costly, it encourages larger inventories, which can raise prices in the short-term but reduces price volatility. Overall, he argues that these changes are "salutary" because they "reflect a more efficient allocation of risk."[76]

Speculation, in the broadest sense of the term, is an essential part of how a well-functioning market responds to changes in participants' perceptions of supply and demand. In March 2012, CFTC Commissioner Bart Chilton asked several commodities analysts in the financial sector to give their view on whether speculation affects retail oil prices.[77] The analysts' response makes several important points:

We do find that buying and selling in the oil futures markets exerts an influence on oil prices. Buying and selling is how information about current and expected future oil supply and demand conditions is transmitted through the market, allowing the oil market to adjust the oil price in order to balance supply and demand. This is how a market works.

They continue:

Commissioner Chilton characterizes this as "speculation", with the suggestion it is unrelated to supply and demand conditions in the oil market. We disagree. In our view, this is the mechanism by which the oil market becomes better informed and reaches a consensus on issues such as the likely impact of the improving world economic outlook on oil demand and the increasing tensions with Iran on crude oil supplies.

Price shifts that come from changing market perceptions, whether of potential supply disruptions or economic recessions, have helpful implications. Fears of a future disruption can drive price higher, for instance, which tempers demand and calls for greater production. Both dynamics help prices cool off. The analysts go on:

To say that "speculation" is contributing to higher oil prices is no different than to say that oil prices are rising on the expectation that the improving world economic outlook will lead to more oil demand and that tensions with Iran could lead to a disruption in crude oil supplies.

In a well-regulated market, speculative buying and selling play a vital and constructive role, even if they mean temporarily higher or volatile prices.

---

[76] Craig Pirrong, *Commodity Price Dynamics: A Structural Approach* (New York, NY: Cambridge University Press, 2012).

[77] ABC News, "Goldman Sachs Response to Congress Members' Claim Gas Prices Spiked by Speculators," March 5, 2012.

CONCLUSION

The study of the role and effect of financial speculators on commodity markets has come under intense scrutiny from scholars and policymakers over the past decade. Similar concerns from government officials date back centuries. Even after extensive testing, however, scholars have not yet been able to uncover convincing evidence that excessive speculation has been occurring or has pushed spot commodity prices beyond their bounds for extended periods. Investor participation in these markets has grown enormously since 2003, and yet that influx of capital does not in itself provide any evidence that these funds are to blame for higher or more volatile prices than in earlier periods. There is, however, compelling evidence to suggest that this so-called financialization of the oil market has had other effects, such as changing risk premia in futures markets and altering commodities' futures prices correlations with each other and with other asset classes.

This vein of inquiry is a dynamic one. Today's conclusions of the role of speculators in oil markets may yet be challenged. As one analyst put it, "the absence of proof" of a "causal relationship between oil prices overshooting and speculative behavior . . . does not imply a proof of absence."[78] Better data about trading activity or more powerful statistical methodologies may uncover yet-hidden relationships between speculative length or trading volume and spot prices. The ultimate question for regulators is not whether the increased presence of non-commercial speculators have altered how futures markets behavior in any respect, but whether any changes that have occurred have improved or worsened the efficient functioning of the market and broader economic welfare. With the Dodd-Frank legislation taking effect, legitimate questions are arising about whether lost liquidity in commodity markets, in addition to fixed-income markets, is detrimental to market performance. It may be that the question that regulators will need to answer next is not whether there is too much speculation in these markets, but too little.

---

[78] Daniel P. Ahn, Improving Energy Market Regulation: Domestic and International Issues, CGS/IIGG Working Paper (New York: Council on Foreign Relations, 2011): 13.

5

The Implications of Oil Prices for the U.S. Economy and Lessons Learned from the 2011 Strategic Petroleum Reserve Release*

For the United States and other net importers of oil, the past two years have the dubious distinction of featuring the highest average annual crude oil prices, in both real and nominal terms, since the beginnings of the modern oil industry in the 1860s.[1] Such elevated prices for oil, marked by extreme volatility at times, pose risks to the still-anemic U.S. and global economies, even though they have proven a boon to the domestic oil industry and the regions of the country where oil and gas are produced. Still, the U.S. economy is much less affected by changes in oil prices today than it was in the 1970s, for instance, when the first modern oil crises wreaked havoc on the national economy.

Understanding how oil prices affect the economy of the United States is crucial to sensible domestic policymaking. The consequences of the dramatic collapse in oil prices in 2014, for instance, vary tremendously across the country's geographic regions, economic sectors, and population segments. Pinpointing the exact dynamics at play, as well as measuring their magnitudes, is difficult to do with precision. But several decades of research have yielded critical insights. These findings can help inform policy decisions in realms as diverse as economic sanctions, strategic petroleum reserve releases, and gasoline taxes, limiting any negative implications their effects on oil prices might cause to the broader economy and maximizing their potential benefits.

One of the policy tools that many countries have at their disposal as a means of mitigating harmful spikes in oil prices is releasing oil from strategic reserves. The major oil release undertaken in 2011, coordinated by the IEA,

---

* A version of a portion of this chapter appeared in the *Georgetown Journal of International Affairs*, Summer/Fall 2013, Volume XIV, Number 2.
[1] BP, *BP Statistical Review of World Energy 2012* (London: BP, June 2012).

provided policymakers with valuable lessons about three critical aspects of these emergency interventions: (1) their effect on oil prices and market perception, (2) their implications for international cooperation, and (3) the logistical issues they raise about the U.S. Strategic Petroleum Reserve (SPR). Energy officials in IEA countries should bear in mind those market-imposed constraints when structuring future releases, tailor their cooperation with influential oil-producing and -consuming countries to evolving geopolitical realities, and address potential operational impediments to the U.S. SPR, informed by the experience of the 2011 release.

HOW DO OIL PRICES AFFECT THE U.S. ECONOMY?

The primary channel through which higher oil prices reduce U.S. economic activity is by squeezing consumers, taking away discretionary income. Higher oil prices, which result in higher bills for essential goods like gasoline, heating oil, and to a much smaller extent, food, function like a tax on U.S. households. Because demand for oil is highly inelastic (i.e., even a large increase in the price does little to discourage consumption), particularly over the short term, more costly oil means that Americans tend to put more of their income toward it. Consumers, rather than businesses, bear the brunt of this income effect. The outflow of wealth from the United States overseas to pay for imported oil, only a fraction of which is eventually recycled back by net oil-exporting countries, means less spending on domestic goods and services, thereby reducing U.S. purchasing power and aggregate demand.

Less significantly, a change in oil prices affects aggregate output and labor productivity, so-called supply-side mechanisms. Oil is a vital input to production. The more expensive oil is, the more costly it is for firms to produce goods and services. This damping effect on productivity puts downward pressure on real growth rates and tends to increase the unemployment rate. Moreover, if consumers expect the oil price increase to be temporary, they will save less and borrow more, which also puts upward pressure on real interest rates and prices. This effect is partially offset by the fact that, thanks to a rise in revenues, greater savings in oil-exporting countries tend, in theory, to lower global interest rates and boost demand in the United States for interest-rate-sensitive assets, such as housing, during the boom years.

But the effects of higher oil prices extend beyond the constraints on the physical process of production or on national income.[2] There are several

---

[2] Christopher L. Foote and Jane S. Little, "Oil and the Macroeconomy in a Changing World: A Conference Summary," Federal Reserve Bank of Boston Public Policy Discussion Paper

reasons why. Higher prices carry adjustment costs for firms and consumers as they struggle to reallocate their capital, which can weigh on short-term aggregate demand and thus retard growth. Consumers shy away from purchasing durable goods complementary with oil usage, particularly automobiles, almost immediately after a significant oil price rise. Labor and capital will tend to flow out of relatively oil-intensive sectors into more fuel-efficient ones, but this switch is costly.[3] In the meantime, capital equipment can go idle or be retired prematurely, and workers must find jobs in new companies or industries. As a result, sudden oil price increases tend to cause a rise in frictional unemployment. Jobs in energy-intensive industries (such as manufacturing) are hit especially hard, with the least-skilled and least-experienced members of the workforce bearing the brunt of the change. Employment opportunities for skilled workers can actually rise following oil price increases, as managers substitute their productivity for more energy-intensive production inputs.[4]

There are other amplifying mechanisms as well. Oil price increases can cause uncertainty about the future, leading to a rise in precautionary saving among consumers and lower capital investment by firms as they wait to see how prices play out.[5] Higher oil prices also risk harming consumer sentiment. According to James Hamilton of the University of California at San Diego, an increase in energy prices that reduces consumer spending power by as little as 1% can prompt a dramatic decline in consumer sentiment.[6] Oil price changes may also lead to coordination problems among firms. Competing firms, lacking information about how their peers' output and pricing decisions will be affected, may be more hesitant about expanding their operations, causing a drag on aggregate output. Threshold effects may

No. 11–3 (June 2011): 44. http://www.bostonfed.org/economic/ppdp/index.htm (accessed December 11, 2012).

[3] During the 2007–2008 oil price run-up, for instance, spending on domestic cars and trucks suffered quickly in response to rising prices, though sales of small foreign cars went up. Had the U.S. auto industry not suffered this drop in demand, one study finds, the domestic economy would have actually grown 1.2% in the first year of the recession, rather than shrunk. See James D. Hamilton, "Oil Prices, Exhaustible Resources, and Economic Growth," in Roger Fouquet (ed.), *Handbook of Energy and Climate Change* (Northampton: Edward Elgar Publishing, 2013), 29–57.

[4] Michael P. Keane and Eswar S. Prasad, "The Employment and Wage Effects of Oil Price Changes: A Sectoral Analysis," *The Review of Economics and Statistics* 78 no. 3 (August 1996), 389–400; James D. Hamilton, "Causes and Consequences of the Oil Shock of 2007–08," *Brookings Papers on Economic Activity* (Spring 2009), 215–282.

[5] Lutz Killian, "Oil Price Volatility: Origins and Effects," World Bank Staff Working Paper ERSD-2010–02, World Bank (1 December 2009): 8.

[6] Christopher L. Foote and Jane S. Little, "Oil and the Macroeconomy in a Changing World: A Conference Summary," Federal Reserve Bank of Boston Public Policy Discussion Paper No. 11–3 (June 2011): 44.

also come into play. When prices rise to very high or very low levels, relative to the historical norm, they may pass a critical limit whereby their influence on areas like consumer confidence and spending or capital investment far exceeds the usual impact at milder price levels.[7]

A jump in oil prices tends to do the U.S. economy more harm than a drop in prices of the same magnitude does it good. A drop in oil prices may lead to small gains in economic growth, but the response tends to be a fraction of the size of the losses that tend to follow an equal rise in prices.[8] The macroeconomic frictions associated with rising energy costs, such as consumer uncertainty and the reallocation of resources across sectors, appear to be behind this asymmetry.[9] This nonlinearity has also been shown to apply when it comes to the effects of changes in oil prices on domestic employment levels and industrial production.[10]

Moreover, volatile oil prices, even when they move downward, are not ideal for economic growth. Oil price volatility has been shown to predict slower U.S. GDP growth, implying that even falling prices can have contractionary consequences.[11] Predictability in oil price changes allows consumers to shift their decision-making to prepare themselves for what the future might hold. When prices swing wildly, defying forecasts, their bounce can stymie attempts by affected businesses and households to adjust as seamlessly as possible, whether through reducing their consumption, increasing the efficiency of their consumption, or hedging their exposure.

It is also important to note that various parts of the country experience the economic consequences of changing oil prices very differently. The benefits of high prices in terms of employment, output, and public revenues overwhelmingly accrue to the producing regions (though the lattermost

---

[7] Hillard G. Huntington, "The Economic Consequences of Higher Crude Oil Prices," EMF SR 9, Energy Modeling Forum (3 October 2005): 20.

[8] For a review of the literature on the asymmetric response of economic activity to oil price changes, see James D. Hamilton, "Nonlinearities and the Macroeconomic Effects of Oil Prices," Working Paper (December 9, 2009; Revised November 15, 2010), http://dss.ucsd .edu/~jhamilto/oil_nonlinear_macro_dyn.pdf, 1–6. Accessed December 11, 2012.

[9] James D. Hamilton, "This is What Happened to the Oil Price-Macroeconomy Relationship," *Journal of Monetary Economics* 38 no. 2 (October 1996): 215–220.

[10] Steven J. Davis and John Haltiwanger, "Sectoral Job Creation and Destruction Responses to Oil Price Changes," *Journal of Monetary Economics* 48 (2001): 465–512; Ana María Herrera, Latika Gupta Lagalo, and Tatsuma Wada, "Oil Price Shocks and Industrial Production: Is the Relationship Linear?," *Macroeconomic Dynamics* 15, S3 (November 2011): 472–497.

[11] J. Peter Ferderer, "Oil Price Volatility and the Macroeconomy: A Solution to the Asymmetry Puzzle," *Journal of Macroeconomics* 18 no. 1 (Winter 1996): 1–16; John Elder and Apostolos Serletis, 2010. "Oil Price Uncertainty," *Journal of Money, Credit and Banking* 42, no. 6 (2010): 1137–1159.

blessing also applies to the federal government); for other regions, such prices hinder economic activity more than help it, on the net. The sensitivity of a net-producing state's economy to oil prices depends largely on share of the total economy consisting of the energy sector and related areas like petrochemicals. For Texas, a hub of domestic oil-related industry, research by the Federal Reserve Bank of Dallas found that a 10% increase in oil prices led to a 0.5% rise in GDP and a 0.36% rise in employment between 1997 and 2010.[12] However, prolonged periods of low oil prices also weigh disproportionately on economic activity in these regions. The oil crash in 1986 caused a recession in Texas, though the state's economy appears less sensitive to prices now than it was then.[13] Public revenues in states like Alaska, which derives 64% of its state tax revenue from severance taxes, and Oklahoma, which takes in 19% of its labor income from the oil and natural gas industry, are also affected by changes in oil prices.[14]

OIL PRICES AND U.S. MONETARY POLICY

Fluctuations in oil prices carry important ramifications for the Federal Reserve. In a robust economy, a rise in oil prices can distort wages and prices and discourage growth. Wages and prices can be inflexible in the face of changes to energy prices, which can weigh on the demand for capital and labor in the short run. Higher oil prices can put upward pressure on labor costs, as the workforce tries to maintain purchasing power, and labor productivity can temporarily fall. Firms then pass on these higher costs to consumers by raising prices for their products. In theory, this could result in an uptick in inflation and tighter monetary policy, which could weaken growth.[15] This effect is likely less applicable under current economic conditions, where low resource utilization means that upward pressure on wages from rising oil prices is limited. Perhaps more relevant, however, is

---

[12] Mine K. Yücel and Jackson Thies, "Oil and Gas Rises Again in a Diversified Texas," *Southwest Economy* (First Quarter 2011): 10–13.

[13] This more muted relationship is a result of greater diversification of the state's industrial base and oilfield activity more immune to price fluctuations. See Steven P.A. Brown and Mine Yücel, "Do High Oil Prices Still Benefit Texas?," *Face of Texas* (October 2005): 33–36.

[14] Sean O'Leary, "Investing in the Future: Making Severance Tax Stronger for West Virginia," West Virginia Center on Budget and Policy (December 2011); and PricewaterhouseCoopers, "The Economic Impacts of the Oil and Natural Gas Industry on the U.S. Economy in 2009: Employment, Labor, Income, and Value Added," Prepared for the American Petroleum Institute (May 2011), http://www.api.org.

[15] Hillard G. Huntington, "The Economic Consequences of Higher Crude Oil Prices," EMF SR 9, Energy Modeling Forum (October 3, 2005): 28.

the risk that an increase in energy prices could spill over into the prices of other goods and thus filter into core inflation, with similar implications for central bankers.

In practice, however, the relationship between oil prices, core inflation, and monetary policy is less straightforward. Jumps in oil prices did appear to contribute to higher core inflation in the case of the 1970s oil price shocks but little since then, as suggested by empirical research based on backward-looking Philips curves.[16] This change in core inflationary effects speaks in part to the progress that increasingly technocratic central bankers have made in credibly keeping market expectations of long-term inflation in check. Global core and headline inflation were stable through 2006 despite rising oil prices, though they did turn upward in 2007–2008. That uptick was likely partly attributed to robust global resource utilization rates, though it may also have been the delayed, cumulative effect of several years of rising oil prices. Still, the U.S. experience since the recession demonstrates that consecutive years of high oil prices need not necessarily translate into materially higher core inflation, though their impact on headline inflation is definitional. This change is fortunate, given that it reduces the likelihood that higher oil prices force central bankers to raise short-term rates, which weighs on economic activity. High inflation can generate uncertainty in an economy that drags down capital investment and adds an inflation risk premium to interest rates. Ultimately, conditions in the broader economy as well as public policy decisions influence the degree of pass-through.[17] In the case of the United States, long-term inflation expectations appear capable of remaining firmly anchored in spite of increasing energy costs owing to an increase in the Federal Reserve's anti-inflation credibility since the 1970s, as well as to structural changes in the domestic economy.[18]

---

[16] James D. Hamilton, "Oil and the Macroeconomy," Working Paper (August 24, 2005), 10. Chapter prepared for Steven N. Durlauf and Lawrence E. Blume (eds.), *The New Palgrave Dictionary of Economics*, Second Edition (U.S. and UK: Palgrave Macmillan, 2008); Ethan S. Harris, Bruce C. Kasman, Matthew D. Shapiro, and Kenneth D. West, "Oil and the Macroeconomy: Lessons for Monetary Policy, Proceedings of the U.S. Monetary Policy Forum," The Initiative on Global Markets at The University of Chicago Booth School of Business and The Rosenberg Institute of Global Finance at the Brandeis University International Business School (February 2009, revised November 2009): 13.

[17] Ethan S. Harris, Bruce C. Kasman, Matthew D. Shapiro, and Kenneth D. West, "Oil and the Macroeconomy: Lessons for Monetary Policy, Proceedings of the U.S. Monetary Policy Forum," The Initiative on Global Markets at The University of Chicago Booth School of Business and The Rosenberg Institute of Global Finance at the Brandeis University International Business School (February 2009, revised November 2009): 13.

[18] Ibid.

HOW MUCH DO HIGHER OIL PRICES MATTER TO
THE U.S. ECONOMY?

How large and long-lasting are these effects on important economic outcomes such as gross domestic product, employment, and inflation? And how might broader economic conditions, as well as the drivers and contours of the oil price change, offset or amplify these effects?

There is little question that structural changes to the U.S. economy have made the effects of oil prices on growth, inflation, and employment much less pronounced than they were prior to the mid-1980s, for several reasons. For one thing, oil's value share in domestic production and consumption has fallen, reducing the effect of a price change on spending patterns. Labor markets have become more flexible. Lower wage rigidity has mitigated the trade-off between stabilizing inflation versus a gap in output. Monetary policymaking has also improved. Central bankers have gained greater credibility in inflation targeting, which has enabled them to anchor inflation expectations in the face of a commodity price increase without the same risks to output growth.[19] The United States economy is also less energy intensive than it was decades ago, reducing the sensitivity of output to an unforeseen change in oil prices.[20] Moreover, rationing may have magnified the ill effects of oil price changes on the U.S. economy during the 1970s.[21] As a result of these altered conditions in the domestic economy, according to one estimate, a change in oil prices may bring about roughly one-third the impact on output and price levels after 1984 as they did prior to that time.[22]

Various studies have been done over the past decade aiming to quantitatively relate real GDP growth, employment growth, and changes in consumer price levels to oil prices.[23] Some of these studies employ

---

[19] Olivier J. Blanchard and Jordi Gali, "The Macroeconomic Effects of Oil Shocks: Why are the 2000s So Different from the 1970s?," NBER Working Paper No. 13368, National Bureau of Economic Research (September 2007): 1–5.

[20] Jorg Decressin, "Global Economy Learns to Absorb Oil Price Hikes," *International Monetary Fund Survey* (May 25, 2012).

[21] Valerie A. Ramey and Daniel J. Vine, "Oil, Automobiles, and the U.S. Economy: How Much Have Things Really Changed?," in Daron Acemoglu and Michael Woodford (eds.), *NBER Macroeconomics Annual 2010* (Chicago: University of Chicago Press, 2010): 333–367.

[22] Olivier J. Blanchard and Marianna Rigg, "The Oil Price and the Macroeconomy: What's Going on?," VoxEU.org (December 7, 2009).

[23] These studies generally utilize one of two approaches. The first type uses complex, disaggregated macroeconomic models of the U.S. economy. These models try to dynamically replicate the interrelationships among important macroeconomic variables, drawing on

disaggregated models of the U.S. economy; others rely on regression analysis to try to isolate the effect of oil price volatility on another facet of the economy. There are several recent studies of the effects of an oil price increase on U.S. GDP and the GDP price deflator (a measure of inflation) (see Table 2). These studies do not offer a perfect apples-to-apples comparison, given their differences in methodology and reference year.[24] Nevertheless, there is some degree of cohesion across the results – if not in the magnitude of the effects, then at least in their direction and size.

Recent model-based analyses imply that a $10 per barrel increase in the price of oil sustained over one or two years generally reduces real GDP by somewhere between −0.2 and −0.3% relative to the baseline over the first year and between −0.3 and −0.6% the following year. As for inflation, the impact is estimated at between +0.2 and +0.5% over the first year and then +0.3 and +0.5% in the second year relative to the baseline. In terms of unemployment (not included in the table), the Global Insight's 2005 study and the 1999 U.S. Federal Reserve study both estimate a departure from the baseline of +0.1% in year one and +0.2% in year two for a $10 per barrel oil price increase. The lone time-series study surveyed, by Jimenez-Rodriguez and Sanchez in 2004, implies that a 10% increase in prices would cause real GDP to fall by roughly −0.5% in year one then again in year two. It judges the effects of a drop in prices of the same magnitude to be only roughly a quarter of that size, in line with the asymmetric dynamic explained earlier. Other dynamics can partially offset these economic impacts. Feedbacks between the U.S. current account deficit and the value of the dollar can increase demand for U.S. exports and thus moderate the drag on aggregate output. Similarly, a rise in external receipts to the United States from net oil exporters enjoying higher incomes and savings are partially recycled into demand for U.S. goods, though emerging-market countries have received the lion's share of these funds.[25] Additionally, other macroeconomic events

---

historical data to estimate the strength of these relationships. The second approach uses time-series analysis. Typically the simpler method, it tries to isolate the effect of a change in crude oil prices on another economic outcome, like changes in GDP or inflation, based on historical experience.

[24] Of these six, all but one rely on some form of macroeconomic model, with the outlier being the 2004 European Central Bank study. Most of the model-based studies report broadly similar findings. with regard to the economic effects of an oil price increase.

[25] Between 2002 and 2007, exports from emerging market countries to OPC rose by $186 billion, $5 billion more than the increase in imports, for a ratio of 103% in new imports to exports. Developed countries, where this ratio was only 52%, saw far less money flowing back from OPEC. See Ethan S. Harris, Bruce C. Kasman, Matthew D. Shapiro, and Kenneth D. West, "Oil and the Macroeconomy," 13–15.

Table 2. *Effect of an oil price increase on U.S. GDP and the GDP price deflator (inflation): A survey of recent estimates.*

Study	Approach	Type of Price Increase	Impact on Real GDP		Impact on Inflation	
			Year 1	Year 2	Year 1	Year 2
Carabenciov et al. (2008), IMF	Macro- econometric model	(Permanent) 10% increase		−0.20		0.27
Barrell and Pomerantz (2004), NIESR	NiGEM Macro- econometric model	(Permanent) $10 increase	−0.2	−0.48	0.3	0.52
OECD Global Model, Hervé et al. (2010)	Macro- econometric model	(Permanent) $10 increase		−0.31		0.41
Jimenez-Rodriguez and Sanchez (2004), ECB	Vector autoregression (VAR)	Impulse response to a 1% oil price shock^	−0.05	−0.05	–	–
Global Insight, Inc. (2005)	Macro-econometric model	(Permanent) $10 increase	−0.3	−0.6	0.2	0.5
U.S. Federal Reserve Bank (1999)	FRB/US macro-economic model	(Permanent) $10 increase	−0.2	−0.4	0.5	0.3

^ Accumulated response of GDP growth to a 1% oil price shock, asymmetric case.
Source: OECD, U.S. EIA

well outside the oil market can mask the effects of exceptional oil market conditions, as occurred during the Asian financial crisis in the late 1990s and the onset of the global recession in 2007.

The suddenness, unexpectedness, persistence, and historical context of the price change also influence its macroeconomic effects. All things equal, the more jarring and unforeseen the volatility, the more pronounced its implications, which can be much stronger or milder than the estimates provided. When businesses and consumers do anticipate a change in prices, they may begin to undertake precautionary saving, leading to an especially protracted economic pullback that can predate the actual market disruption. Additionally, an increase in oil prices that consumers expect to persist tends to be more disruptive to the broader economy than a jump they believe will fade fast, even a large one.[26]

When oil prices jump, the broader economic consequences depends in part on whether they have broken new ground, rising higher than any time in the recent past, or whether they stay in familiar territory. Econometric modeling suggests that net oil price increases only have a significant effect when they exceed their level over the past three years.[27] An increase that simply reverses a previous trend tends to be mostly ineffectual, as consumers have likely already adjusted their behavior. The public also becomes accustomed to sudden price fluctuations and takes steps to reduce their vulnerability, which mitigates the implications of a future change.[28] These dynamics are likely partly why the triple-digit oil prices appear to have had a milder impact on the economy over the past few years than they would have had in previous eras.

The source of an increase in oil prices – whether it is caused by swelling demand or interruptions to supply – makes a critical difference to its larger effects on the economy. Not all oil price changes are alike in their implications. This is intuitive: oil prices are not exogenously determined but are in part a function of economic growth, on which they then feedback. A jump in oil prices that comes about as a result of a rise in aggregate demand

---

[26] Ray Barrell and Olga Pomerantz, "Oil Prices and the World Economy," National Institute of Economic and Social Research Discussion Paper 242 (December 2004), http://goo.gl/H09FN (accessed April 2013).

[27] James D. Hamilton, "What is an Oil Shock?," *Journal of Econometrics* 113, no. 2 (2003): 363–398.

[28] Kiseok Lee, Shawn Ni, and Ronald A. Ratti, "Oil Shocks and the Macroeconomy: The Role of Price Variability," *The Energy Journal* 16 no. 4 (September 1995): 39–56; Hillard G. Huntington, "The Economic Consequences of Higher Crude Oil Prices," Energy Modeling Forum, EMF SR 9 (October 3, 2005): 8–9.

actually tends to correspond to no change or even an increase in net economic output over the short term. The same economic growth that lifts oil prices also lifts the economy in other ways, such as by stimulating demand for U.S. exports, which can entirely offset the negative shock of greater energy costs for a stretch. Yet over time these effects appear to wear off, and more expensive oil begins to take its toll on aggregate demand. This dynamic may help partly explain why the U.S. economy weathered rising oil prices so well for much of the 2000s, given that the bull market was mostly a result of global demand growth. On the other hand, when higher oil prices are sparked by an unanticipated supply interruption, real GDP tends to fall immediately. It remains negatively impacted at statistically significant levels for two years. Consumer prices, however, are not significantly affected.[29]

Domestic economic conditions at the time of the price change, as well as the response by monetary authorities, also affect the magnitude of the economic impacts. If inflationary pressures prior to the shock are running high, the Federal Reserve may face constraints in allowing money supply to expand, which will make it more difficult to offset the drag on output. The monetary response to rising oil prices is an important determinant of the economic impact. For example, the oil price shocks of the 1970s were followed by recessions partly because they coincided with tightening monetary policy, another negative shock.[30] High unemployment can also tie central bankers' hands. Like inflation, it heightens the tradeoff they face in attempting to navigate their dual mandate between inflation and output. Price trends in other commodity markets besides oil also matter; rising prices for other raw materials compound the challenge for monetary authorities to keep inflation expectations well anchored without resorting to raising benchmark rates.

WHAT NEXT FOR THE U.S. OIL ECONOMY?

The links between the U.S. macroeconomy and the price of oil are complex and multifaceted. Often, these ties are ambiguous in nature: The picture is never of a change in oil prices being uniformly good or bad, but rather of a

[29] Lutz Killian, "Not All Oil Price Shocks are Alike: Disentangling Demand and Supply Shocks in the Crude Oil Market," *The American Economic Review* 99, no. 3 (June 2009): 1053–1069.

[30] James D. Hamilton, "Will Gas Prices Trigger Another Recession?," CNN.com, May 5, 2011 (accessed May 2012).

diverse set of trade-offs as well as winners and losers. Much of the country might cheer on declining oil prices, but for some parts of the country (and, pointedly, for some other countries in the world) they can be devastating. The linkages are also dynamic. The magnitude of the effects of a change in oil prices on subsections of the country, whether demographic or geographic, vary over time as technology, the location of oil production, and other aspects of the national economy evolve.

The U.S. oil landscape is undergoing a period of profound change, in terms of supply patterns as well as demand. Tight oil production is ramping up in places far beyond the traditional epicenter of domestic oil production, such as North Dakota, which has widened the geographic locus of economic growth associated with more drilling sparked by higher oil prices. This evolving geography expands the economic pie in new production centers, but also exposes their economy to new vulnerabilities caused by downturns in prices or disappointed expectations of future abundance. The same trend is playing out even more dramatically in natural gas, with booming production in Pennsylvania and other states that were previously far removed from the action. Meanwhile, a combination of high prices at the pump, increasingly fuel efficient cars and trucks, a weak economy, and an aging population, which tends to drive less, has led to a secular downshift in U.S. oil consumption.

Many of these factors are likely to persist for some time, given the outlook for the American economy over the next decade, and some will be here to stay even after the recovery gains traction. The evolution that has occurred since the 1970s – of a national economy less sensitive to unexpected changes in oil prices since that tumultuous decade – continues to this day. With such tectonic changes in the country's oil economy, the nature of the domestic economy's ties to oil prices will no doubt continue to evolve.

LESSONS LEARNED FROM THE 2011 STRATEGIC PETROLEUM RESERVE RELEASE

One action that national governments can take to attempt to mitigate a rise in oil prices that could prove harmful to the broader economy is via a release from strategic oil stockpiles. On June 23, 2011, the International Energy Agency (IEA) announced plans to coordinate the release of emergency oil stockpiles in an attempt to offset an ongoing loss of crude oil production in Libya. In the six months prior, oil prices had jumped more than 20%, as political upheaval in Libya had prevented an estimated 132 million barrels of oil from reaching the market.[31] IEA member country policymakers feared that high oil prices risked undermining a nascent global economic recovery. To combat that threat, twelve IEA member countries made roughly 60 million barrels of crude oil and refined oil products, such as diesel and gasoline, available to the market. The release, which the IEA referred to as the "Libya collective action," lasted from July 23, 2011, until September 15, 2011. It was only the third time in its nearly thirty-year history that the IEA, which was founded after the 1973 oil crisis, has undertaken a coordinated release, though the United States has unilaterally released strategic stocks on several occasions for reasons that include raising revenue and countering rising heating oil prices.

The 2011 IEA release provided policymakers with valuable lessons about three critical aspects of these emergency interventions: their effect on oil prices and market perception, their implications for international cooperation, and the logistical issues they raise about the U.S. Strategic Petroleum Reserve (SPR).

MARKET PERCEPTION AND EFFECT ON OIL PRICES

Policymakers should be modest about expecting an emergency release to lower oil prices in absolute terms. Although oil prices may fall sharply immediately after a release is announced, they are liable to rebound quickly if market conditions warrant a release. That is exactly what occurred following the June 23, 2011, announcement of an impending release. No sooner had the IEA made the media aware that it would be holding a major press conference than prices began tumbling. The price of Brent crude oil, a benchmark for global oil prices, fell 6% the day of the announcement and an additional 2% the next day (see Figure 37). Policymakers in Washington, DC, who had favored the release were privately delighted by how responsive prices were to the news.[32]

But the immediate collapse in prices proved short lived. By the first week of July 2011, oil prices had reclaimed all their lost ground and then some, closing $4 per barrel higher than they had the day of the announcement (see Figure 38).

---

[31] International Energy Agency, "FAQs: IEA Collective Action," http://www.iea.org/files/faq .asp. Accessed June 2012.

[32] Information from an anonymous former U.S. energy official.

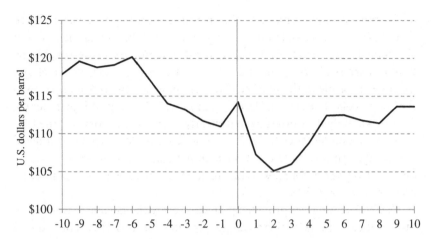

Figure 37. ICE Brent Crude Oil Prices Ten Trading Days Before and After the IEA Announcement on June 23, 2011. *Source:* Bloomberg

The rally in oil prices in the two weeks following the IEA announce-ment reflected a surge in economic optimism, propelling oil prices higher alongside financial markets. The Dow Jones Industrial Average leaped more than 6% between June 24, 2011, and July 7, 2011, on signs of an improving economic outlook for the United States and China. A decline in the value of the dollar relative to the euro also contributed to the bounce in oil prices,

Figure 38. Brent Crude Oil Prices (June–December 2011). *Source:* Bloomberg

as oil is priced in dollars. Had the market's outlook for the global economy not brightened following the IEA announcement, oil prices may very well have not rebounded to their preannouncement levels so quickly. But that counterfactual only underscores the larger point: broader market forces – in this case, economic data – can quickly overwhelm the immediate price impact of an IEA-coordinated boost to world oil supply.

Yet this does not necessarily mean that the IEA action was unhelpful. Another measuring stick, by which the IEA later justified the release, is what it might have helped avoid: a large spike in oil prices in the second half of 2011. An IEA statement in July 2011 defended the release as helping mitigate the risk of a "renewed, damaging and sustained surge in international prices" in the third quarter of the year.[33] Later, IEA deputy executive director Richard Jones reiterated this view. Testifying to the U.S. Senate in January 2012, he defended the IEA's action on the grounds that it "played at least a partial role in helping avoid a damaging price spike during summer 2011."[34] Many market analysts agreed. "The SPR releases did help since prices would have been higher without them," said Olivier Jakob of Petromatrix in September 2011. Edward Morse of Citigroup felt it was "pretty clear" that "things would have been worse without the releases."[35]

The collapse of Libyan production in the spring of 2011 created a severe shortage, primarily in Europe, of light sweet crude oil – the kind prized by refiners for the ease of processing and generous yield of valuable refined products. No other producers, including Saudi Arabia, were able to provide the market with a suitable replacement for Libya's light sweet crude oil. Nearly all of OPEC's spare production capacity is held by Saudi Arabia. At the time of the Libyan disruption, Saudi production stood at around 8.8 mb/d. Even conservative estimates of total Saudi production capacity suggest that the country could come close to making up for the lost Libyan exports.[36] The problem, however, was that Saudi Arabia's spare production capacity was too heavy and sour (viscous and high in sulfur) to provide refiners with a like-for-like replacement for Libyan

[33] International Energy Agency, "Providing Liquidity to a Tighter Market," *Oil Market Report: 13 July 2011*, July 13, 2011.

[34] John Kemp, "RPT-COLUMN-Libya is Template for Releasing Oil Stocks in 2012: Kemp," *Reuters*, February 22, 2012.

[35] Joshua Schneyer, "Analysis: Oil Releases a Gamechanger, Despite Price Bounce," *Reuters*, September 16, 2011.

[36] Barbara Lewis, "Saudi Oil Capacity Depleted: Goldman," *Reuters*, June 13, 2011.

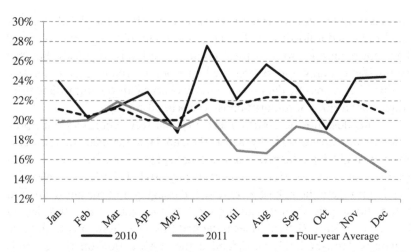

Figure 39. Percentage of U.S. Light Crude Imports (API gravity over thirty-five degrees).
Source: U.S. Energy Information Administration

oil. The best available substitute was the light sweet crude oil in the U.S. SPR.

Partial evidence that the release did help keep a lid on prices was the way in which the intervention altered global trade flows. The 30.6 million barrels of light sweet crude oil drawn from the U.S. SPR during the summer of 2011, which stayed within the United States, reduced the country's need for light sweet crude imports. By releasing light sweet crude to U.S. refiners, the SPR release was able to divert waterborne imports from the Gulf of Mexico to Europe (see Figures 39 and 40). All the while, commercial oil inventories did not decline beyond their normal seasonal patterns (see Figure 41). Light sweet crude imports that ordinarily would have flowed to the United States, typically from West Africa, were freed up for other buyers (see Figure 42).[37] This rearrangement of global trade flows helped relieve the shortage of light sweet crude oil in Europe and cooled buying in the Brent market.

Important indicators in the oil market also suggest that the IEA release helped alleviate supply strain. Libya's crude oil exports are among the lowest in sulfur in the world. When the exports dried up in early 2011, the price spread between low-sulfur Brent crude and high-sulfur Dubai crude oil

---

[37] West African crude oil imports to the United States are undergoing a secular decline. So far, in 2012, less than one mb/d has come to the United States from West African countries. The 2011 SPR release appeared to accelerate this long-term decline during the months that it was in force.

Figure 40. U.S. Crude Oil Refinery Runs. *Source*: U.S. Energy Information Administration

swelled (see Figure 43), reflecting the growing scarcity of low-sulfur oil in the marketplace. The price gap largely disappeared over the second half of the year, as low-sulfur crude oil from the U.S. SPR and elsewhere helped offset the shortfall. Movement in the forward curve for Brent crude oil also suggested that the IEA action helped quench the market's thirst for oil. By April 2011, the loss of Libyan exports had put a premium on oil for immediate delivery (see Figure 44). That premium all but evaporated

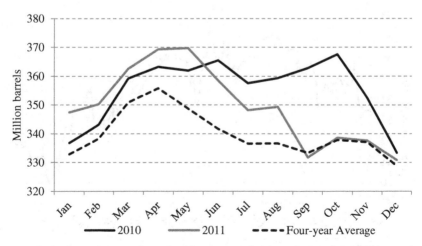

Figure 41. U.S. Commercial Crude Oil Inventories. *Source*: U.S. Energy Information Administration

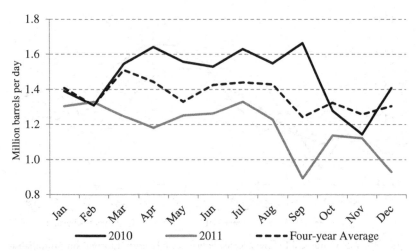

Figure 42. U.S. Crude Imports from West Africa. *Source:* U.S. Energy Information Administration

when the IEA announced the upcoming release (though it returned with a vengeance once all of the emergency oil had been delivered that fall). Both of these effects were only temporary, yet they are clear evidence that global supplies benefited from greater supplies.

It is tempting to attribute the downtrend in oil prices that took place over the second half of 2011 to the IEA release, but, again, larger forces in the

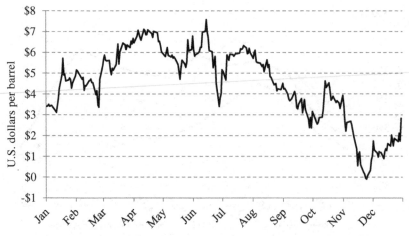

Figure 43. Price Spread Between Brent and Dubai Spot Crude Oil for 2011. *Source:* Bloomberg

Figure 44. Price Spread Between One- and Six-Month Brent Crude Oil Futures for 2011.
Source: Bloomberg

market were likely much more responsible for that outcome than the IEA
release. On the supply side of the ledger, Libyan oil production, which many
analysts thought might stay offline for the remainder of the year, surprised
the market by reaching half its prewar level by December 2011. That flow
of oil slowly removed what had been the chief catalyst of rising prices in the
spring (see Figure 45). Saudi Arabia also helped by raising production to
just under ten mb/d, its highest level in more than three decades.

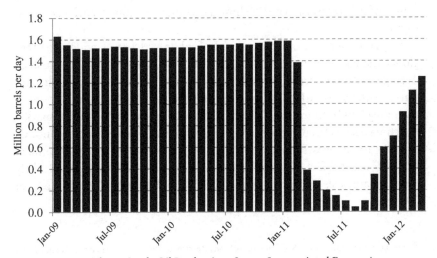

Figure 45. Libyan Crude Oil Production. *Source*: International Energy Agency

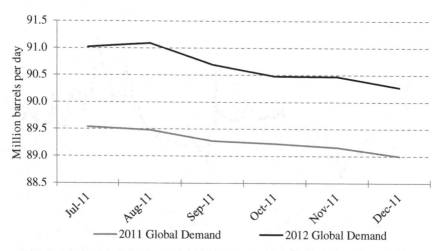

Figure 46. IEA Global Oil Demand Forecasts for 2011 and 2012, July–December 2011
Source: International Energy Agency

On the demand side, the market's growing belief in the second half of 2011 that global economic growth – and hence oil demand growth – would prove slower than anticipated also weighed on prices. From July through December 2011, the IEA continually revised down its world oil demand forecasts for 2011 and 2012 in light of the ongoing European economic crisis and worries that emerging market economies were cooling off (see Figure 46). Even a 0.5 mb/d decrease in global demand, maintained over the course of two years, can easily eclipse a onetime 60-million-barrel addition to supply.

The darkening economic mood in the middle of 2011 was evident in other global financial indicators as well (see Figure 47). The Dow Jones Industrial Average and Brent crude oil prices experienced many of the same fits and starts in the second half of the year, both about 3% lower in December than they had been in June. The close correlation between the two market benchmarks has been common during periods of intense macroeconomic uncertainty, as was the case in 2011. This high degree of synchronicity underscores the fact that shifting expectations for global demand likely played a large role in driving oil prices through the summer and autumn of 2011.[38]

---

[38] See James D. Hamilton, "Strategic Petroleum Reserve to the Rescue," Econbrowser, March 18, 2012, http://www.econbrowser.com/ (accessed May 2012).

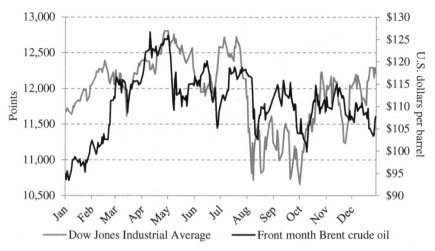

Figure 47. Dow Jones Industrial Average and Brent Crude Oil Prices, June–December 2011. *Source*: Bloomberg

UNINTENDED CONSEQUENCES OF RELEASING STRATEGIC STOCKS

Policymakers should remember that releasing oil from strategic stocks is hardly a free lunch. Tapping emergency inventories may dampen prices in the short term (though even that effect can be highly transient), but it can cause prices to rise soon thereafter.

There are two likely reasons why. First, market participants know that national governments will probably buy oil in the future to replace what they just released. Second, an emergency release also tends to increase the market's skepticism that oil producers are well equipped to satisfy global demand. As Lawrence Eagles of JPMorgan explained, a release can "send the message that consumer governments have little faith that there is any spare capacity within the producer group, and/or there are concerns over OPEC's short and long term price aspirations."[39] Market participants tend to be highly skeptical of official estimates of countries' spare production capacity. Any signal from IEA countries that appears to reinforce those doubts can send prices higher. As analysts at Pacific Investment Management Company (PIMCO) later wrote, a "temporary release aimed at influencing short-term prices could actually send an unintended bullish signal to the market that long-term spare capacity in OPEC producers is insufficient to meet

[39] Barbara Lewis, "OPEC, IEA Clash over Oil Reserves Weapon," *Reuters*, June 24, 2011.

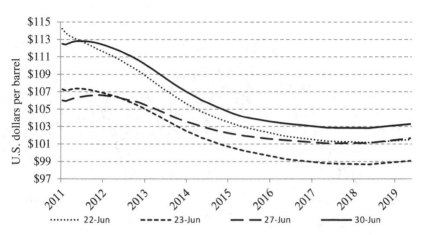

Figure 48. Forward Curve for Brent Crude Oil Around the June 23, 2011, IEA Announcement. *Source:* Bloomberg

supply losses." Because oil prices are a "function of both near-term supply and demand and perceived long-term balances," concern among market participants that the market may tighten up later can immediately feed back into higher prices.[40]

Thus, a release can make markets more anxious, not less, about future conditions in the oil market. Market expectations about higher prices tomorrow can spark higher prices today.

Fluctuations in the forward curve for Brent crude oil around the time of the IEA's June 23 announcement provides support for these views (see Figure 48). Prices all along the curve fell sharply during trading on June 23, the day of the announcement. But by June 27, just two trading days later (June 25–26 was a weekend), long-term prices had already rebounded to their preannouncement levels. Three days later, the price of oil for delivery after January 2012 was higher than it had been prior to the IEA's announcement. This jump in prices, though driven in part by a bounce in economic sentiment, suggests that the market may have indeed interpreted the IEA release as putting upward pressure on longer-term prices. It is also broadly consistent with the notion that market fears about long-term conditions are liable to feed back into near-term prices.

---

[40] Greg E. Sharenow and Mihir P. Worah, "Release Oil from the SPR? Better to Take the Long View," Pimco: Viewpoints, April 2012, http://www.pimco.com/ (accessed May 2012).

NEED FOR PUBLIC UNITY AMONG IEA MEMBER COUNTRIES

IEA member countries should present a unified front after the IEA secretariat announces a release. They failed on this score in the 2011 release. What is more, press leaks about internal dissention among IEA members may have exacerbated oil price volatility that summer.

When the IEA issued a press release announcing the upcoming emergency release, it drew attention to the fact that its governing board would "review the impact of [its] coordinated action and decide on possible future steps" within thirty days.[41] This language suggested to the market that the initial 60 million barrels of oil made available could be followed by a second release, should officials decide to act. Many analysts interpreted the statement as an attempt by the IEA to mitigate speculative buying by telegraphing that more oil might be on the way.[42]

Shortly after the press release, however, reports began to surface suggesting that Germany and Italy had gone into the IEA release dragging their heels and were strongly disinclined toward, and perhaps even firmly opposed to, a second one. One French government official leaked to Reuters that "Germany and Italy were not much in favor of the decision back in June." The decision was unanimous, he conceded, but "not all were committed." The two European countries, among the world's top holders of strategic reserves, were "likely" to resist any call for a second release, the source confided.[43] A senior official at Erdolbevorratungsverband (EBV), Germany's national petroleum stockholding agency, also let slip that "the word from Berlin is that there won't be a second release." Other European officials were reported as making similar remarks.[44]

These leaks may have contributed to price volatility in July. When news got out that some countries were opposed to further action, many market participants felt a second release was much less likely, though they did not rule it out.[45] Any IEA member country could still have acted unilaterally, as some speculated the United States might, but the likelihood of another

---

[41] International Energy Agency (IEA), "IEA Makes 60 Million Barrels of Oil Available to Market to Offset Libyan Disruption," Press Release, June 23, 2011, http://www.iea.org/ (accessed June 2011).

[42] Interview with anonymous North American energy traders.

[43] Muriel Boselli, "Exclusive: Germany, Italy May Resist Second IEA Oil Release," *Reuters*, July 15, 2011.

[44] Javier Blas, "Italian and German Resistance on IEA Release Sends Oil Higher," *Financial Times*, July 20, 2011.

[45] Interviews with anonymous North American energy traders.

large-scale release appeared much dimmer. As traders tried to make sense of the leaks, oil prices whipsawed. Some commentators attributed an unusually large jump in oil prices, occurring the same day news broke about Germany and Italy not favoring another release, as attributed in large part to market guessing about the IEA's next move.[46]

Any power the IEA may have to tamp down short-term oil prices by threatening to draw down emergency stocks is undercut by the appearance of divisions among IEA member countries. In practice, the extent to which the IEA is able to discourage market participants from speculative buying is difficult to gauge. Some analysts have suggested that the IEA might be able to discourage speculative buying by credibly threatening to tap emergency stocks if prices go too high. In the words of Amy Jaffe of Rice University, if the IEA shows it is "willing to use the strategic reserves," then speculators "have to worry that extra oil may come if prices reach a certain level."[47] That policy tool is only likely to affect market participants' decision-making if they believe that officials will actually wield it. The more unified IEA member countries appear in their determination to use emergency stocks to contain the market, the more effectual the threat of joint action.

OPTIMIZING THE STRUCTURE OF AN IEA RELEASE

In a joint IEA emergency release, each member country has the prerogative of deciding what form its participation will take (e.g., how much oil the country will make available, what type of oil, and by what means it will be released).[48] IEA officials do not impose their own preferences. This process allows every national government to tailor its participation in an IEA release to suit its own interests. But it also runs the risk that the release will be ill-suited to the market's needs.

---

[46] Javier Blas, "Italian and German Resistance on IEA Release Sends Oil Higher," *Financial Times*, July 20, 2011.

[47] Joshua Schneyer, "Analysis: Oil releases a gamechanger, despite price bounce," *Reuters*, September 16, 2011.

[48] There is an important difference between how much emergency oil an IEA release "makes available" to the market versus how much it actually adds to the market. In the 2011 release, for example, IEA member countries made about 60 million barrels of oil available to the market. That number represented the amount of emergency oil that market participants had a chance to put into circulation, either by buying them at auction (as occurred in the United States and Germany) or via lowered stockholding requirements for industry (as in France and the United Kingdom). Thus, an IEA release sensibly does not force the market to take on more oil than it can bear. But by the same token, all of the oil made available commonly ends up not being released, as occurred in 2011.

Table 3. *Emergency Stocks Made Available from the IEA Release*

	Total	Public	Industry	Crude Oil	Refined Product	Of which: Gasoline	Diesel	Residual Fuel Oil	Jet Fuel/ Kerosene
United States	30,640	30,640		30,640					
Total IEA North America	30,640	30,640		30,640					
Japan	7,915		7,915	3,958	3,957				
Korea	3,467	3,467		1,998	1,469	300	1,169		
Total IEA Pacific	11,382	3,467	7,915	5,956	5,426	300	1,169		
Belgium	797	95	702		797	43	654	6	95
France	3,242		3,242		3,242	476	2,375	64	327
Germany	2,770	2,770		1,620	1,150	500	650		
Italy	2,524		2 ,524		2,524	1,183	373	968	
Netherlands	1,173	1,173		1,023	150		150		
Poland	959		959	310	650	139	510		
Spain	2,274		2,274		2,274	331	1,799	144	
Turkey	1,071		1,071		1,071	176	895		
United Kingdom	3,000		3,000	600	2,400				
Total IEA Europe	17,811	4,038	13,773	3,553	14,258	2,848	7,407	1,181	422
Total IEA	59,833	38,145	21,688	40,149	19,684	3,148	8,576	1,181	422

* The breakdown in crude and product has been estimated; overall stockholding obligations on industry, which include both crude and refined products, have been lowered in these countries.

Source: International Energy Agency

143

Of the roughly 60 million barrels of oil the IEA authorized for release, nearly one-third of the oil that was made available to industry came from relaxing industry stockpiling requirements of refined products in Europe.[49] That was unfortunate. In these countries, governments require refiners to hold a certain amount of oil. Once a government reduces this officially mandated level of storage, refiners are free to sell or refine some of their stocks, though they are under no obligation to do so. Given conditions in the European oil market at the time, refiners had little incentive to release additional products onto the market. The release would likely have been more effective if it had consisted of more light sweet crude, ideally auctioned from public stocks, as opposed to refined products. Had that been the case, a greater percentage of the 60 million barrels of oil that was made available by the IEA release would have reached the market.

Altering the release in this way, however, would have required asking more of those countries with sizable national stockpiles of high-grade crude oil. The United States holds the lion's share of the sweet crude reserves held within IEA member countries, with some 262 million barrels (or 38% of total IEA holdings) as of July 2012.[50] Washington would have had to increase its role in the release if significantly more light sweet crude were to have been supplied. As it was, the United States was already providing more than half of the total oil made available in the 2011 IEA release, and may have resisted expanding its role.

European and Asian governments could very likely have also taken on a much larger role in supplying sweet crude oil. Indeed, they likely released much less of this type of crude, as a percentage of their total public holdings, than the United States did in 2011. The IEA does not keep comprehensive data on the grade of its member countries' crude stockpiles, so it is difficult to know for certain which countries may have been able to increase the amount of sweet crude they supplied.[51] Yet public inventories of crude oil in Europe amounted to 186 million barrels in May 2011. Assuming the ratio of sweet to sour crude oil in European public stockpiles is similar to that of

---

[49] As the IEA explained, "Five countries (Belgium, Germany, Korea, the Netherlands, and the United States) are releasing stocks from public reserves via tender, auction or direct sale. Eight countries (Belgium, France, Italy, Japan, Poland, Spain, Turkey, and the UK) lowered the emergency reserves obligation on market operators (Belgium is using both public and industry stocks in this action)." See International Energy Agency, "The IEA's Libya Collective Action Explained," *Oil Market Report: 13 July 2011*, July 13, 2011, 31.

[50] See U.S. Department of Energy, "Current SPR inventory as of July 18, 2011," Strategic Petroleum Reserve Inventory, July 18, 2011, http://www.spr.doe.gov/dir/dir.html (accessed July 2011).

[51] Correspondence with Martin Young of the IEA.

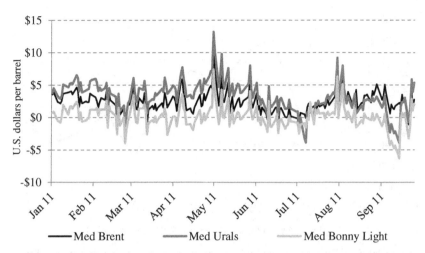

Figure 49. Oil Refining Margins in Southern Europe (Select Grades). *Source:* Bloomberg; International Energy Agency

the United States, European IEA members could have more than doubled the amount of sweet crude they made available in 2011 and still not have surpassed Washington's contribution as a percentage of sweet crude stocks. It would have been sensible for Europe, whose physical market was affected most directly by the disruption, to have shouldered more of the burden. It is also likely that Japan has sizable strategic stocks of sweet crude that it withheld, as its government-held reserves – about 323 million barrels – consist entirely of crude oil. But the Japanese government chose not to release any of the stockpiles in the 2011 IEA action.

Paltry demand for diesel in Europe, as a result of severe economic weakness, coupled with high crude oil prices had pushed refiners' profit margins into abysmally low, even negative, territory (see Figure 49). Releasing more fuel would only have made things worse. "Far from depressing prices and rescuing a fragile economic recovery in the industrialized world," one news report observed, the prospect of more refined products in the European market would "[pile] more misery on refiners, and has raised expectations of increased supply [of crude oil] that may not be realized."[52] Not coincidentally, industry stockpiles of refined products in Europe at the time were well above the levels mandated by the IEA. Had companies had an economic rationale for releasing more products at prevailing prices, they would have

---

[52] Christopher Johnson, "Analysis: Oil Stock Release Looks Chaotic, Could Backfire," *Reuters*, June 30, 2011.

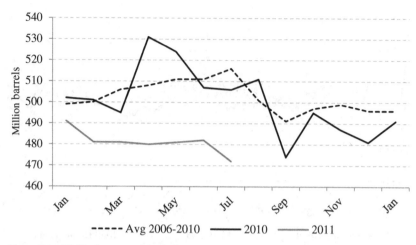

Figure 50. OECD Commercial Crude Oil Inventories Outside North America. *Source:* Bloomberg; International Energy Agency

already done so. Thus, lowering storage mandates for refined products likely did little to help improve supply conditions in the European market.

Outside of North America, where oil supplies in the Midwestern United States were at all-time highs, commercial inventories in the Organization for Economic Cooperation and Development (OECD) countries were far lower than the historical norm, reflecting a global crude oil market that was tight (see Figure 50). It was no coincidence that all of the 30.6 million barrels of crude oil auctioned from the U.S. SPR found their way to the market, albeit indirectly by diverting waterborne imports away from the United States to Europe. Priced at a discount to prevailing market prices, SPR crude was attractive to market participants. It also attacked the root of the global supply problem by allowing those European refiners most hurt by the loss of Libyan crude to take advantage of newly freed light sweet crude from West Africa, which no longer flowed to the United States.

Oil analysts' expectations for what the IEA release could accomplish would have been far more positive had the release favored crude oil over fuel and government-held oil over reduced stockholding requirements on industry. Shortly after details of the release were announced, Goldman Sachs analysts argued that the reduction in stockholding requirements would "have an almost negligible impact on oil prices," noting that commercial stocks in IEA countries were above mandated levels. Lowering the mandate "might result in very little additional oil being made available," making the "price impact from those measures" likely "very limited."[53] Oil analysts at JPMorgan took a similar view, arguing that "the method of sale, and the lack of guidance on refilling, work against the barrels being used."[54] A European oil trader predicted that "the 15 million barrels of products should mean that refinery margins get pummeled and runs are cut, seeing as demand is already poor."[55]

This line of criticism was common enough to prompt IEA officials to address it directly in the following month's *Oil Market Report*, a regular IEA publication:

> While relaxing the stock obligation on operators might be a less visible response, or be seen as a more diluted measure, since no formally announced sales or physical movements may occur, it is no less effective. The lowered obligations give operators the opportunity to make additional oil available over the coming months, and they will use this greater flexibility according to market circumstances.[56]

Although this argument is true in theory, given the particular issues facing the oil market in the summer of 2011, policymakers in IEA member countries would have been more effective at offsetting any global supply shortage by restructuring the specifics of the release.

THE DIFFICULTY OF NEGOTIATION AND CONSENSUS BUILDING

International politics lie at the center of any IEA decision to jointly tap member countries' emergency oil inventories. The 2011 release highlighted the challenges to, as well as the changing nature of, cooperation among IEA member countries, major non-IEA members like China, and pivotal producers such as Saudi Arabia. It can be far harder and take far longer for IEA member countries to form a consensus to authorize a joint release than the policymakers involved might expect or desire. Alas, delay can also compromise the effectiveness of a release.

Officials from the Obama administration, which made the initial push for the release, learned this lesson in the months prior to the June 2011 agreement. Although senior U.S. officials reportedly began lobbying their IEA peers for a release as early as March, it took nearly four months to

---

[53] Guy Chazan, "IEA Defends Oil Release," *Wall Street Journal,* July 4, 2011.

[54] Christopher Johnson, "Analysis: Oil Stock Release Looks Chaotic, Could Backfire," *Reuters,* June 30, 2011.

[55] Zaida Espana and Emma Farge, "Analysis: IEA Stock Release Wounds Europe's Refiners," *Reuters,* June 28, 2011.

[56] International Energy Agency, "The IEA's Libya Collective Action Explained," *Oil Market Report: 13 July 2011,* July 13, 2011, 31.

reach a decision. The Obama administration's early attempts at persuasion were met with "nothing but resistance."[57] By late April, talks among the twenty-eight IEA nations had begun. On May 6, President Barack Obama called King Abdullah of Saudi Arabia and Kuwaiti emir Sheikh Sabah al-Ahmad al-Sabah to discuss a possible release. The president then sent a secret delegation of senior administration officials to Saudi Arabia, the United Arab Emirates (UAE), and Kuwait.[58]

By May 19, after a meeting of the IEA's governing board, international buy-in for a release was strong enough for the agency to publicly announce that member nations were ready to use "all tools" at their disposal to settle the market.[59] Later that month, President Obama pressed his peers at a G8 summit in France to take joint action.[60] After the OPEC meeting in June ended without an agreement to raise production quotas, IEA member countries made a final decision to intervene, announcing their intention two weeks later.

The slowness of the decision-making process likely worsened the timing of the release in at least three ways. First, rampant speculation in the market press about the possibility of an imminent release – and possibly leaked information from political insiders – may have amplified price volatility that rattled the markets from April through the first half of June. Rumors abounded that the enormous $10 drop in crude oil prices on May 5 was attributable to a tip-off that Obama had "started to consult seriously" about tapping the U.S. SPR.[61] Second, announcing a release as early as March or April may have helped calm oil's stampede to $125 per barrel, as the market anticipated peak demand in the Northern Hemisphere amid a dire Libyan supply crunch. Third, the time elapse between the collapse of Libyan exports and IEA's June announcement provided ammunition for critics who claimed that the Libyan production stoppage was only a pretext for

---

[57] Information from an anonymous former U.S. energy official.

[58] Keith Johnson and Guy Chazan, "World Oil Reserves Tapped," *Wall Street Journal*, June 24, 2011.

[59] David Sheppard and Joshua Shneyer, "Traders Abuzz at Timing of U.S.-led Oil Talks, Price Swings," *Reuters*, June 30, 2011.

[60] Keith Johnson and Guy Chazan, "World Oil Reserves Tapped," *Wall Street Journal*, June 24, 2011.

[61] Rumors abounded that the $10 drop in crude oil prices on May 5 stemmed from the fact that it was the first day that President Obama "started to consult seriously on using the SPR in this way," in the words of one analyst. Some analysts also attributed the dramatic collapse in the LLS-Dated Brent spread to under $6 to leaked information about an impending release of LLS from the SPR. The spread quickly rebounded to normal levels the following week. See David Sheppard and Joshua Shneyer, "Traders Abuzz at Timing of U.S.-led Oil Talks, Price Swings," *Reuters*, June 30, 2011.

a decision that was politically motivated.[62] Had the release followed more closely on the heels of the Libyan disruption, IEA policymakers would have been able to avoid that accusation.

THE SHIFTING PERCEPTIONS OF CRITERIA FOR IEA EMERGENCY INTERVENTIONS

The IEA's decision to tap emergency stocks immediately met with intense skepticism among media and policy analysts who questioned whether conditions in the market warranted the intervention. The 2011 decision "proved particularly controversial" within the IEA, according to one report, "dividing the agency's members and whipping up a firestorm of criticism from senior oil analysts and traders." Some felt that the agency had overstepped its bounds. "They (the IEA) have given themselves justification to do just about anything they want. I'm sure it will be a lively debate internally," said Mike Wittner, an oil analyst at Société Générale and former IEA official.[63] Some market analysts surmised that the United States was exhibiting a newfound willingness to deploy its strategic reserves for nonemergency purposes.[64]

For some, the IEA decision evidenced that the agency's mission had drifted from providing emergency supplies to trying to proactively manage prices. "By influencing short term sentiment," wrote an analyst in the *European Energy Review*, "the IEA is playing a very dangerous game."[65] It is true that IEA policymakers, particularly in the United States and the European Union, were desperate to buoy a nascent economic recovery. Fierce opposition to any additional fiscal or economic stimulus had largely rendered such measures politically impossible. Some saw the IEA release as an attempt by Western policymakers as stimulus by other means. "An economic stimulus... in oil dollars," one analyst somewhat derisively described it.[66] The release, in other words, was a "reach by member countries for the remedy

---

[62] See, for example, "Editorial: The Wrong Reason for Depleting the Strategic Oil Reserve," *Washington Post*, June 23, 2011.

[63] Muriel Boselli, "Exclusive: Germany, Italy May Resist Second IEA Oil Release," *Reuters*, July 15, 2011.

[64] See, for instance, the Barclays Capital note cited in Keith Johnson and Cassell Bryan-Low, "U.S., U.K. Discuss Tapping Oil Stocks," *Wall Street Journal*, March 15, 2012.

[65] Matthew Hulbert, "A Strategic Slip from The IEA," *European Energy Review*, June 30, 2011.

[66] *Reuters*, "IEA Releases Oil Reserves: What the Analysts Say," *Financial Post*, http://business.financialpost.com/2011/06/23/iea-releases-oil-reserves-what-the-analysts-say/ (accessed June 2011).

of last resort to high oil prices."[67] The IEA was foolishly trying to assume Saudi Arabia's role as the "central bank" of world oil, intervening in the market to suit its own economic objectives. The timing of the release, some months after Libyan production first began to collapse, raised some analysts' suspicions that Libya was nothing more than "good cover" for the attempt to lower fuel prices.[68]

At the heart of the debate was the question of what market conditions justify as an emergency IEA intervention. Some policy analysts wondered whether IEA intervention was needed, as oil refineries worldwide appeared to be well supplied, despite the loss of Libyan exports. As Guy Caruso of the Center for Strategic and International Studies put it: "We're already several months into the Libyan disruption and a lot of the logistical rearrangement of supplies has already taken place. Most refiners I've talked to appear to be adequately supplied."[69] Yet inventory data were showing signs of rapidly depleting industry crude oil stockpiles in Europe. By March, these stocks in OECD Europe had fallen well below normal seasonal levels owing to the combined effects of the Libyan disruption and production outages in the North Sea.

The real question was not whether light sweet crude supplies were running low – they clearly were, particularly in southern Europe – but whether the shortage was severe enough and global enough in nature to justify an IEA collective action. Opinions differed sharply. The release raised other legitimate points of contention, including who bore primary responsibility for combating the shortage (some in Washington saw the European Union as the obvious candidate, given that its refiners were most harmed and U.S. commercial inventories remained high); whether the criteria for deciding to release stocks was too ad hoc and politicized; and whether the failure of the release to drive prices lower in the weeks following the June 23, 2011, announcement eviscerated the fundamental economic logic of the release.[70]

---

[67] Ibid.

[68] Ibid.

[69] Keith Johnson and Guy Chazan, "World Oil Reserves Tapped," *Wall Street Journal*, June 24, 2011.

[70] For a study of the dynamics of present-day global oil supply, see Hakim Darbouche and Bassam Fattouh, "The Implications of the Arab Uprisings for Oil and Gas Markets," Oxford Institute for Energy Studies (September 2011). Questions about the release come from interviews with North American and European energy traders and analysts, as well as from industry press sources cited elsewhere.

Facing sharp criticism over the release, IEA officials defended their decision in the July 2011 edition of the *Oil Market Report*: "Much ink has been spilt subsequently suggesting that the IEA action comes three months too late, depletes emergency stockpiles and has failed to reduce rampant crude and motor fuel prices. However, we feel compelled to point out that critics cannot have their cake and eat it too." IEA officials rejected the argument that influencing prices was the goal of the action or the measuring stick by which it should be judged, calling it "blinkered" to "focus on specific price levels." The authors pointed out that a lack of "major OPEC production increases up until June implied a real possibility that commercial stocks could fall to the bottom of their seasonal range, risking a renewed, damaging and sustained surge in international prices" later in the year. The emergency action was not a dangerous depletion of oil stocks, they argued. After all, it entailed only 1% of total IEA inventories.[71] The bottom line, as the IEA officials saw it, was that the "impact of the collective action will only be truly evident in hindsight."

THE NEED FOR COOPERATION WITH SAUDI ARABIA

For IEA countries, cooperation with Saudi Arabia (and its Gulf allies, to a much lesser extent) is critical for a release to meet its objective of helping relieve a shortage of oil in the market. Saudi Arabia acts as the world's major swing producer of oil, continually raising and lowering its output in response to market conditions. Without some degree of cooperation from Riyadh, any attempt by IEA member countries to offset supply losses by drawing on strategic stocks is almost certain to be ineffective. The reason is straightforward: were the Saudis to choose to dial back their production to offset emergency IEA supplies, they could easily neutralize a release.

Some analysts saw Riyadh's unwillingness to aggressively discount the oil it offered to the market after Libyan production went down in early 2011 as a failure in Saudi-IEA cooperation.[72] Traditionally, consumer governments view releasing oil from emergency stockpiles to combat a supply disruption only as a second resort. Instead, they would prefer to see OPEC, which has historically kept some of its production capacity idle, make up for any

---

[71] International Energy Agency, "Providing Liquidity to a Tighter Market," *Oil Market Report: 13 July 2011*, July 13, 2011.

[72] Insight thanks to an anonymous reviewer.

harmful shortfalls in global supplies. But judging by its production levels, Riyadh appeared unwilling to play this critical role in the early spring of 2011, prior to the IEA announcement, even as prices shot higher. For Saudi Arabia, putting more oil on the market inevitably would have meant offering it at a discount. Only then would its additional production attract interest from European buyers, who would have preferred the kind of light sweet crude they lost when Libya went offline.

IEA secretariat officials were aware of the need for cooperation from Saudi Arabia from the start of the planning process. Saudi Arabia has long held its current pivotal role in the global market. As the IEA saw it, the release would not substitute for Saudi oil, but rather supplement it in two ways. The emergency oil would serve as a backstop in case the expected increase in Saudi production did not arrive as quickly as planned or fell short. After an inconclusive OPEC meeting in early June 2011, the Saudis publicly declared their intention to ramp up their output that summer to help stem rising oil prices. When IEA officials announced their emergency release a few weeks later, they acknowledged the Saudis' promises, saying that the IEA "warmly welcomes the announced intentions to increase production by major oil producing countries," notably Saudi Arabia and its Gulf peers.[73] The purpose of the release, as the IEA described it, was to create a "bridge to higher supplies from other OPEC producers ... and to try to prevent a potentially abrupt drawdown in OECD inventories ... if other OPEC supplies did not increase."[74]

The IEA intervention also supplemented Saudi production by offering a grade of oil that was closer to the missing Libyan crude than Riyadh had provided. Saudi Arabia was unable to replace ultra-high-quality crude oil exports from Libya with its own common grades, all eight of which are sour (i.e., high in sulfur content). As Libyan export volumes began to dwindle early in the year, Saudi Aramco, Saudi Arabia's national oil company, announced in March 2011 that it would help remove the deficit of light sweet crude in the global marketplace by offering higher-quality synthetic versions of its own crude. These hybrid Saudi grades met with only tepid interest from refiners. The market's lack of interest was likely because the oil was still an imperfect substitute for the missing Libyan

---

[73] International Energy Agency, "IEA Makes 60 Million Barrels of Oil Available to Market to Offset Libyan Disruption," Press Release, June 23, 2011, http://www.iea.org/ (accessed June 2011).

[74] John Kemp, "RPT-COLUMN-Libya is Template for Releasing Oil Stocks in 2012: Kemp," *Reuters*, February 22, 2012.

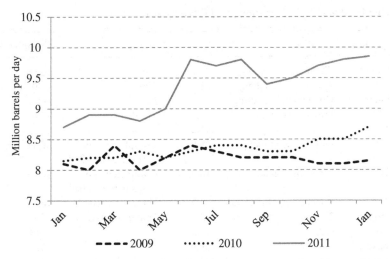

Figure 51. Saudi Arabian Crude Oil Production. *Source:* International Energy Agency

crude, and the Saudis offered them to the market at too high an asking price to attract buyers, given the quality of the oil.[75]

Cooperation between IEA member countries and the Gulf states, notably Saudi Arabia, was strong during and after the release. Riyadh lifted its crude output to the highest level in more than three decades, notwithstanding the IEA intervention (see Figure 51). Kuwait and the UAE also increased production. As Libya started to pump more oil in September 2011, the Gulf States trimmed back their supplies accordingly.[76] Ultimately, European refiners relied on higher-than-usual imports of oil from Saudi Arabia, Nigeria, Iraq, and Angola as the best available substitute for lost Libyan exports. Nigerian and Angolan crude proved especially valuable, given their low sulfur content and low viscosity. Many southern European refineries, unable to process the relatively high-sulfur crude oil common in the Middle East, could easily process this crude oil from West Africa.[77]

---

[75] Izabella Kaminska, "What Price is Saudi Arabia's New Special 'Blend'?," FT Alphaville, http://ftalphaville.ft.com/.

[76] See IEA Oil Market Reports from 2011, especially International Energy Agency, "OPEC Crude Supply," *Oil Market Report: 12 October 2011*, October 12, 2011, 18.

[77] "European Refiners Tapped Other OPEC Supply to Replace Lost Libyan Barrels," *Oil Market Report: 14 March 2012*, March 14, 2012.

Table 4. *China's SPR Expansion (as of February 2012)*

Operator	Location	Capacity	Status	Completion
Sinopec	Zhenhai, Zhejiang	32.7	Filled	3Q06
Sinchem	Zhoushan, Zhejiang	31.4	Filled	4Q07
Sinopec	Huangdao, Shandong	20.1	Filled	4Q07
CNPC	Dalian, Liaoning	18.9	Filled	4Q08
Phase 1		**103.2**		**2008**
CNPC	Dus hanzi, Xinjiang	18.9	Completed and ready to be filled	3Q11
CNPC	Lanzhou, Gansu	18.9	Completed and ready to be filled	4Q11
CNPC	Jinzhou, Liaoning	18.9	Under construction	1Q12
Sinopec	Tianjin	22.0	Under construction	1Q12
	Other	90.3		2013
Phase 2		**169.0**		**2013**
Phase 3		**227.8**		**2016**
Total SPR		**500.0**		

Source: International Energy Agency

THE NEED FOR COOPERATION WITH CHINA

China's strategic petroleum reserves, still in the early phases of construction at the time of the 2005 IEA release, are now among the largest in the world. The IEA should continue to attempt to coordinate future releases with China and eventually with other non-IEA countries such as India.

China has been actively constructing and filling its strategic reserves in recent years. According to IEA reports, Beijing completed phase one of its SPR in 2008, building and filling four storage facilities with a combined capacity of 103 million barrels of crude oil (see Table 4). As of June 2012, China was working on phase two of its SPR development. At capacity, these additional sites, which are due for completion in 2013, will house another 169 million barrels of crude. All in all, the buildup of Chinese emergency stockpiling capacity might be ready to receive as many as 79 million barrels of oil in 2012.[78]

Oil purchases by the Chinese government have become a significant force in the global market. Analysts believe that China's efforts to begin filling these growing emergency coffers in the first quarter of 2012 boosted the

---

[78] International Energy Agency, "China's SPR Expansion," *Oil Market Report: 10 February 2012*, February 10, 2012: 31.

country's crude oil imports and contributed to a sharp rise in oil prices over that time frame.[79] In March 2012, oil traders and analysts estimated that China had been adding as much as 250 thousand barrels per day (kb/d) to 500 kb/d to its national stockpiles.[80]

Planning the 2011 release, IEA officials almost certainly realized that China's ongoing efforts to fill its own SPR could interfere with an IEA emergency stock draw. The IEA thus risked oil effectively moving out of IEA strategic stocks into the Chinese SPR, neutralizing the release. Trying to avert that outcome, IEA officials contacted Chinese officials prior to the release. The contents of their discussion have not been disclosed.[81] Chinese energy officials publicly voiced support for the IEA intervention shortly after the announcement. China's National Energy Administration released a statement giving the IEA's move a "very positive evaluation and support." Chinese officials promised to "pay close attention to the impact and usefulness of oil stock releases on international oil prices and international oil markets."[82] It is unclear whether China did in fact cooperate with the IEA's release by slowing down the rate at which it was filling its SPR. The Chinese government does not release regular data about the flow of oil into its strategic reserves.

This type of coordination between IEA policymakers and their Chinese counterparts is essential. The Chinese economy, like those of the large Western consumer nations, is highly vulnerable to global oil supply shortages and the high prices they bring about. Although China will not cede its sovereignty over its own national oil stockpiles, the IEA should attempt to persuade Chinese officials to assist them in an emergency release based on both parties' shared interest in low, stable oil prices and reliable supplies. This assistance might take one of two forms. Ideally, China would supplement an IEA release by drawing down its own stocks in conjunction with IEA member countries. If that is not possible, China would at least refrain from filling its SPR (if applicable) in the months prior to, during, and after an IEA release.

The need for the IEA to develop effective ways to work with the strategic reserve policies of major non-IEA consumers like China will grow more

---

[79] Carolyn Cui, "China Seen Bolstering Oil Reserves," *Wall Street Journal*, April 11, 2012.

[80] Javier Blas, "Fears over Conflict Fuelling Oil Hoarding," *Financial Times*, March 22, 2012.

[81] Thanks to Aad Van Boheman of the IEA for this insight.

[82] Correspondence with Aad Van Boheman of the IEA, who I also owe for providing the Chinese National Energy Administration's June 24, 2011 press release (and the IEA's unofficial translation).

urgent in the years ahead. As emerging-market countries become more dependent on oil imports, their demand for emergency supplies will grow.[83] China, for its part, plans to expand its strategic reserves by a further 228 million barrels by 2016, lifting its capacity to 500 million barrels.[84] At that scale, China's reserves would be roughly 70% the size of the U.S. SPR. Moreover, India unveiled plans in late 2011 to increase the size of its proposed national stockpile to 132 million barrels by 2020. India's top oil official has said that the country may use SPR stocks to combat "price fluctuations," rather than only to address emergency shortages.[85] That distinction suggests India might intervene in the market more actively than other countries have. All signs point to the need for IEA member countries to coordinate more closely with countries outside their ranks if future releases are to be effective.

Effect on relations with OPEC member countries

An IEA emergency stock release risks causing diplomatic friction between IEA member countries and their allies within OPEC, particularly if the latter group does not see the circumstances as meriting extraordinary intervention.

This dynamic played out in the 2011 release. Predictably, both the OPEC secretary general and Iran's representative to OPEC roundly criticized the IEA intervention.[86] But even OPEC countries that are allies of the United States and other Western nations seemed to resent what they perceived to be an unwarranted intrusion by the IEA. One Gulf delegate later said he saw "no reason" for the IEA release, accusing the agency of "playing politics" by acquiescing to a White House–directed release driven more by electoral than market considerations.[87] A recent statement by Saudi oil minister Ali al-Naimi suggests that Riyadh may have a dim view of the 2011 release, despite Saudi leaders' apparent acquiescence during consultations with U.S. policymakers prior to the release. Speaking to reporters on March 29, 2012, about another possible IEA action, al-Naimi derided the 2011 release, saying: "What I can tell you is that they have done it

---

[83] Javier Blas, "Fears over Conflict Fuelling Oil Hoarding," *Financial Times*, March 22, 2012.

[84] International Energy Agency, "China's SPR Expansion," *Oil Market Report: 10 February 2012*, February 10, 2012, 31.

[85] Rakesh Sharma, "India Unveils Strategic Oil Stockpile Plans," *Wall Street Journal*, December 21, 2011.

[86] "Iran says IEA Oil Stock Release a 'Dangerous Game,'" *Platts*, June 27, 2011.

[87] Barbara Lewis, "OPEC, IEA Clash over Oil Reserves Weapon," *Reuters*, June 24, 2011.

before and it didn't do anything. You saw what happened in the last release? Nothing."[88]

It is difficult to know whether al-Naimi's statement reflects disapproval that Saudi officials harbored privately at the time of the release or whether they had grown more critical in the intervening months. Some analysts believe it may have been prompted by Riyadh's desire to avoid giving Tehran the impression of total solidarity with Washington. Either way, IEA member countries should be aware that the Saudis may not be as supportive in the future as they appeared to be in 2011. The new era of cooperation between Riyadh and the IEA that the release seemed to many to herald may be more tenuous than it initially looked.

Such a negative reaction from OPEC countries should not come as a surprise. After all, the IEA was devised after the 1973 energy crisis to give Western powers a means of leverage against OPEC's dominance in the oil market. For many OPEC countries, oil exports represent the source of the vast majority of their public revenues. Saudi Arabia enjoys special prominence by acting as the figurative central banker to the global oil market, adding and draining liquidity to keep prices within a range that suits its strategic objectives. To the extent that an IEA release places downward pressure on oil prices or signals incredulity among consumer governments that OPEC is able to manage the market, deploying emergency stocks runs counter to the economic and political interests of OPEC countries, and thus is likely to draw their ire. Fear of a diplomatic backlash against IEA countries is hardly a reason not to tap emergency stocks when conditions warrant. Still, the diplomatic friction in the wake of the 2011 release serves as a reminder that tapping IEA stockpiles can also have ramifications for international politics, not just economics.

Dealing with Jones Act restrictions

President Obama's authorization to tap the U.S. SPR as well as the Department of Homeland Security's decision to grant numerous waivers to the Merchant Marine Act of 1920 (commonly known as the Jones Act, which curtails the use of non-U.S. vessels for domestic transport of oil) provoked sharp, if somewhat predictable, criticism from various groups. The Jones Act requires that all shipping vessels traveling between U.S. ports sail under the U.S. flag, be built in the United States, and be crewed by mostly U.S.

---

[88] Richard Mably, "Exclusive: West Wants Saudi Arabia to Keep Up Oil Production," *Reuters*, March 29, 2012.

citizens. Conventional wisdom holds that the Jones Act impedes the efficient release of oil from the U.S. SPR to maritime trade, but granting waivers to the act is politically fraught. The experience of 2011 confirmed this view.

Exporting crude oil from the SPR is effectively prohibited by U.S. law unless there is a "compelling national interest."[89] As a result, oil released from the SPR must flow to U.S. refiners in one of several directions: within the Gulf of Mexico, where the storage facilities that hold SPR oil are located; to inland refineries via pipelines; and to other coastal refineries reachable by sea.

Only fifty-six ocean-going oil tankers meet that standard – less than 1% of the world's tanker capacity.[90] Even in normal times, Jones Act restrictions have a material effect on the flow of oil between U.S. ports. They thwart the transfer of refined fuels from the U.S. Gulf Coast to the East Coast, for example, a route that could often be profitable using foreign vessels but that is not economically feasible using more costly U.S.-flagged vessels. In emergencies, however, the impact of Jones Act restrictions is much larger. Baker & O'Brien, an energy consulting firm, estimates that shipping refined oil products from Houston to New York Harbor on a Jones Act–compliant tanker increases the cost by about four dollars per barrel.[91]

The process of issuing waivers to the Jones Act in conjunction with the 2011 U.S. SPR release was not entirely smooth. On June 23, 2011, the Department of Energy announced the sale of crude oil from the SPR. The Department of Homeland Security issued a blanket waiver of the Jones Act for the marine delivery of oil purchased in the SPR sale. Similar general, time-limited waivers of the Jones Act had been issued in conjunction with the 1991 and 2005 SPR releases, the latter of which was followed by a case-by-case consideration of waiver requests.[92] Proponents of the Jones

---

[89] See U.S. House of Representatives Subcommittee on Energy and Power, Committee on Commerce, *Testimony of the Honorable R. Roger Majak*, Hearing on "Strategic Petroleum Reserve: A Closer Look At The Drawdown Petroleum Short Supply Export Controls," October 19, 2000.

[90] Matthew Robinson, "Insight: Obama's Oil Tanker Dilemma: Vex Unions to Win Pennsylvania?," *Reuters*, March 12, 2012.

[91] See Baker & O'Brien Inc., "U.S. Refining Margins Decline as Mid-Continent Crude Oil and Light/Heavy Differentials Narrow," Press Release, March 1, 2012, http://www.marketwire.com/. Accessed March 2012. Note that the figure assumes no back-haul opportunity and is based on charter rates in early 2012.

[92] See Richard Farmer, *Rethinking Emergency Energy Policy* (Washington, DC: Congressional Budget Office, 1994), 29. Also Keith Hennessy, "How to Waive the Jones Act," June 10, 2010, http://keithhennessy.com/ (accessed May 2012).

Act, upset by the announcement, convinced the Obama administration to release an amended notice of sale the next day. Instead of a universal waiver, the notice specified that exemptions would be issued on a case-by-case basis. No public explanation was given for the change in policy.[93]

The Department of Homeland Security, in consultation with the Obama administration and other federal departments, made extensive use of its prerogative to waive Jones Act restrictions. At the time, to issue a waiver, the secretary of homeland security had to determine that the allowance was in the interest of national defense and the Maritime Administration at the Department of Transportation needed to certify that U.S. shipping capacity was insufficient.[94] In the 2011 SPR release, most purchasers bought oil in large volumes, seeking to take advantage of economies of scale. Transporting such massive quantities of oil using the available fleet of U.S.-flagged vessels – many of them coastal barges that hold no more than 150,000 barrels – would have made the release unfeasibly slow and expensive. In the end, these considerations were enough for the Department of Homeland Security to grant fifty-two Jones Act waivers, the most issued under any U.S. administration. Only one U.S.-flagged vessel was used in the release.[95]

These exemptions to the Jones Act were crucial to enabling a speedy, cost-effective release, but they sparked criticism from the U.S. maritime industry, labor unions, and public officials from coastal states. This reaction was not surprising. "Whenever someone takes on the Jones Act it is usually to their peril," said Charles Ebinger of the Brookings Institution.[96] In the case of the

---

[93] See U.S. House of Representatives Subcommittee on Coast Guard and Maritime Transportation, Committee on Transportation and Infrastructure, *Testimony of Thomas Allegretti*, Hearing on "A Review of Vessels Used to Carry Strategic Petroleum Reserve Drawdowns," June 27, 2012. For the original Notice of Sale, see Department of Energy, "Notice of Sale DE-NS96–11PO97000," June 23, 2011. For the amended Notice of Sale, see "Notice of Sale DE-NS96–11PO97000 Amendment 001," June 24, 2011, http://fossil.energy.gov/ (accessed May 2012).

[94] For a concise description of the law governing Jones Act waivers, see U.S. Department of Homeland Security, Letters Regarding Merchant Marine Act of 1920 (Jones Act) Waivers from Secretary Janet Napolitano, July 8, 2011, http://www.dhs.gov/xlibrary/assets/foia/ jones-act-3.pdf (accessed May 2012). The letter to Shell Oil grants a waiver in connection with the SPR release.

[95] Nathan Harvey of the U.S. Department of Energy, Meghan Gordon of Platts, and Erlinda Byrd of the Department of Homeland Security provided very helpful insight on this issue. See also John M. Broder, "Oil Reserves Sidestep U.S. Vessels," *New York Times*, August 23, 2011; and Meghan Gordon, "Feature: Oceangoing Barges Could Meet Gap in U.S. Northeast Gasoline, ULSD Supply," *Platts*, March 23, 2012.

[96] Matthew Robinson, "Insight: Obama's Oil Tanker Dilemma: Vex Unions to Win Pennsylvania?," *Reuters*, March 12, 2012.

2011 waivers, a spokesman for the American Waterways Operators accused President Obama of "violating the spirit, if not the letter, of Jones Act by ignoring the availability of Jones Act ships and barges."[97] Likewise, Senator Mary Landrieu (D-LA) and a bipartisan group of seven other members of Congress, mainly from coastal states, issued a joint statement decrying the waivers.[98] The AFL-CIO Maritime Trade Department, which represents maritime workers, lamented the impact of the waivers on blue-collar jobs.[99]

The fallout over the Jones Act waivers was enough to prompt new legislation, passed in 2012, that raised the hurdles that U.S. federal agencies must meet to issue waivers. These toughened rules prohibit the Department of Homeland Security from approving a waiver without taking "adequate measures to ensure the use of U.S.-flagged vessels." Before granting waivers, the Department of Transportation will also be required to assess whether Jones Act–compliant vessels "with single or collective capacity" are capable of lifting SPR crude oil. The Department of Homeland Security must also "provide a written justification" for all waivers granted.[100]

Despite the opposition, the Obama administration has continued to defend the Jones Act waivers granted in conjunction with the 2011 SPR release, citing the exceptionally large volumes of oil requested by the purchasing companies and the "focus on getting this oil to U.S. markets as quickly as possible."[101] These arguments are well-founded. Without the waivers, transportation constraints would have almost certainly prevented the United States from sticking to the sixty-day release window agreed upon by the IEA. It would also have required bidders for U.S. SPR oil to lower their bids significantly to compensate for higher transportation costs. Facing lower bids, the Department of Energy would have then had to consider releasing less oil (if the bids did not meet government-determined minimum price thresholds) or selling it at a much lower price.

[97] R.G. Edmonson, "Jones Act Carriers Furious over Fed Oil Contracts," *Journal of Commerce*, August 19, 2011, http://www.joc.com/ (accessed May 2012).

[98] Office of Senator Mary Landrieu, "Landrieu Sends Bipartisan Letter to President Criticizing Repeated Waivers of Jones Act," Press Release, August 26, 2011, http://www.landrieu.senate .gov (accessed May 2012).

[99] Matthew Robinson, "Insight: Obama's Oil Tanker Dilemma: Vex Unions to Win Pennsylvania?," *Reuters*, March 12, 2012.

[100] See U.S. House of Representatives Subcommittee on Coast Guard and Maritime Transportation, Committee on Transportation and Infrastructure, *Testimony of Thomas Allegretti*, Hearing on A Review of Vessels Used to Carry Strategic Petroleum Reserve Drawdowns, June 27, 2012.

[101] John M. Broder, "Oil Reserves Sidestep U.S. Vessels," *New York Times*, August 23, 2011.

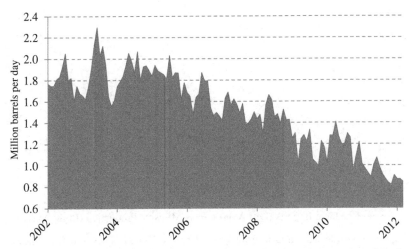

Figure 52. Crude Oil Shipped by Pipeline from the Gulf Coast (PADD III) to the Rest of the United States. *Source*: U.S. Energy Information Administration

POSSIBLE OPERATIONAL COMPLICATIONS FACING THE U.S. SPR

The U.S. SPR release ignited a debate about whether recent changes in North American oil flows and pipeline configurations have greatly reduced the rate at which these stockpiles can be released to the market. If true, the SPR may be far less able to combat a sudden, major oil shortage than it was in past eras.

Edward Morse, a former U.S. State Department official who is now head of commodities research at Citigroup, has argued that the release suggested that the U.S. SPR is "significantly less usable than advertised."[102] He notes that the U.S. SPR was designed to transport oil from Gulf Coast storage facilities inland on pipelines, rather than outward via seaborne trade. But most of the pipelines that once brought crude oil from the Gulf of Mexico northward had to be reversed – a process that can take months –to funnel oil southward to the Gulf (see Figure 52).

The pipeline reversals were the result of surging oil production in the Midwestern United States in addition to increasing imports from Canada (see Figure 53).

These changes in the U.S. logistical system, Morse argues, have vastly reduced the speed at which oil can be distributed to industry from the U.S.

---

[102] Edward Morse, "Cushions to Stem Iran Oil Price Spike are Proving Elusive," *Financial Times*, February 27, 2012.

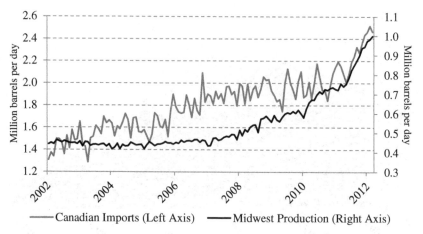

Figure 53. Crude Oil Imports from Canada to the United States and U.S. Midwest (PADD II) Crude Oil Production. *Source*: U.S. Energy Information Administration

SPR. Oil can still be loaded onto tankers, but not nearly as quickly it once could into pipelines, because of port congestion in the Gulf of Mexico. In his estimation, the rate at which oil flowed out of the U.S. SPR in the summer of 2011 (around 500,000 barrels per day) was likely closer to the peak evacuation rate than the 4.4 mb/d that the Department of Energy claims.[103]

The Department of Energy disputes Morse's conclusions, insisting that it would have no problem executing a drawdown and distributing oil at a rate of 4.25 mb/d in the event of a major supply disruption. (The slight 0.15 mb/d reduction from its usual claim of 4.4 mb/d capacity is because of a storage tank that is out of service at the Bryan Mound site.) The slow pace at which oil was moved out of the SPR during the 2011 emergency release was not indicative of mounting infrastructure constraints, U.S. officials argue. Instead, the pace reflected the fact that most of the U.S. SPR crude was delivered to vessels via only some of the SPR sites and marine terminals, and that the distribution utilized only a fraction of the available tanker loading docks to avoid disrupting commercial trade flows. The Department of Energy defends the reliability of its figures based on "routine and thorough analysis of commercial distribution capabilities" that the department conducts in order "to ensure accurate assessments,"

[103] Ibid.

according to an anonymous official cited by Platts, an industry news source.[104]

Policymakers in the United States should investigate this issue via a test drawdown and sale and publicly disclose their findings. If market participants harbor doubts about the flow capacity of the U.S. SPR, they may discount its ability to help offset any sudden supply shortages, rendering it a less effective tool for calming the market. Greater transparency about the SPR's capabilities, particularly in light of profound recent changes in the North American oil landscape, would be sensible.

CONCLUSION

The 2011 release provides an important case study for understanding the political and market consequences of deploying emergency oil inventories. These lessons are outlined here.

Market perception and effect on oil prices

The 2011 IEA release shed light on how such emergency interventions can affect oil prices as well as how oil market participants and analysts perceive them. A few of the lessons for policymakers:

- Emergency oil releases may have only a modest impact on prices, and broader market forces can easily overwhelm them. Ultimately, emergency releases may be more effective at preventing harmful price spikes than actually lowering prices.
- Market participants may view an emergency release as signaling future tightness in the oil market, which risks raising long-term prices and can feed back into higher short-term prices.
- The threat of releasing stocks may be useful to policymakers as a tool for tamping down prices in the short term, but only if that threat appears credible. Mixed signals from energy officials about a possible future release, as in July 2011, can make oil prices even more volatile.
- A release's effectiveness hinges on how it is structured. The better IEA member countries tailor a release to the market's needs at the time, the greater its chances of influencing prices.

---

[104] Meghan Gordon, "U.S. Defends SPR's Potential for Quick Response to Oil-Supply Emergencies," Platts, March 1, 2012. See also Philip K. Verleger, Jr., "Impact of a Middle East Oil Export Disruption," *Business Economics* 47 (2012), 197–201. Additional details were provided by an anonymous reviewer.

International cooperation

The 2011 IEA release highlighted the challenges, as well as the changing nature, of cooperation among IEA member countries, major non-IEA consumers like China, and pivotal producers such as Saudi Arabia. Among the lessons for policymakers are:

- Negotiating a release can be time consuming and difficult, particularly when some member countries are skeptical that supply conditions warrant intervention. A delayed decision, however, can undermine the release, in terms of both its market impact and public reception.
- The circumstances surrounding a release – its timing and perceived economic objective, for instance – have a decisive impact on its critical reception among analysts and in the popular press. Many analysts were skeptical that the supply shortage in June 2011 was severe enough to warrant the release, instead viewing the move as an unwise attempt by the IEA, under pressure from the United States, to manage prices.
- Cooperation with Riyadh is essential for an IEA release to help relieve a major shortage of crude oil, although the Saudis may only be able to offer an imperfect substitute for the missing oil and may be hesitant to discount their crude sufficiently to attract buyers.
- The IEA must continue to attempt to coordinate future releases with China, whose strategic petroleum reserves are now among the largest in the world, and eventually with other non-IEA countries such as India.
- An IEA emergency stock release risks causing diplomatic friction between IEA member countries and their allies within OPEC, particularly if the latter do not see the circumstances as meriting the intervention.

The logistics of the SPR in the United States

President Obama's authorization to tap the U.S. SPR, as well as the U.S. Department of Homeland Security's decision to grant numerous waivers to the Merchant Marine Act of 1920 (commonly known as the Jones Act), prompted debate on legal and operational aspects of U.S. SPR releases. Lessons for U.S. policymakers from the 2011 SPR release include the following:

- Granting waivers to the Jones Act is essential for a speedy large-scale release, but this strategy is likely to meet sharp opposition from the maritime industry, labor unions, and some U.S. officials.

- The Department of Energy should investigate the merit of the argument that surging North American oil production and mismatched infrastructure have limited the speed at which oil can be released from the U.S. SPR. It should publicly disclose its findings to allay any fears among market participants about the functionality of these reserves.
- Energy officials, both in the United States and other IEA member countries, should act on these findings to improve policy decisions when considering a future release.

Policymakers in the United States and other IEA member countries should act on these lessons when the inevitable need to tap emergency oil stockpiles returns. Heeding them will help ensure that these reserves help mitigate the economic disruption caused by a severe shortage of oil in the global marketplace.

6

The Gold Standard as an Alternative
Monetary Regime

Revived enthusiasm in some corners of U.S. politics for a return to the gold standard as a monetary system has renewed debate over the fitness of precious metals as a medium of exchange, highlighting the significance that these commodities have played at times in the global economy beyond their physical value. The Republican Party's 2012 platform suggested that the United States consider a return to a gold standard. Although it did not mention the standard by name, the statement noted that President Reagan, "shortly after his inauguration, established a commission to consider the feasibility of a metallic basis for U.S. currency." It called for a similar taskforce in 2012 to "investigate possible ways to set a fixed value for the dollar."[1] The proposal hearkens back to the pan-Atlantic classical gold standard era that existed in the decades prior to World War I. Then, the leading industrial economies, as well as many smaller agrarian ones, defined the value of their currencies in terms of a specified amount of gold.[2] Paper currency as well as other forms of money, such as bank deposits, could then be converted into gold at will (and vice versa) at the set price.[3]

The gold standard as a monetary system has seen various iterations over the course of U.S. history. The last official vestige of the gold standard

---

[1] "2012 Republican Platform: We Believe in America," GOP.com, http://www.gop.com/2012-republican-platform_home/ (accessed November 2012).

[2] Ronald McKinnon, "The Rules of the Game: International Money in Historical Perspective," *Journal of Economic Literature* 31, no. 1 (March 1993): 3.

[3] Different countries have operated different forms of the gold standard at various times. Moreover, the term "gold standard" could be construed to include simply gold bullion or coins as specie, while others would advocate for a narrower definition, limited to paper currency backed by and fully convertible into physical gold.

in the United States vanished in 1976, when the legal statute defining the dollar in terms of gold was eliminated.[4] The Nixon administration had effectively put the nail in the coffin five years earlier by closing the so-called gold window, announcing that it would no longer freely convert dollars for bullion at the official exchange rate. Now, several decades later, enthusiasm for ditching fiat currency for commodity-backed money has begun to seep back into the conservative mainstream.[5] "The international gold standard shimmers from the past like the memory of a lost paradise," one historian has written of generational interest in gold-backed money. It "[embodies] all the nostalgia of the Victorian and Edwardian eras – stability, harmony, respectability."[6]

Yet the wisdom of returning gold to a position of privilege within the U.S. or global monetary system is controversial. Top American economists oppose the idea.[7] Milton Friedman called a neo-gold standard "neither desirable nor feasible."[8] Advocates of the standard disagree, arguing that it is the only defense against the government monopoly of the creation of money, a power they argue strips citizens of control over their own wealth and foments economic instability.[9] It is an irony of history that the gold standard – in its heyday a century ago, a symbol of financial rectitude for participating nations – has fallen so out of favor among elite scholars.[10] No serious economist in London or New York, at the turn of the twentieth century, would dared to have advocated abrogating it. As the Russian economist A.N. Gurjev remarked, "[m]embership in worldwide civilization is unthinkable without membership in the worldwide monetary economy," in which gold was the lynchpin.[11] Those countries that abided by the rules of the game most closely (among them the United States, Australia,

---

[4] *An Act to Provide for Amendment of the "Bretton Woods Agreement Act,"* 90 Stat. 2660, October 16, 1976.

[5] Seth Lipsky, "The Gold Standard Goes Mainstream," *Wall Street Journal,* August 29, 2012.

[6] Peter L. Bernstein, *The Power of Gold: The History of an Obsession* (New York: John Wiley & Sons, 2000): 239.

[7] "IGM Forum: Gold Standard," The Initiative on Global Markets at the University of Chicago Booth School of Business, January 12, 2012.

[8] Milton Friedman, "The Resource Cost of Irredeemable Paper Money," *Journal of Political Economy* 94, no. 3, part 1 (June 1986), 646.

[9] Lewis E. Lehrman, "A Road to Prosperity," The American Spectator, September 14, 2012.

[10] Michael D. Bordo and Hugh Rockoff, "The Gold Standard as a 'Good Housekeeping Seal of Approval,'" *Journal of Economic History* 56, no. 2 (June 1996), 389–428.

[11] Cited in Giulio M. Gallarotti, *The Anatomy of an International Monetary Regime: The Classical Gold Standard, 1880–1914* (New York and Oxford: Oxford University Press, 1995): 144.

and Canada) earned the right to borrow internationally on the best terms, while habitual strays from the golden fold, such as Brazil and Argentina, were punished by creditors accordingly.[12]

Is a return to the gold standard a sensible or feasible policy? For one thing, the likelihood of a return to the classical gold standard, requiring as it would a concert of nations to profoundly change their monetary order, is extremely remote, barring a catastrophic rupture in the current regime. Moreover, the very conditions that made the system successful no longer exist, which calls into question whether an attempt at resurrecting the standard would achieve the objectives for which its proponents are searching. There is no denying that the gold standard as a rule-based system of monetary governance had certain significant macroeconomic and trade-related benefits. Yet, by the same token, it is easy to romanticize the gold standard, forgetting the downsides of its rigidities and the chronic challenges its upholders faced in unsuccessfully trying to maintain it.

THE HISTORY OF THE GOLD STANDARD IN THE UNITED STATES

What is a gold standard? As Bordo and Schwartz define it, a gold standard has three essential features. First, a national monetary authority "defines the weight of gold coins, or alternatively fixes the price of gold in terms of national currency." The government maintains this fixed price via its "willingness [to] freely buy and sell gold at the mint price." The system also requires that private citizens be unrestricted in owning and using gold for commerce. Although a gold standard could consist purely of the use of gold coins as money, the more common iteration in modern times was the more feasible one: a "mixed standard," which combined paper money, including

---

[12] Benn Steil, "The End of National Currency," *Foreign Affairs* 86 no. 3 (May/June 2007): 83–96. A January 2012 survey by the University of Chicago asked forty of the nation's most prominent economists, including those who have served in Republican and Democratic administrations, if reinstituting a gold standard in the United States would mean that "price-stability and employment outcomes would be better for the average American." Not a single one thought so. The majority strongly disagreed (53%). The kindest respondent acknowledged that the lapsed regime did have some limited advantages. It "would have avoided the policy mistakes of the 2000s, but still likely that discretionary policy is useful during recessions," opined Daron Acemoglu. Most were flatly dismissive. "This proposal," wrote William Nordhaus, "makes no sense in the modern world." Others were even less sympathetic. "Eesh. Has it come to this?" asked Austan Goolsbee. His Chicago colleague, Richard Thaler, mockingly wondered "Why tie to gold? why not 1982 Bordeaux?" And some were downright harsh: "Love of the [gold standard] implies macroeconomic illiteracy," one economist responded.

notes and deposits issued by commercial and central banks backed by and freely convertible into gold.[13]

Six of the yellow metal's characteristics make it well suited to use as money. It is durable, divisible, storable, portable, recognizable, and easy to standardize.[14] Because the supply of gold is highly inelastic in the short term, by pledging not to increase its money supply beyond its gold stocks (or some multiple thereof) a government makes a credible commitment to curtail its money supply. Backing money with a commodity, whether gold or otherwise, tends toward long-run price stability in that currency. Its purchasing power reverts to the cost of producing the physical commodity over the long run – though the short-run can be much bumpier, and long-term drift in the price of the underlying commodity can cause problematic fluctuations in the goods and services the money can buy.[15]

Although exchanging gold as money dates backs back millennia, the modern originator of the gold standard as a monetary regime was Great Britain.[16] It was Britain that pioneered a full legal gold standard in 1821, though the practice had been unofficially operative there for roughly a century before. In 1717, the Master of the Mint, Sir Isaac Newton, had missed the price of gold relative to silver, causing sterling to disappear from circulation. Other countries, including Germany, the United States, and France, flocked to the gold standard in the 1870s. Their turn to gold, however, was more a rejection of bimetallism than it was an embrace of gold. Up until that time, silver (and sometimes copper) had served well for everyday transactions, whereas gold was reserved for the bigger buys. Central monetary authorities had set a fixed mint price ratio between the two metals.

The United States had maintained a bimetallic standard throughout the first decades of the country's existence.[17] The nation's first secretary of the

---

[13] Michael D. Bordo and Anna J. Schwartz, "Monetary Policy Regimes and Economic Performance: The Historical Record," in *Handbook of Macroeconomics*, ed. John B. Taylor and Michael Woodford (The Netherlands: Elsevier B.V., 1999): 154–155.

[14] Michael D. Bordo, "The Classical Gold Standard: Some Lessons for Today," *Federal Reserve Bank of St. Louis Review* 63, no. 5 (1981): 2.

[15] Ibid., 3.

[16] This historical overview is based in large measure on information provided in a report by Craig K. Elwell, *CRS Report for Congress: Brief History of the Gold Standard in the United States* (Washington, DC: Congressional Research Service, June 23, 2011).

[17] The recitation of the monetary history of the United States in this section of the chapter draws heavily on a report by Craig K. Elwell, *CRS Report for Congress: Brief History of the Gold Standard in the United States* (Washington, DC: Congressional Research Service, June 23, 2011).

treasury, Alexander Hamilton, helped formulate the first coinage act in 1792. It defined the dollar as equivalent to 371.25 grains of silver, with gold being set at a 15 to 1 ratio to silver. But that ratio soon fell out of step with the world market, where silver's parity weakened to around 15 ½ to 1. Americans took advantage of the arbitrage by sending gold abroad and keeping silver at home, which left the country's everyday commerce dominated by silver. Although it is hard to imagine today, the United States initially recognized certain foreign coinage as legal tender, a policy that remained in place for the next half-century. Gold and silver coins from Britain, Portugal, France, Spain, and the Spanish colonies were among those accepted by Washington, helping quench the thirst of a growing domestic market for a means of exchange.

Congress took action to stop the outflow of gold in 1834, when it reset the fixed silver-to-gold mint ratio to 16:1. But this time they overshot in the opposite direction: it was now gold, not silver, that soon dominated domestic exchange. The discovery of massive amounts of gold in California and Australia in the 1840s, in addition to large quantities being mined in Russia, accelerated the trend. At the time, some prominent economists grew worried that this boom in world supplies could provoke catastrophic inflation. Yet their fears turned out to be misplaced; growth in worldwide economic activity was happening quickly enough to keep pace with the additional gold supplies, helping curtail the grinding deflation that had engulfed the United States economy since the Napoleonic Wars.[18]

No legal tender paper money circulated in the United States prior to the Civil War. Paper money did circulate, though Washington did not formally declare it a legal requirement that parties to a transaction must accept it as money. What money was issued took other forms, such as commercial bank notes, Treasury notes, and bills of exchange. In antebellum America, all were freely convertible for gold or silver through the issuer. It was not until the Civil War that the U.S. government first issued legal tender not backed by gold or silver. These "greenbacks," as they were known, were the first fiat paper money – in other words, "money or coins of little or no intrinsic value and not convertible into gold or silver, but made legal tender by order of the government" – the country had ever seen.[19] Abandoning a metal standard allowed Washington more flexibility to borrow to pay for the war, and caused significant inflation. By 1879, Congress, determined to restore

---

[18] Roy Jastram, *The Golden Constant: The English & American Experience, 1560–1976* (New York: John Wiley & Sons, 1977), 32.

[19] "Financial Times Lexicon," *Financial Times*, lexicon.ft.com (accessed October 2012).

metallic money, was able to claw enough greenbacks out of circulation to restore the antebellum metal-dollar ratios. But American money was irrevocably changed: the federal government would henceforth be an issuer of paper legal tender redeemable for gold or silver.

The heyday of the gold standard in the United States was from 1879 to 1933. During these years, the federal government issued pure gold coins as well as gold certificates, good for a certain amount of gold on demand. Legislation passed in 1873 excluded silver from the legal definition of the dollar, even though it continued to be used as a fractional currency at the margins. (The Sherman Silver Purchase Act of 1890, which was repealed in 1893, gave silver greater prominence in domestic money supply for three years.) The passage of the Gold Standard Act of 1900 firmly established the gold standard as the law of the land. It defined the gold-back U.S. dollar as the country's standard unit of account, and called for the creation of a physical gold reserve to back the nation's legal tender. Other existing forms of money, such as greenbacks and silver dollars, were henceforth also redeemable by gold. The creation of the Federal Reserve in 1913 did not, at the time, impinge on the operation of the gold standard. In fact, the mandate of the Reserve was to help maintain it. This it did, even during World War I, when every country other than Great Britain suspended the standard.[20] In reality, there is little need for a central bank for a country strictly abiding by a gold standard; all that is needed is some public institution to maintain the gold-to-currency ratio by buying and selling gold and that is willing to hold sufficient gold reserves to do so.[21]

The gold standard operated in its most "pristine" form on an international level between 1879 and 1914, the period known as the classical gold standard among historians.[22] By 1879, the standard was "inclusively international" in the sense that it had been adopted by all major advanced economies and many smaller ones outside the Atlantic basin. Countries in Western Europe and the United States managed to maintain their fixed exchange rates

[20] Barry Eichengreen and Marc Flandreau, "Editors' Introduction," in Barry Eichengreen and Marc Flandreau (eds.), *The Gold Standard in Theory and History* (Oxford and New York: Routledge, 1997): 19.

[21] Michael D. Bordo, "The Classical Gold Standard: Some Lessons for Today," *Federal Reserve Bank of St. Louis Review* 63, no. 5 (1981): 5.

[22] Ben Bernanke and Harold James, "The Gold Standard, Deflation, and Financial Crisis in the Great Depression: An International Comparison," in *Financial Markets and Financial Crises*, ed. R. Glenn Hubbard (Chicago: University of Chicago Press, 1991), 36; Michael D. Bordo, "The Classical Gold Standard: Some Lessons for Today," *Federal Reserve Bank of St. Louis Review* 63, no. 5 (1981): 2.

"without significant interruption" for these three and a half decades.[23] During these years, a set of implicit rules, both active and passive, governed how participating central banks and treasuries operated, whether in Washington, London, or farther afield. These so-called rules of the game, imperfectly followed, nevertheless provided gold-standard nations with "a kind of fraternity . . . whose members protected one another from the hazards and uncertainties imposed on them by the world beyond their borders."[24] The years of the classical gold standard were ones of rapid economic growth and technological progress. Relatively free trade in labor, capital, and goods predominated.[25] The gold standard helped make it possible. The use of a single, predictable (at least in good times) trans-border monetary system facilitated one of the most impressive periods of economic globalization ever experienced before or since.[26]

Economic historians debate some of the functional details of the operation of the international gold standard regime as well as member countries' actual fidelity to the so-called rules of the game by which they were to abide. The general mechanism underlying the monetary order, known as the price-specie-flow mechanism, is straightforward. It was through this balance-of-payments adjustment process that global prices were tied together under the fixed exchange rate regime. One economist explains the concept, in its simplest form:

Suppose that a technological innovation brought about faster real economic growth in the United States. Because the supply of money (gold) essentially was fixed in the short run, U.S. prices fell. Prices of U.S. exports then fell relative to the prices of imports. This caused the British to demand more U.S. exports and Americans to demand fewer imports. A U.S. balance-of-payments surplus was created, causing gold (specie) to flow from the United Kingdom to the United States. The gold inflow increased the U.S. money supply, reversing the initial fall in prices. In the United Kingdom, the gold outflow reduced the money supply and, hence, lowered the price level. The net result was balanced prices among countries.[27]

[23] Ronald McKinnon, "The Rules of the Game: International Money in Historical Perspective," *Journal of Economic Literature* 31, no. 1 (March 1993): 3.

[24] Ibid., 3–4; Peter L. Bernstein, *The Power of Gold: The History of an Obsession* (New York: John Wiley & Sons, 2000): 240.

[25] Michael D. Bordo, "Gold Standard," Concise Encyclopedia of Economics, http://www .econlib.org/ (accessed October 2012).

[26] Benn Steill, "Monetary Sovereignty as Globalization's Achilles" Heel," *Cato Journal* 27, no. 2 (Spring/Summer 2007): 208–210.

[27] Michael D. Bordo, "Gold Standard," Concise Encyclopedia of Economics, http://www .econlib.org/ (accessed October 2012).

The peace that prevailed during the decades leading up to World War I, the high degree of homogeneity in political and economic philosophy in the European countries at the core of the system (Britain, France, and Germany), and the buy-in of the peripheral countries, which sought access to the trade and capital markets that came with being part of this community of nations, all contributed to the smooth functioning of the regime during these prosperous years.

Even during the classical period, the form in which the gold standard operated across participating countries varied. Gold coins circulated in six countries, including France, Germany, and the United States, while other countries stuck to token coins and paper money freely convertible into gold. Some countries, the United States among them, declared the right of citizens to convert into gold inviolate, while others, such as France and Belgium, reserved the right to hand out silver instead. Many countries on the standard did not fully back their paper currency and base-metal coin with gold reserves. Some countries, Britain and Russia among them, gave the central government the right to issue a certain amount of currency not backed by gold held in reserve, which was designated as such. Other countries also allowed for a fixed percentage of currency not to be backed by gold reserves though all currency was treated equally.[28]

But Eden – for present-day goldbugs, at least – could not last. The Great Depression, the severity of which many economists believe was worsened markedly by the federal government's intransigent adherence to the gold standard, set in motion the chain of events that would see the United States go off the standard in 1933. (The relationship between the Depression and the gold standard will be discussed later.) A newly inaugurated President Franklin Roosevelt took decisive action to break the gold link so as to allow more expansive monetary policy, a push that that Congressional legislation furthered and Supreme Court rulings allowed. An executive order issued in April 1933 banned the "hoarding" of gold, effectively nationalizing the country's private gold inventories by requiring citizens to turn them over to the government at a predetermined price. Just a month earlier, by passing the Emergency Banking Act, Congress had handed Roosevelt the power to prohibit the use of gold for commercial transactions, which he exercised.

The 1934 Gold Reserve Act was the nail in the coffin. Reinforcing the President's nationalization of gold, it turned over the title to all domestic gold

---

[28] Barry Eichengreen and Marc Flandreau, "Editors' Introduction," in Barry Eichengreen and Marc Flandreau (eds.), *The Gold Standard in Theory and History* (Oxford and New York: Routledge, 1997): 7–8.

stocks to the U.S. government and pulled all gold coins out of circulation. The dollar would continue to be legally defined in terms of gold, but it was largely symbolic. Only the Federal Reserve retained the right to settle transactions in gold, and those were with other central banks; for ordinary Americans, a robust gold standard was no more. Although critics howled, the Supreme Court obliged, granting the federal government as well as private citizens via two decisions in February 1935 the right to pay down any outstanding debts in paper fiat money.[29] The rulings provided a crucial path for funding the New Deal, and soon thereafter, the war effort.

The wreckage of World War II ushered in the Bretton Woods agreement, struck in 1944, which kept gold on the periphery of the international monetary system. It was now the U.S. dollar, not gold, that was the bedrock currency in which the value of its global counterparts was defined via pegged exchange rates. Only the dollar was freely convertible for gold, at the fixed price of $35 an ounce, though only other national treasuries and central banks had the privilege, not ordinary citizens as in the earlier times. These rules were intended by Britain and the United States, the two most prominent architects of the Bretton Woods system, to ensure open trade, with the dollar essentially "as good as gold."[30] They also provided for the creation of the International Monetary Fund, which was tasked with being a lender of last resort to countries unable to maintain their fixed exchange rate, or alternatively to help oversee an orderly reduction in the par value of their currency.

A slow, persistent inflation in the United States as a result of its overly accommodative monetary policy and worsening fiscal problems put the viability of gold-dollar convertibility under serious strain less than two decades later. By 1960, the country's gold-backed foreign liabilities of around $20 billion had outrun the government's gold stock, putting the Federal Reserve in a vulnerable position.[31] Domestic prices were rising as close as 6% annually by the close of the decade, as fiscal deficits mounted. Congress began to pull back on its commitments to back Federal Reserve holdings with gold. It had did away with the requirement to hold gold reserves in line with the Fed's deposits in 1965, then extended the repeal to Fed notes three years later. Meanwhile Washington's gold stockpiles

---

[29] See U.S. Supreme Court, Norman v. Baltimore & Ohio Railroad Co., 294 U.S. 240 (1935) and U.S. Supreme Court, Perry v. United States, 295 U.S. 220 (1935).

[30] Peter L. Bernstein, *The Power of Gold: The History of an Obsession* (New York: John Wiley & Sons, 2000): 349.

[31] Ibid., 334.

continued to flow overseas as the country began to chalk up a sizeable trade deficit.

Unwilling to curb its fiscal or monetary policy to curb the rising tide of inflation, the Nixon administration took a drastic measure in 1971 to stem the outflow of gold. It declared that the United States would no longer hold up the promise of freely redeeming dollars for gold. Such conversion would henceforth be available by negotiation only. The gold window, which had extended the option to convert at a fixed price to at least certain groups for nearly two centuries, was now shut. At first Nixon conceived of convertibility suspension as a temporary measure, devaluing the dollar in terms of gold several times between 1971 and 1973 in a failed effort to right the ship. But it soon became apparent that defending even those looser pegs against rampant speculation would prove enormously difficult. By late 1973, the Bretton Woods consortium no longer made any attempt to reach a new monetary agreement stipulating a par value for the dollar in gold terms.

The final remnant of the gold standard in the United States died in October 1976, when President Ford signed an amendment to the Bretton Woods Agreements Act. It eliminated the legal definition of the dollar in gold terms (by that time $42.22 per ounce), which had been defunct for several years anyway. Ford heralded the act as providing "increased flexibility, resilience, and reliance on market mechanisms which today's monetary relationships require, replacing the exchange rate rigidity and gold emphasis of the Bretton Woods system."[32] The United States has operated on pure fiat money with a floating exchange rate ever since.

THE CONTEMPORARY POPULAR CASE FOR A RETURN TO THE GOLD STANDARD IN THE UNITED STATES

The intellectual scaffolding on which contemporary calls rest in the United States for a return to the gold standard is based largely on the works of mid-twentieth-century economists identified with the Austrian school of economics, particularly Friedrich Hayek and those of this tutor, Ludwig von Mises. Drawing on their work, Texas Rep. Ron Paul, who has advocated a return to the gold standard since he first entered national politics in the 1970s, has tried to rally fresh enthusiasm for hard money. The financial collapse of 2008 aided his cause. The crash forced many Americans normally agnostic about monetary policy to come to terms with the origins of the

---

[32] Gerald R. Ford, "Statement on Signing Amendments to the Bretton Woods Agreements Act," October 21, 1976.

crash. The Austrian understanding of the business cycle found a wave of new adherents, who have articulated what they see as the potential benefits of a new gold standard in the United States.

In a U.S. context, today's gold-standard advocacy – almost exclusively a Republican or Libertarian position – fits within a broader range of alternative monetary policy arrangements that have received increased attention from activists and legislators since the 2008 financial panic, though a consensus appears to favor the status quo of active discretionary rate management by the Federal Reserve. Some economists have stressed the virtues of rule-based monetary policy, such as an adoption of the Taylor Rule, which would link rates to observed macroeconomic conditions.[33] They point to studies that have shown that if the Federal Reserve had hewed more closely to what the rule had implied during the 2000s, both the asset price inflation of the mid-2000s and its reversal, along with the ensuing financial market turmoil, might have been avoided.[34] To the political right of these proposals are those who argue for a return to the classical gold standard, where the dollar is defined in and fully convertible into gold, which must be backed by public bullion stocks. James Grant of *Grant's Interest Rate Observer* and Steve Forbes fall into this bucket. Further along the spectrum stands Rep. Ron Paul who likewise calls for a neoclassical gold standard but who, like Hayek, also advocates private coinage to compete with or replace the federal monopoly on currency issue. At the final end of the spectrum fall advocates of doing away entirely with paper money, substituting it for gold coinage.[35]

How does the work of Hayek and von Mises inform the arguments of those like Forbes and Paul, who would like to see some form of the gold standard restored? In *The Denationalization of Money*, published in 1976, Hayek made the case that government monopoly over a nation's money supply gives it a lever of control over private citizens that limits their freedoms and undermines the value of the their property.[36] Central banks, subject to pressure from powerful special interest groups, are chronically unable to

---

[33] International Monetary Fund, "Monetary Policy Implementation at Different Stages of Market Development," Accessed at www.imf.org/ (October 26, 2004): 13–14.

[34] Pier Francesco Asso, George A. Kahn, and Robert Leeson, "The Taylor Rule and the Transformation of Monetary Policy," Research Working Paper, The Federal Reserve Bank of Kansas City Economic Research Department (December 2007): 34–35.

[35] This spectrum of views is summarized well in Seth Lipsky, "The Gold Standard Goes Mainstream," *Wall Street Journal*, August 29, 2012.

[36] F.A. Hayek, *The Denationalisation of Money: The Argument Refined*, 3rd ed. (London: The Institute of Economic Affairs, 1990).

keep a lid on the creation of money and hence on inflation. Once sparked, inflation only prompts greater central bank and other government meddling in the economy, invariably most harmful to the poorest members of society, until the entire easy-money-fuelled boom eventually collapses. The bust triggers a newfound round of government intrusion into the economy in the name of stabilization, crimping the free market's ability to allocate goods in the most growth-producing way and paving the way for the next round of government-induced economic instability. Control over money, in other words, is the engine that fuels creeping government intrusion in other areas of private life and leads to economic unrest.

Hayek's solution to this problem was to allow for private currency, thereby imposing market competition on currency issuers that would discipline the supply of money. Here classical gold standard advocates and those who see denationalization of money as the answer part ways. But Rep. Paul's case for why metal-based money should be restored draws inspiration from Hayek's thinking in other respects. In his 2009 book, *End the Fed*, he argues that "ending the Fed would be the single greatest step we could take to restoring American prosperity and freedom and guaranteeing that they both have a future." He sees Nixon's decision in 1971 to renege on Washington's commitment to freely convert gold for dollars as the root of the country's ills. It set the stage for the devolution of U.S. currency to a pure fiat currency, giving it unmitigated control over the national money supply. That prerogative, in turn, gave spendthrift Washington policymakers the monetary rope by which they would fiscally hang themselves in the ensuing decades, casting aside the fetters that had stopped the Fed from underwriting continual federal budget deficits.

The answer, for Paul, is to return to gold-backed money. The fact that gold has been used as money historically is evidence of its suitability: it "became money because it had all the properties people look for in good money. Government had nothing to do with it." The dollar would once again be redeemable in gold, thanks to the federal government's holdings. This new gold standard would impose "discipline," and a "new culture would quickly emerge in Washington."[37] Paul ticks off a list of economic ills that he believes would end if the Federal Reserve's "money monopoly" were gone, via a return to the gold standard:

It would bring an end to dollar depreciation. It would take away from the government the means to fund its endless wars. It would curb the government's attacks on the civil

---

[37] Ron Paul, *End the Fed* (New York: Grand Central Publishing, 2009): 203–204.

liberties of Americans, stop its vast debt accumulation that will be paid for by future generations, and arrest its massive expansion of the welfare state. . . . It is the first step to restoring constitutional government. Without the Fed, the federal government would have to live within its means. . . . There are other benefits as well, such as stopping the business cycle, ending inflation, building prosperity for all Americans, and . . . would put the American banking system on solid footing. . . . Ending the Fed is the one sure way to restore sanity to economic and political life in this country.[38]

It was the federal government's abandonment of the gold standard, Paul argues, that gave the Federal Reserve its position of prominence in national life; only by returning to the standard can these problems be remedied.

One of the most detailed articulations of the case for gold to appear in the popular press was made by Lewis Lehrman, a member of Reagan's U.S. Gold Commission in 1981, in *The American Spectator* in September 2012.[39] For Lehrman, the decision between a gold standard and a floating exchange rate could not be of greater import: To choose or to reject the true gold standard," Lehrman argues, "is to decide between two fundamental options: on the one hand, a free, just, stable, and objective monetary order; and on the other, manipulated, inconvertible paper money" guilty of a host of ills. Fiat currency is "the fundamental cause of a casino culture of speculation and crony capitalism, and the incipient financial anarchy and inequality it engenders." It was the gold standard, in Lehrman's view, to which the United States owed its ascendance from "13 impoverished countries by the sea in 1789 to leadership of the world in little more than a century."

Gold as money is more than just sensible policy, for Lehrman and the like-minded; it is a natural law, and an ancient and venerable order. After "two millennia of market testing," gold remains the "single, inde-structible . . . natural currency," able to do what all money should: pro-vide a "standard unit of account, a stable medium of exchange, a stable store of value, and a stable deferred means of payment." Gold's "natural properties" – a significant real cost of production chief among them – make it superior to inconvertible paper money, where supply is only limited by the privileged whims of "insiders." Lehrman extols gold money was "endowed by nature with profound but simple national and international network-ing effects," so that "even hostile nations" could do business with each other. Small wonder, then, that gold or gold-backed money emerged as the

---

[38] Ibid., 6–8.

[39] Lewis E. Lehrman, "A Road to Prosperity," *The American Spectator*, September 14, 2012, http://spectator.org/ (accessed October 2012).

"preference of tribal cultures, as well as ancient and modern civilizations."
By using it, they were able to avoid fiat money's tendency "toward depreciation and inflation, interrupted by bouts of austerity and deflation."

There is a moral hue to Lehrman's case for gold, as there is to Ron Paul's.
Adopt the gold standard, both argue, and "a just social order and economic
growth" will ensue. Restoring Americans' ability to convert dollars into
gold would mean an array of good things for the economy: more "savings,
investment, and entrepreneurial innovation," boosting employment and
wages. The underdogs and heroes of American capitalism – "workers, savers,
investors, and entrepreneurs" – receive their "just and lasting compensation." The gold standard brings about nothing short of a "major mutation in
human behavior." It requires that "every able-bodied person and firm must
first make a supply before making a demand . . . effectively alter[ing] human
conduct. It weeds out hangers-on and spendthrifts by "encourag[ing] production before consumption." The gold standard removes the "exorbitant
privilege" of the American government, trims the influence of the moneyed
class, and helps hold borrowers accountable for excessive leverage and the
trouble that it brings.

Another blessing of the gold standard, Lehrman explains, is the way in
which it rebalances the global economy. He explains:

> Until recent times the gold standard also underwrote, indeed required, global trade
> rebalancing, now the subject of exhortations by the International Monetary Fund
> and political authorities. But to desire a goal without the effective means to attain
> it – namely the true gold standard – is to court political and financial disaster. In
> the absence of prompt balance-of-payments settlements in gold . . . the result has
> been increasing trade imbalances, ever-rising debt, and credit leverage at home and
> abroad. . . . The true gold standard, without official reserve currencies, is the sole
> rule-based monetary order that reliably and systematically rebalances worldwide
> trade and exchange among all participating nations.

Lehrman cites "systemic inflation" in the United States over the past half
century as a result of the country's chronic balance-of-payments deficit,
which he attributes to the dollar's status as the world's reserve currency. This
"perverse" arrangement, which grants Washington the ability to print its
own money and thus finance its own fiscal deficits, tends to spark increases
in domestic prices for goods and services. The gold standard would not
allow such a problem. By forcing countries to settle balance-of-payment
deficits promptly in gold, the "exponential debt increases" in the United
States he sees as structurally inherent to the post-Bretton Woods system,
would disappear. Returning to gold, and thus ending the use of the dollar as
the world's reserve currency, is the only way to "gradually end the long era of

extreme global trade imbalances, secular debt accumulation and inflation, and currency depreciation."

THE ADVANTAGES AND DISADVANTAGES OF A GOLD STANDARD

Economists continue to debate certain practical aspects of how the classical gold standard as a monetary system functioned, as well as the credit or culpability, depending on one's point of view, it deserves for the positive and negative elements of the global economy during that period.[40] Although the regime did offer certain pronounced benefits, such as ensuring long-term price predictability and lessening transaction costs for cross-border trade and investment, these strengths were coupled with significant drawbacks, which make a return to the gold standard as unadvisable as it would be unfeasible.

To proponents of a return to the gold standard, one of its chief attractions is its long-term anti-inflationary bias. By limiting the rate at which money supply can increase by the rate of growth in gold supply (where in theory new production only slightly adds to the existing stock), and obligating participating governments to pay gold on demand at a fixed price, the system exerts a built-in discipline over money creation unknown to national currencies in flexible exchange rate regimes. The mechanism by which the gold standard achieves price stability is market-driven, and hence in theory immune from the vagaries of central banking conducted by mere mortals.[41] As Anna Schwartz explains, in theory, the "rate of increase in the gold money supply" varies "automatically with the profitability of producing gold, assuring "a stable money supply and stable prices in the long run."[42]

In this sense, the gold standard helps overcome the time-inconsistency problem inherent in flexible rate setting, whereby policymakers' short-run

[40] For a sampling of recent analyses, see Benn Steil, *The Battle of Bretton Woods: John Maynard Keynes, Harry Dexter White, and the Making of a New World Order* (Princeton, NJ: Princeton University Press, 2013); Steven Bryan, *The Gold Standard at the Turn of the Twentieth Century: Rising Powers, Global Money, and the Age of Empire* (New York: Columbia University Press, 2010); Douglas A. Irwin, "Anticipating the Great Depression? Gustav Cassel's Analysis of the Interwar Gold Standard," NBER Working Paper No. 17597 (National Bureau of Economic Research, November 2011); and Gabriel Fagan, James R. Lothian, and Paul D. McNelis, "Was the Gold Standard Really Destabilizing?," *Journal of Applied Econometrics* 28 no. 2 (March 2013), 231–249.

[41] Frederic S. Mishkin, "International Experiences with Different Monetary Regimes," NBER Working Paper No. 6965, (National Bureau of Economic Research, February 1999): 2–3.

[42] Anna J. Schwartz, "Alternative Monetary Regimes: The Gold Standard," in Anna J. Schwartz (ed.), *Money in Historical Perspective* (Chicago: University of Chicago Press, 1987): 371.

objectives can lead them to pursue overly expansionary monetary policy, causing people to adjust their wage and price expectations upward, which can undercut long-run price stability.[43] Political pressure on central bankers to juice the economy through too-easy money is a structural temptation in a flexible rate regime, though the Federal Reserve is arguably less susceptible to this sort of pressure today than are central bankers in other countries.[44] A credible gold standard, in contrast, offers a built-in check on inflation-inducing increases in government-issued paper currency that rules out political manipulation of the money supply as long as participants abide by the rules of the game.

The historical evidence shows that the gold standard did provide the United States with greater long-run price stability than it has experienced since World War II. Between the adoption of the standard in 1834 and 1913, wholesale prices declined on average just 0.14% annually. During the classical period, from 1880 to the advent of World War I, inflation (per the GDP inflator) averaged 1.7%.[45] Under the present fiat money regime, since 1968, it has averaged just shy of 4.0% annually.[46] The difference is even starker when viewed across the major world economies at the time: 0.9% average annual inflation during the classical gold standard years compared to 5.3% since 1968.[47] This ability to stabilize purchasing power over long periods of time was among the major macroeconomic accomplishments of the classical gold standard era.

The behavior of prices during the nineteenth-century gold standard, prior to the classical gold standard era, was more mixed. Many modern-day opponents to a neo-gold standard cite the frequent economic crises, both

---

[43] See Finn E. Kydland and Edward C. Prescott, "Rules Rather Than Discretion: The Inconsistency of Optimal Plans," *Journal of Political Economy* 85, no. 3 (June 1977), 473–492; Guillermo A. Calvo, "On the Time Consistency of Optimal Policy in a Monetary Economy," *Econometrica* 46, no. 6 (November 1978), 1411–1428; and Robert J. Barro and David B. Gordon, "Rules, discretion and reputation in a model of monetary policy," *Journal of Monetary Economics* 12, no. 1 (1983), 101–121.

[44] For a discussion, see Sylvester C.W. Eijffinger and Jakob de Haan, "The Political Economy of Central-Bank Independence," Special Papers in International Economics No. 19 (Princeton University, May 1996).

[45] Michael D. Bordo, Robert D. Dittmar, and William T. Gavin, "Gold, Fiat Money and Price Stability," Working Paper 2003–014D (June 2003 Revised May 2007). See Table 1: Measures of Price Stability Average Inflation and Persistence in the Price level.

[46] Author's calculation.

[47] Michael D. Bordo, Robert D. Dittmar, and William T. Gavin, "Gold, Fiat Money and Price Stability," Working Paper 2003–014D (June 2003; Revised May 2007). See Table 1: Measures of Price Stability Average Inflation and Persistence in the Price level. Note the latter figure is based on data through 2001.

real and financial, in the United Kingdom and the United States as evidence of gold's failings, and yet this is unfair: many of these episodes, such as the crisis of 1847, were neither rooted in nor exacerbated by the monetary system.[48] Wholesale prices did fluctuate dramatically for stretches over that time period, these secular movements driven in part by sizeable gold discoveries in the mid-1800s and a general price decline in the 1870s as the gold standard expanded internationally. Changes in prices were often reversed only after a long lag. Notwithstanding this variability, adherence to the gold standard did allow for a high degree of long-term price *predictability*, if not stability.[49] Like gravity, prices were ultimately pulled back to trend over the long term thanks to the self-regulating mechanisms of the gold standard regime. Such predictability in long-term domestic and international prices provided incentive for the formation of long-term contracts, which increase the efficiency of a market economy.[50]

Some analysts convincingly argue that the gold standard, had it been in place, would have helped smooth the boom-and-bust that continues to define the path of the world economy. "The discipline imposed by a gold standard on monetary policy," a 2012 Chatham House taskforce found, "might have served as a brake on the imprudent banking and massive debt accumulation of the past decade."[51] Barry Eichengreen, though no advocate of a revived gold standard, concurs that the Austrian understanding of credit cycles, which to a large extent animates neo-gold-standardism in the United States, "bears more than a passing resemblance" to the pattern of recent monetary history:

Our recent financial crisis had multiple causes, to be sure – all financial crises do. But a principal cause was surely the strongly procyclical behavior of credit and the rapid growth of bank lending. The credit boom that spanned the first eight years of the twenty-first century was unprecedented in modern U.S. history. It was fueled by a Federal Reserve System that lowered interest rates virtually to zero in response to the collapse of the tech bubble and 9/11 and then found it difficult to normalize them quickly. The boom was further encouraged by the belief that there existed

---

[48] Rudiger Dornbusch and Jacob A. Frenkel, "The Gold Standard and the Bank of England in the Crisis of 1847," in Michael D. Bordo and Anna J. Schwartz (eds.), *A Retrospective on the Classical Gold Standard, 1821–1931* (Chicago: University of Chicago Press, 1984), 233–276.

[49] Benjamin Klein, "Our New Monetary Standard: The Measurement of Effects of Price Uncertainty, 1880–1973," *Economic Inquiry* 13, no. 4 (December 1975), 461–484.

[50] Anna J. Schwartz, "Alternative Monetary Regimes: The Gold Standard," in Anna J. Schwartz (ed.), *Money in Historical Perspective* (Chicago: University of Chicago Press, 1987): 376.

[51] André Astrow (Rapporteur), "Gold and the International Monetary System," A Report by the Chatham House Gold Taskforce (London: Chatham House, February 2012): 29.

a "Greenspan-Bernanke put" – that the Fed would cut interest rates again if the financial markets encountered difficulties, as it had done not just in 2001 but also in 1998 and even before that, in 1987.[52]

In an international gold standard regime in which central banks abide by the rules of the game, the price-specie-flow mechanism imposes a form of self-regulation. When a credit expansion begins, domestic prices rise and gold flows out. In response, the central bank must contract credit, which cuts the expansion short. A central bank with a freer hand, if undisciplined, can give rise to the conditions that make for unsustainable booms and unnecessarily severe busts.[53] To those who argue a gold standard problematically constrains policymakers from using the monetary toolkit to revive a collapsed national economy, gold standard advocates reply that were the standard adhered to, calamities such as the Great Depression or a Great Recession would not have occurred in the first place.[54] The gold standard, in other words, is the ounce of prevention unequaled by a pound of Keynesian cure. Yet excess debt, both sovereign and private, and credit crises it can spawn have existed for centuries, long before the rise of the modern fiat currency regime. Expecting any monetary system to be a panacea for public bad behavior is too tall an order.[55]

One of the chief attractions of a gold standard is its power to reduce transaction costs, particularly in cross-border capital flows. This is true of fixed exchange rate regimes in general, given the predictability they provide. In its heyday, between the closing decades of the nineteenth century and the outbreak of World War I, the use of gold (or a credible claim on it) as money in a wide swath of the world helped facilitate a boom in international trade and investment that rivaled the economic globalization that began in the late twentieth century. Gold's function as a nominal anchor helped integrate financial markets, thanks to a reduction in devaluation risk.[56] As long as their commitment to participating in the international system was credit, countries in crisis were more likely to promptly receive emergency funds because their peers were confident that the gold link would be restored. As a

[52] Barry Eichengreen, "A Critique of Pure Gold," *The National Interest*, August 24, 2011.

[53] Lawrence H. White, "A Gold Standard with Free Banking Would Have Restrained the Boom and Bust," *Cato Journal* 31, no. 3 (Fall 2011): 500.

[54] Lawrence H. White, "Recent Arguments against the Gold Standard," *Policy Analysis* no. 728 (Cato Institute, June 20, 2013).

[55] Carmen M. Reinhart and Kenneth S. Rogoff, *This Time Is Different: Eight Centuries of Financial Folly* (Princeton, NJ: Princeton University Press, 2009).

[56] Michael D. Bordo, "The Gold Standard: The Traditional Approach," in Michael D. Bordo and Anna J. Schwartz (eds.), *A Retrospective on the Classical Gold Standard, 1821–1931*, (Chicago: University of Chicago Press, 1984), 23–120.

result, currency crises were less frequent during the classical gold standard, and when they did occur, they were shorter-lived and less severe than those of the present floating exchange rate era.[57]

The intuitive sense behind the use of a universal money as a means of catalyzing commerce across borders was self-evident at the time of the classical gold standard, even among its critics. "Nothing else but commodity money could serve" to strengthen world trade, Karl Polanyi argued, "for the obvious reason that token money, whether bank of fiat, cannot circulate on foreign soil."[58] Polanyi was ultimately proven wrong on that score, but the logic behind the indisputable advantages of an international system defined by a unified, credible commitment to fixed rates of exchange, backed by a universal store of value, remains sound. It offers the advantage of avoiding the possibility of central bankers deviating from a rule of sensible money supply growth or a lack of commitment to long-term price stability, both of which are possible in the current fiduciary system.

Yet there are significant drawbacks to reverting to a gold standard, both theoretical and practical, which outweigh the benefits of a likely ill-fated attempt at trying to restore the lapsed regime. While in practice, a gold standard was neither as effective at avoiding the kind of negative outcomes that its advocates long for, such as greater macroeconomic stability, nor was it ultimately enough of a shackle to stop governments from behaving badly when faced with hard choices. On top of these drawbacks, it is far from clear that the conditions that made the standard feasible in its fullest form prior to World War I exist today; and even in if they did in the United States, reimposing a functional international gold standard akin to the classical era would require a broader global agreement, which further reduces its likelihood anytime soon.

Perhaps the most straightforward drawback to a pure gold standard was the resource cost of maintaining it. As Anna Schwartz explains: "For prices to remain stable under a gold standard, the monetary gold stock must increase at the same rate as the demand for money rises in response to real income growth plus or minus any change in the ratio of GNP to the money stock (a change in velocity)."[59] How large would this increase in gold stocks need to be to maintain a full gold coin standard? In 1960, Milton

---

[57] Benn Steil, "The End of National Currency," *Foreign Affairs* 86 no. 3 (May/June 2007): 83–96.

[58] Quoted in Benn Steil, "The End of National Currency," *Foreign Affairs* 86 no. 3 (May/June 2007): 83–96.

[59] Anna J. Schwartz, "Alternative Monetary Regimes: The Gold Standard," in Anna J. Schwartz (ed.), *Money in Historical Perspective* (Chicago: University of Chicago Press, 1987): 379.

Friedman estimated that monetary gold inventories would have had to be increased at a rate of 4% per year between 1900 and 1950 to maintain price stability, based on the average rate of real income growth and declining money velocity. All in all, an enormous 2.5% of the gross national product would be required to increase monetary gold to keep prices stable.[60] At 2011 levels, that would amount to $380 billion being absorbed into keeping a full gold-coin standard afloat. The exceedingly high costs involved in such a system are what drove the adoption of proxies for gold in everyday transactions and in reserves, such as paper currency. But even with dollars in circulation, Washington was obliged to keep sizeable gold inventories on hand to fulfill, if not inspire, credibility in the gold-dollar link and provide convertibility when necessary.

Despite its benefits for long-run price stability (at least during the 1890–1914 era), the gold standard fostered problematic short-run fluctuations in crucial aspects of the larger economy like output and employment, not to mention in consumer prices. Yes, prices may have been kept constant over long stretches, or at least predictable – but to what end, if the regime is less dependable in terms of supporting economic growth and job creation? Without the discretion of targeting rates in response to monetary or real shocks to the domestic economy, U.S. officials saw real output fluctuate more sharply during the classical gold standard years than during the present-day rate regime. Between 1879 and 1913, the coefficient of variation for real output nationally was 3.5, compared to just 0.4 in the half-century following World War II. The gold standard regime's single-minded focus on price stability also meant less flexibility to mitigate increases in unemployment. Joblessness was higher during the classical gold standard period, averaging 6.8% between 1879 and 1913 compared to 5.7% between 1947 and 2011.[61] Short-term prices also oscillated much more sharply. The coefficient of variation of annual changes in the price level during the classical gold standard era in the United States was a multiple of what it has been over the past fifty years, the oil shocks of the 1970s and 2000s notwithstanding.[62] The long-term stability in purchasing power that the now-obsolete regime was able to achieve was made possible by periods of inflation being offset by

---

[60] Michael D. Bordo, "Gold Standard," Concise Encyclopedia of Economics, http://www .econlib.org/ (accessed October 2012).

[61] Author's calculations based on Bureau of Labor Statistics data; also drawn from "Gold Standard," Concise Encyclopedia of Economics, http://www.econlib.org/ (accessed October 2012).

[62] Michael D. Bordo, "The Classical Gold Standard: Some Lessons for Today," *Federal Reserve Bank of St. Louis Review* 63, no. 5 (1981): 14–15.

years of wrenching deflation, which contributed to more halting aggregate growth, upward pressure on unemployment, and longer recessions.

Whatever its virtues, the gold standard was a not a guarantee of the kind of fiscal discipline or limited government that many gold standard advocates desire. Sovereign debtors can still fall prey to excessive external debt issuance and with it the risk of default and devaluation. Debt crises did not originate with fiat currency; shunning the latter would not banish the former. That said, during the years of the international gold standard, the number of countries in external default or restructuring weighted by share of world income was the lowest it has consistently been in the past two centuries. Ironically, the serenity of those two decades was matched only by the period from 2003 to 2008. Both periods were ultimately followed by a new wave of defaults.[63] Even under a gold standard, bank lending can be highly procyclical, fomenting the boom-and-bust pattern that some would like to associate only with fiat currencies. Although its critics see it as a regime that shuns accountability, in reality, flexible exchange rates based on fiat currencies can deter fiscally irresponsible governments more quickly and reliably than in other arrangements. Markets can continuously devalue a currency in response to bad behavior. Yet under a gold standard, where exchange rates are fixed, the feedback mechanism is slower to operate, which raises the risk of market discipline coming more suddenly and unpredictably.[64] Like other fixed-rate regimes, it also heightened the risk of real and monetary shocks reverberating across international borders.[65]

Moreover, the lack of flexibility in the regime problematically curtails the federal government's ability to respond to economic downturns. The same rigidity over money supply expansion required by strict adherence to an international gold standard precludes the possibility of a central bank taking expansionary measures to boost output after a negative shock to growth. Many gold standard advocates would object to this concern, arguing that under such a regime, thanks to its ability to prevent excessive debt accumulation and risk taking in the financial sector, crises and panics would not happen in the first place. They are right to the extent that debt crises leading to a sovereign default among leading countries were almost unheard of during the classical gold standard era from 1879 to 1913. But looking

[63] Carmen M. Reinhart and Kenneth S. Rogoff, *This Time Is Different: Eight Centuries of Financial Folly* (Princeton, NJ: Princeton University Press, 2009): 71–72.

[64] Sebatian Edwards and Eduardo Levy Yeyati, "Flexible Exchange Rates as Shock Absorbers," NBER Working Paper No. 9867 (National Bureau of Economic Research, July 2003).

[65] Michael D. Bordo and Anna J. Schwartz, "Transmission of Real and Monetary Disturbances Under Fixed and Floating Rates," *Cato Journal* 8 no. 2 (Fall 1988), 451–475.

back at the credit crisis of the past decade, it is difficult to say with certainty how the global economy would have performed under the lapsed monetary regime. Maintaining gold convertibility at a fixed dollar price throughout much of the nineteenth and into the twentieth century did not preclude numerous and repeated banking crises and macroeconomic turmoil, not to mention more frequent and longer recessions. The panics of 1857, 1873, 1893, 1896, and 1907 all occurred under some form of metallic standard. The frequency of financial panics has declined since the creation of the Federal Reserve System, thanks in part to its ability to help stabilize interest rates.[66] The chronic deflation wrought by a badly managed gold standard regime appears to have contributed to the Great Depression. Not coincidentally, those countries that were quickest to abandon dollar convertibility at a fixed gold price in the 1930s were also the earliest to see their economies rebound.[67]

The desire for long-term price stability that animated calls for a return to the gold standard in the United States were perhaps unsurprising in the early 1980s, given the recent history at the time of runaway inflation, and the still-nascent grip on monetary policymaking it reflected.

When some were advocating a return to the gold standard in the early Reagan days, headline CPI was running as high as 15%. It had stayed well north of 6% for much of the 1970s (see Figure 54). But inflation rates have hardly seen a return to such runaway levels since that time, as monetary policymaking has improved. Ten-year expected inflation has trended steadily downward over that period (see Figure 55), though some prominent U.S. economists, including former Federal Reserve Chairman Alan Greenspan, have long forewarned it might move higher in the near term, perhaps problematically so.[68] So far such a problematic scenario has not materialized. Many gold advocates are skeptical of common measures of consumer price levels, like the Bureau of Labor Statistics' CPI index. But other measures of broad consumer prices, unmediated by the government, such as MIT's Billion Prices Project, document very similar changes.[69]

---

[66] Jeffrey A. Miron, "Financial Panics, the Seasonality of the Nominal Interest Rate, and the Founding of the Fed," *The American Economic Review* 76, no. 1 (March 1986), 125–140.

[67] Ben Bemanke and Harold James, "The Gold Standard, Deflation, and Financial Crisis in the Great Depression: An International Comparison," NBER Working Paper No. 3488 (National Bureau of Economic Research, October 1990).

[68] Charlie Rose, "Charlie Rose Talks to Alan Greenspan," *Bloomberg Businessweek Magazine,* June 23, 2011, http://www.businessweek.com/.

[69] The MIT Billion Prices Project daily online price index is available at http://bpp.mit.edu/usa/ (accessed May 2012).

Figure 54. Year-on-Year Percentage Change in U.S. Urban CPI, All Items (1970–2012).
Source: Bloomberg

There are also a host of technical problems that would complicate any attempt to reintroduce a gold regime, either domestically or on a joint basis with other developed countries. Such challenges include, as Anna Schwartz identifies them, "choosing the right price of gold, deciding what to do with the profits of gold devaluation, arranging for the pegging of the new gold price, linking the domestic money supply to gold reserves, assuring the

Figure 55. Ten-Year Expected Inflation (1982–2012). *Source*: Federal Reserve Bank of Cleveland

adequacy of gold output, and fixing sustainable foreign exchange rates."[70] Resolving these issues would not be sufficient, but would certainly be necessary, to put a gold standard back in place. They are not insuperable, but mistakes could be quite costly. Assigning too high a price for gold, for instance, can lead to an extended bout of deflation. Given that real interest rates difficult to push below the zero bound, falling price levels will translate into higher real interest rates. In light of current sovereign and consumer debt levels in the United States, and deflation's punishing effect on net-debtors as it increases the real burden of servicing those obligations, the risk of a deflationary trap that a return to the gold standard entails is hard to reconcile with robust employment and output growth.

CONCLUSION

Ultimately, resolving the technical issues associated with a resumption of the regime are eclipsed by more difficult problem: convincing countries to put the standard in place, and once they do, to keep it in place. The political will to put the regime in place simply does not exist. The United States, arguably the chief sovereign beneficiary of the post-Bretton Woods monetary order, given the dollar's ongoing status as the world's predominant reserve currency, would be loath to relinquish its exorbitant privilege.[71] Even should it decide to adopt the regime, doing so without other countries' participation accomplishes little. As Michael Bordo explains:

Perhaps of paramount importance for the successful operation of the managed gold standard was the tacit cooperation of the major participants in (ultimately) maintaining the gold standard link and its corollary, long-run price stability, as the primary goal of economic policy. This suggests that one country alone on the gold standard would likely find its monetary gold stock and hence its money supply subject to persistent shocks from factors beyond its control.[72]

Yet convincing other nations to join the regime was not the central structural problem faced by its members during the international gold standard era – it was staying on it when there was incentive to defect. It was the credible commitment of the core European countries during the prewar classical gold standard to preserve convertibility, buttressed by a fear among

---

[70] Anna J. Schwartz, "Alternative Monetary Regimes: The Gold Standard," in Anna J. Schwartz (ed.), *Money in Historical Perspective* (Chicago: University of Chicago Press, 1987): 389.

[71] Barry Eichengreen, *Exorbitant Privilege: The Rise and Fall of the Dollar and the Future of the International Monetary System* (New York: Oxford University Press, 2011).

[72] Michael D. Bordo, "The Classical Gold Standard: Some Lessons for Today," *Federal Reserve Bank of St. Louis Review* 63, no. 5 (1981): 15–16.

peripheral countries like the United States that infidels would be shunned in London's all-important capital markets, which gave the order of what success it enjoyed. Yet the unique historical conditions that defined the era, and made the monetary regime flourish in the decades leading up to 1913, largely vanished with the Great War.[73]

---

[73] Barry Eichengreen, *Golden Fetters: The Gold Standard and the Great Depression, 1919–1939* (New York: Oxford University Press, 1992).

7

Conclusion

Analyzing the future direction of the market requires understanding the four sets of opposing forces that define the global commodity trade: (1) net importing and net exporting countries, in search of economic gains; (2) sovereign states (and state-owned enterprises) and private-sector companies vying for competitive advantage; (3) international cooperation and nationalism as opposing means of addressing failures in resource markets; and (4) the physical and financial aspects of the modern commodity trade. These pairs of forces form the critical context in which the competition for relevancy among countries, companies, and consumers negotiate in the commodities marketplace for economic and political advantage will take place. They are the critical context in which the broad range of policy- and investment-related issues discussed in this book, from debates over speculators in commodities markets to mitigating harmful energy and food market volatility, will be settled.

The dive in crude oil prices in late 2014 underscores the potential for sudden reversals that are intrinsic to commodity markets – particularly to those like oil with long project lead-times – and their capacity for confounding even the best attempts by analysts to predict long-term price paths. Brent crude oil, trading at roughly $60 per barrel at year-end, appeared to many observers to be locked firmly in the $100 to $120 dollar range, where it had traded over the preceding three years, for the foreseeable future. And yet the suppositions that had formed the basis for such predictions – that the Saudis would put a floor under prices no lower than $90 per barrel to protect the fiscal feasibility of their social spending programs, that a still-recovering developed-world economy would sputter at prices above that range, and that an uptick in worldwide consumption should prices fall below that threshold would cause any dip below it to be short-lived and contain the seeds of its own undoing – now look feeble. Regardless of where one sits with regard to if and when prices will regain lost ground, it is clear that the relative tranquility that had marked commodities broadly since their rebound in 2009 to 2011 was a transitory state of affairs. We have not reached the end of oil market history. Volatility and structural shifts, difficult to detect far in advance, are still ahead, continue to define these markets.

Index